||||| || |||| |||||||||||||||||||||||||||||| | |||

Environmental Victims

Wor
De

Classifi

To r
Books shoul

5 MAY

Environmental Victims
New Risks, New Injustice

Edited by Christopher Williams

Earthscan Publications Ltd, London

First published in the UK in 1998 by Earthscan Publications Ltd

A catalogue record for this book is available from the British Library

ISBN: 1 85383 524 2 paperback
     1 85383 534 X hardback

Typesetting by PCS Mapping & DTP, Newcastle upon Tyne
Printed and bound by Biddles Ltd, Guildford and King's Lynn
Cover design by Declan Buckley

For a full list of publications please contact:

Earthscan Publications Ltd
120 Pentonville Road
London, N1 9JN, UK
Tel: +44 (0)171 278 0433
Fax: +44 (0)171 278 1142
Email: earthinfo@earthscan.co.uk
WWW: http://www.earthscan.co.uk

Earthscan is an editorially independent subsidiary of Kogan Page Limited and publishes
in association with WWF-UK and the International Institute for Environment and
Development.

Contents

Abbreviations and Acronyms

AHRTAG	Appropriate Health Resources & Technologies Action Group
BCL	Bougainville Copper Limited
BGIA	Bhopal Group for Information and Action
BSE–CJD	bovine spongiform encephalopathy–Creutzfeldt-Jakob disease
CBE	Citizens for a Better Environment (US)
CGG	Commission on Global Governance
CMA	Chemical Manufacturers Association
CRA	Conzinc Rio Tinto Australia
DNA	deoxyribonucleic acid
EC	European Community
EPA	Environmental Protection Agency (US)
ESRC	Economic and Social Research Council (UK)
EU	European Union
G-7	Group of Seven (Canada, France, Germany, Italy, Japan, UK, US)
GATT	General Agreement on Tariffs and Trade
GEC	Global Environmental Change (ESRC)
GMO	genetically-modified organism
GNP	gross national product
ICRP	International Commission for Radiological Protection
ILO	International Labor Organization
IMF	International Monetary Fund
IQ	intelligence quotient
MOSOP	Movement for the Survival of Ogoni People
MPCA	Minnesota Pollution Control Agency
NGO	non-governmental organization
NRPC	Nagarik Rahat Aur Punarvas Committee (India)
OAU	Organization of African Unity
OSHA	Occupational Health and Safety Administration
PAMM	Programme Against Micronutrient Malnutrition
PC	personal computer
PCB	polychlorinated biphenyl
PEM	protein energy malnutrition
PHC	primary health care
PLA	Panguna Land Owners Association
PNG	Papua New Guinea
PPT	Permanent Peoples' Tribunal
PR	public relations
RTZ	Rio Tinto Zinc

TB	tuberculosis
UK	United Kingdom
UN	United Nations
UNHCR	United Nations Office of High Commissioner for Refugees
UNICEF	United Nations Children's Fund
US	United States
USSR	Union of Soviet Socialist Republics
VOC	volatile organic compound
WHO	World Health Organization
ZGKSM	Morcha (Zahreeli Gas Kand Sangharsh Morcha) (India)

List of Contributors

Françoise Barten is a senior lecturer at the University of Nijmegen and since 1991 coordinator of the Nijmegen Urban Health Group – an interdisciplinary working group which brings together scientists from different faculties within the university around a common theme: 'urban health and its determinants in the broadest sense'. She has worked in the Nicaraguan health system for many years and in 1995 received an honorary professorship at the Universidad Nacional Autónoma de Nicaragua for her contribution to academic development of the Public Health School of Nicaragua (CIES).
Contact: Nijmegen Institute for International Health, University of Nijmegen, PO Box 9100, code 103, 6500 HB Nijmegen, The Netherlands.
Email: f.barten@aig.azn.nl

Alicia Fentiman is a social anthropologist currently working with the Partnership for Child Development, Department of Zoology, University of Oxford, on the constraints to education and the health status of children in Africa. She has carried out extensive fieldwork research in southern Nigeria and northern Ghana. She is also a research associate of the African Studies Centre, Cambridge.
Contact: African Studies Centre, University of Cambridge, Cambridge, CB2 3RE, UK. Email: atjl@cus.cam.ac.uk

Suzanne Fustukian completed an MSc in Social Policy and Planning in Developing Countries at the London School of Economics and has been codirector of the Appropriate Health Resources & Technologies Action Group (AHRTAG) since 1988. She is the editor of Health Action, an international newsletter on primary health care.
Contact: AHRTAG, Farringdon Point, 29–35 Farringdon Road, London, EC1M 3JB, UK.

Rosemarie Gillespie is a Barrister at Law and environmental activist with the people of Bougainville.
Contact: 24 Garling Street, Lyneham, Australian Capital Territory 2606, Australia.

Sylvia de Haan is a research fellow in Tanzania on the project Environmental and Occupational Health Hazards Related to Small-Scale Industries in Low-Income Urban Areas in Dar-es-Salaam, Tanzania. She has studied the air pollution caused by local industries and its influence on human health in Niamey, Niger, and Arnhem, The Netherlands, and has taught environmental health to health

science students at the University of Nijmegen.
Contact: Nijmegen Institute for International Health, University of Nijmegen, PO Box 9101, 6500 HB Nijmegen, The Netherlands.
Diane Henkels is a graduate of the School of Law at the University of Vermont.

Sanford Lewis is an environmental attorney and the director of The Good Neighbor Project for Sustainable Industries. In addition, he is an instructor in environmental law at Tufts University.
Contact: The Good Neighbor Project, PO Box 79225, Waverly, MA 02179, USA. Email: gnproject@earthlink.net.

Peter Penz is associate professor in the Faculty of Environmental Studies at York University. His current work is on global environmental and economic justice and on development-induced population displacement. He is co-editor of *Global Justice, Global Democracy.*
Contact: Faculty of Environmental Studies, York University, 4700 Keele Street, North York, Toronto, ON, M3J 1P3, Canada. Email: ppenz@yorku.ca.

Satinath Sarangi is a metallurgical engineer by profession and an activist by choice. He came to Bhopal the day after the Union Carbide disaster and stayed on to work on different issues left in its wake. Since 1996 he has been involved in running a clinic that provides free medical care through modern medicine, ayurveda and yoga to chronically ill survivors of the disaster.
Contact: Sambhavna Clinic, 44 Sant Kanwar Ram Nagar, Berasia Road, Bhopal 462 001. Email: sathyu@bhavna.unv.emet.in.

Meena Singh works with Common Security Forum-South Africa and is a fellow of Clare Hall, University of Cambridge.
Contact: c/o Centre for History and Economics, King's College, Cambridge, CB2 1ST, UK.

Sharon Stephens is an assistant professor in the Department of Anthropology and School of Social Work at the University of Michigan. She is also a senior research associate at the Norwegian Centre for Child Research in Trondheim.
Contact: Department of Anthropology and School of Social Work, University of Michigan, 1020 LS&A Building, Ann Arbor, MI 48103, USA.
Email: sharonks@umich.edu.

Christopher Williams is a lecturer in international education at the Institute of Education, University of London. Previously he held an ESRC research fellowship at the Global Security Programme, University of Cambridge, and is author of *Terminus Brain: the environmental threat to human intelligence* and *Invisible Victims: crime and abuse against people with learning disabilities.*
Contact: Institute of Education, University of London, 20 Bedford Way, London, WC1 0AL, UK. Email: C.Williams@ioe.ac.uk.

Acknowledgements

Thanks are due to the Global Environmental Change programme of the UK Economic and Social Research Council (ESRC), for supporting the research that contributed towards this book, and to the Directors of the programme – Michael Redclift, Jim Skea, and Alister Scott – for their ongoing support and interest. Thanks also go to the authors of each chapter, for co-operating to develop their own ideas around the central theme of environmental victims, and to the editors of *Social Justice: a journal of crime, conflict and world order* – Suzie Dod and Gregory Shank, in particular – for their encouragement and help to produce the first version of this book as a special issue of their journal (volume 23, number 4).

Special mention should be given to a number of individuals at the Global Security Programme, University of Cambridge, namely Dr Gwyn Prins, Director, and Dee Noyes and Alison Suter, administrators, for hosting the study and for providing a way to think about the problem, daily support and encouragement, and Alison Suter, for speedy and impeccable proof reading of first drafts. In addition, particular thanks are due to Sheena Mackenzie, Information Officer at the Norah Fry Research Centre and Scottish Office Education and Industry Department, for her initial data searches, insightful discussion, design work and much else, and Frances MacDermott and Jonathan Sinclair Wilson at Earthscan, for the inevitable but invisible work that turns a manuscript into a book.

Finally, thanks to Trockel Ulmann & Freunde, one of the few cafes in Cambridge that has not become part of the academic theme park, for providing endless coffee, friendship and sanctuary while reading, thinking and correcting drafts.

As always, responsibility for error rests with the editor, who would be grateful to receive constructive comments about factual inaccuracies.

Introduction

Christopher Williams

> *Icky oil all over our feet*
> *Black waters*
> *Our food has run away*
> *Plants have gone bad...*
>
> McGee (1996)

In these few words from her poem, *The Disgrace of Shell Oil*, eight-year-old Mali McGee presents the paradigm of environmental victimization better than many academics. We are not just faced with the consequences of pollution *or* contaminated food *or* land degradation or a loss of biodiversity. Human well-being is threatened in distinct but *related* ways that are complex chemically, although simple conceptually. The threat resides first in the *presence* of environmental agents that injure, such as lead, which we perceive generally as an urban problem. Second, it lies in the *absence* of environmental macro- and micro-nutrients that are vital to human survival, leading to conditions such as protein energy malnutrition (PEM), which is seen mainly as a rural problem caused by land degradation. Most important, yet least considered, it lies in the *synergistic* effects between the two; for example, iron deficiency can precipitate the uptake of lead (see Figure I).

This last aspect is not just relevant in its biological form. Filthy factories are increasingly relocating to remote rural areas where their impact compounds the rural nutritional problems. These rural threats are also apparent in the towns. Micro-nutrient deficiencies are now a concern in relation to pregnant women in many urban settings, including those from poor areas of London. In Denmark, 75 percent of adults lack sufficient iodine in their diet. Urbanized endeavors can also create rural problems that return to haunt urban life. In 1996, there were for the first time outbreaks of a rural disease, cerebral malaria, in urban regions of India.

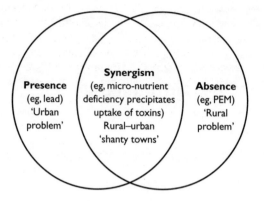

Figure I *Synergistic Effects Between Environmental Agents and Vital Nutrients*

This is linked with the overuse of pesticides, dam-building, and the excessive prescription of curative drugs. More graphically, the ever-burgeoning 'shanty towns' bring together the rural-urban problems creating the social synergism that hosts and precipitates the biological synergism (Williams, 1997).

These threats are not, of course, 'caused' by the environment, but by human beings. So let us start by getting our discourse right. We are talking about environmentally *mediated* hazards. Moreover, the outcomes are not principally diseases and health problems – they are first and foremost injuries and justice problems.

So-called Minamata disease in Japan can neither be caught nor cured. More properly, the term describes an injury resulting from mercury poisoning by known perpetrators. The disease label no doubt contributed to a circumstance whereby it was not until 1995 that compensation was finally awarded. By then, the victims were in their seventies. They received about £16,000 ($26,600) each for injuries that, had they been caused by medical negligence, would have attracted payments of anything up to £7 million ($11,637,500). *Chisso* successfully delayed payment for 22 years after the initial court ruling. It is crucial to conceptualize what is happening via our environment in terms of social justice, instead of through medicalized discourse that favors the interests of the perpetrator, or thoughtless phraseology that creates an impression that 'the environment' is to blame.

Hit a child on the head with a hammer, causing an intellectual impairment, and the event is seen first as a question of justice, with medicine doing its best to mitigate the consequences. Drive a car using leaded gasoline, causing intellectual impairments in countless children, and the outcome is seen only as a medical problem. A court is not the place to deal with medical problems, so redress is unlikely. The purpose of *Environmental Victims* is to challenge the conceptualizations that have created such a warped view of environmentally mediated injury, and to change the perception of those who suffer from that of sick patients who are simply in need of treatment, to that of environmental victims who deserve justice.

Contributors represent a wide range of interested parties. Naturally, an academic input has its place, but this is greatly illuminated by the perspectives of front-line activists and those within related professions, who are putting ideas into action. In Part One, existing concepts are challenged and developed. Part Two provides a set of classic case studies that broadly reflect the initial conceptual arguments. Part Three provides a glimmer of hope, not so much through documenting success in upholding the rights of environmental victims – it is too early for that – as through showing that we are at least able to come up with ideas that might change the world for the better.

The conceptual starting point for Part One is the environmental justice movement. A few decades ago this emergent US movement challenged the white middle-class perception that environmental problems only concerned the natural world. Activists, especially from minority groups suffering the effects of environmentally mediated poisoning, reminded the world that saving humans is as important as saving whales. The impact of the movement has been effective, but it, too, has its limitations. As the introductory article argues, it is time for complementary thinking that moves us from an exclusively activist stance framed in the light of US experience, to a broader and more objective framework that has global relevance. Not least is the need for a definition of 'environmental victim' and 'environmental causation' that does not lead to the dismissal of subsequent arguments as merely concerning a peripheral quality-of-life debate.

Peter Penz develops this baseline through a meticulous discussion in relation to state sovereignty and national borders. 'If you want to get there – I wouldn't start from here' is a common quip, expressing frustration in relation to international agencies, global governance, and cross-border ecopolitics. We must nonetheless start from here – the nation-state – though Penz quickly takes his argument from a succinct appreciation of its benefits to the point at which 'a federal system of divided authority, extended down to the local level and up to the global level' starts to appear feasible.

'Glocal' – the word that reminds of the necessary relationship between the global and the local – is also the theme of Sharon Stephens' article, which deals with that locally omnipresent, but globally invisible minority, children. She further elaborates the starting point of the first article and questions why the environmental justice movement has largely forgotten the specific concerns of children – an inherent problem among social movements, which tend by their nature to be adult-centered. Stephens reminds us that children need not be seen just as vulnerable victims. They can be part of our common fight against environmental injustice. Things are changing. In 1996, the EPA released a much-needed report detailing the health threats faced by children from toxics in the environment, *Environmental Health Risks to Children*.

In Part Two, the case studies cover some of the classic stories from the end of the second millennium. Anthropologist Alicia Fentiman makes a unique contribution to the study of environmental victimization through a culturally informed analysis of the circumstances in the Niger Delta. Her approach is quite distinct from the 'race' perspectives of the US environmental justice literature.

The Bhopal activist Satinath Sarangi provides a current update of circumstances in Bhopal and an insightful assessment of the strengths and weaknesses of the victim movement, displaying a sense of balance that is rare from an observer who has been so closely involved.

The case of RTZ in Bougainville should rank with the Union Carbide (Bhopal) poisoning in importance. Yet Bougainville is an isolated island in the South Pacific, far from the gaze of the media, and events are an embarrassment to responsible states and to the responsible sector of the commercial world. Thus, its problems remain largely unknown. Rosemarie Gillespie is an Australian barrister and environmental activist, who takes great personal risks to assist and monitor the conditions of victims in Bougainville. Her chapter nearly did not make the deadline for the book because she was cut off behind the Papuan blockade. Let us hope that Gillespie's article helps to put Bougainville more firmly on the global human rights agenda.

When nations are in political transition, environmental issues become a low public and state priority. The case of Central and Eastern Europe is an obvious example. There, although environmental activism played a part in bringing about political change leading to the events of 1989, environmental victimization remains rampant. South Africa is the other example. It seems unlikely that there could ever be a public uprising against the Mandela government because of, for instance, a polluting state industry. Yet, despite competing demands, the South African Constitution set a world benchmark in relation to adverse environmental impacts on human beings. Intentionally or not, Article 29 would relate to the whole environmental victimization paradigm (Figure I), not just the *presence* aspect. Moreover, it might even embrace acts by South African citizens that affect others outside South Africa's borders. It states, without qualification, that 'Every person shall have the right to an environment which is not detrimental to his or her health or well-being' (Article 29, Act 200, 1993).

In light of the unique circumstances of this region in transition, Meena Singh, of the South Africa Common Security Forum, outlines current problems and priorities, supporting her arguments with some surprising and little-known facts and figures. Reflecting the discussion by Peter Penz, she does this not only in relation to one nation, but also in the context of the whole Southern African region.

Part Three seeks light at the end of the tunnel. The 'Good Neighbor Agreements' pioneered and documented in this issue by Sanford Lewis with Diane Henkels are one of the most interesting approaches. Working *with*, as opposed to against, potential polluters at a local level must surely be better than constant conflict between environmentalists and industry. Yet the strategy evolved in a rich nation where local communities have at their disposal well-resourced local administrators and educated individuals, able and willing to embark on the often frustrating journey toward better preventive policy. Could this approach be developed in the poorer nations?

Occupational health has long been the flagship of environmental medicine, because the endeavors of the early trade unions brought the problems of workplace hazards to the fore. However, trade unions and occupational health were essentially Western ideas, and many of the resultant approaches are barely relevant in poorer communities. Françoise Barten and Suzanne Fustukian provide an insightful but well-moderated critique of this circumstance, which carries a crucial message if our Western perspective of work-related environmental victimization is not to contribute further to the intellectual imperialism that has so often hampered the efforts of indigenous academics and policymakers in less-wealthy countries.

The final sign of optimism comes in the form of the *Charter of Rights Against Industrial Hazards*. Hope does not derive simply from the Charter itself; if anything, it is further evidence of a seemingly intractable problem. It comes from the extraordinary success of the Permanent Peoples' Tribunal in creating a forum for testing the arguments that underlie the quest for justice for environmental victims. The Tribunal's meetings were not empty talking shops where academics simply reproduced further kilobytes of problematization and prescription, questioned only by other academics from the same intellectual club. It was a dynamic forum in which activists, victims, industrialists, lawyers, medics, and other professionals came together with academics to present individual cases that were then challenged vigorously as in a court of law. The result is not only a cogent and unified view, but also a robust construction of a necessary extension of human rights.

Ultimately, environmental victimization must be seen in the context of the broader global security framework. The traditional security and economic agendas have always dictated the political priorities in relation to environmental concerns. Who better to describe the broader linkages than Ken Saro-Wiwa, Jr (1995: 15):

> *According to* Scorched Earth, *by Williams Thomson, 'in every country except Costa Rica, the military dwarfs secondary sectors such as...environmental protection, whose funding, expertise, and attention are...pre-empted by national security priorities.' The slow destruction of the Ogoni's livelihood by the ecologically careless policies of Shell is of little concern to the Federal government of Nigeria – it's secondary to the need to safeguard the vital oil revenues that provide 90 percent of Nigeria's foreign exchange earnings. Thus, to protest against this devastation is to protest against 'national security priorities.' The instruments for enforcing national security – the armed forces – are turned on law-abiding citizens, because the survival of communities like the Ogoni is effectively judged inimical to the survival of the nation.*

It is time for change. The rethinking of the post-Cold War security agenda to embrace environmental concerns, epitomized by the title of Gwyn Prins' book, *Threats Without Enemies* (1993), increasingly presents environmental victimization as a matter of human security – at the personal, national, and global levels.

As the case of Ken Saro-Wiwa reminds us, however, we must continually question: Security of whom? Security against what? The aim of *Environmental Victims* is to provide better arguments to help us ensure that these questions can be asked more effectively to prevent further events like those perpetrated by the Nigerian government, the oil industry that created the 'black waters' that Mali McGee complains of, and the countless others who are daily implicated in environmental victimization.

REFERENCES

McGee, Mali (1996) 'The Disgrace of Shell Oil.' *Social Justice* 23, 4.

Prins, Gwyn (ed) (1993) *Threats Without Enemies: Facing Environmental Insecurity.* Earthscan Publications: London.

Saro-Wiwa, Ken (1995) 'Man's First Right.' *Amnesty* 75,15.

Williams, Christopher (1997) *Terminus Brain: The Environmental Threats to Human Intelligence.* London: Cassell.

Final Statement to the Tribunal

Ken Saro-Wiwa

My Lord, we all stand before history. I am a man of peace, of ideas. Appalled by the denigrating poverty of my people who live on a richly endowed land, distressed by their political marginalization and economic strangulation, angered by the devastation of their land, their ultimate heritage, anxious to preserve their right to life and to a decent living, and determined to usher to this county as a whole a fair and just democratic system, which protects everyone and every ethnic group and gives us all a valid claim to human civilization, I have devoted all my intellectual and material resources, my very life, to a cause in which I have total belief and from which I cannot be blackmailed or intimidated. I have no doubt at all about the ultimate success of my cause, no matter the trials and tribulations which I and those who believe with me may encounter on our journey. Neither imprisonment nor death can stop our ultimate victory.

I repeat that we all stand before history. I and my colleagues are not the only ones on trial. Shell Oil is here on trial, and it is as well that it is represented by counsel said to be holding a watching brief. The company has, indeed, ducked this particular trial, but its day will surely come and the lessons learnt here may prove useful to it, for there is no doubt in my mind that the ecological war the company has waged in the delta will be called to question sooner than later and the crimes of that war will be duly punished. The crime of the company's dirty wars against the Ogoni people will also be punished.

On trial also are the Nigerian nation, its present rulers, and all those who assist them. Any nation which can do to the weak and disadvantaged what the Nigerian nation has done to the Ogoni loses a claim to independence and to freedom from outside influence. I am not one of those who shies away from protesting injustice and oppression, arguing that they are expected of a military regime. The military does not act alone. They are supported by a gaggle of politi-

---

Ken Saro-Wira delivered this address in Port Harcourt, Nigeria, on September 1, 1995. He was killed by the Nigerian government on November 10, 1995.

cians, lawyers, judges, academics, and businessmen, all of them hiding under the claim that they are only doing their duty, men and women too afraid to wash their pants of their urine. We all stand on trial, my Lord, for by our actions we have denigrated our country and jeopardized the future of our children. As we subscribe to the subnormal and accept double standards, as we lie and cheat openly, as we protect injustice and oppression, we empty our classrooms, degrade our hospitals, fill our stomachs with hunger, and elect to make ourselves the slaves of those who subscribe to higher standards, pursue the truth, and honor justice, freedom, and hard work.

I predict that the scene here will be played and replayed by generations yet unborn. Some have already cast themselves in the role of villains, some are tragic victims, and some still have a chance to redeem themselves. The choice is for each individual.

I predict that the denouement of the riddle of the Niger Delta will soon come. The agenda is being set at this trial. Whether the peaceful ways I have favored will prevail will depend on what the oppressor decides, what signals it sends out to the waiting public.

In my innocence of the false charges I face here, in my utter conviction, I call upon the Ogoni people, the peoples of the Niger Delta, and the oppressed minorities of Nigeria to stand up now and fight fearlessly and peacefully for their rights. History is on their side, God is on their side. For the Holy Koran says in Sura 42, verse 41: 'All those who fight when oppressed incur no guilt, but Allah shall punish the oppressor.' Come the day.

Part One

Concepts

Chapter 1

An Environmental Victimology

Christopher Williams

INTRODUCTION

I do not want to be a victim, and all steps should be taken to
guard against my victimization.

If I am a victim, I want all available help, and expect government, industry, and community to come to my aid.

I do not want to be revictimized by governments, companies,
courts, or the medical and legal professions.

The expression of these demands from the *Permanent Peoples' Tribunal on
Industrial and Environmental Hazards and Human Rights* in Bhopal (PPT,
1992: 13) reflects the urgent need to address environmental victimization,
not only in the form of obvious disasters as at Bhopal, but also the 'creeping
disasters' such as traffic pollution. Law is one form of response, but, as is lucidly
argued by Peter Yeager in *The Limits of Law* (1991), even in state-of-the-art
countries such as the US, statutes alone can never fully address the problems
posed by environmental crime. The difficulties experienced in implementing
statutory compensation in Bhopal provide a poor-nation perspective (BGIA,
1992). There is an obvious need for social justice approaches to parallel formal
legal processes.

THE LIMITS OF 'ENVIRONMENTAL JUSTICE'

The 'environmental justice movement' has provided the most prominent alternative in recent years, at least in the US (see Bryant, 1995; Hofrichter, 1993; Capek, 1993). Yet, although generating valuable insights and an effective basis for informed environmental activism, its broader application is limited, principally for three reasons.

First, 'environmental justice' relies greatly on *subjective (often self-) definitions of victimization*. This may work well in relation to activism, but ultimately the development of justice perspectives, legal or social, requires objective benchmarks. Without objective definitions, how do we apply victim conceptualizations when (i) victims *will not* self-define? What of the 'manic denial' of the Mormons in Nevada, who accept the health problems resulting from nuclear testing as a necessary sacrifice for the good of the state (Gallagher, 1993: 217), or the Indian who attributes lead poisoning to *karma*, not to the illegal smelter next door? How do we accord victim status when (ii) victims *cannot* self-define, for example, with the unborn child or when the outcome is severe intellectual disability from radiation or lead pollution (Williams, 1997). How do we formally identify victims when (iii) national or community leaders will not acknowledge the victimization of those they govern? In the case of cross-border acid rain and the nuclear power disaster at Chernobyl, European governments did not argue for redress because they did not want to encourage precedents that might later be applied in reverse. What of the individuals among the Mescalero Apaches in New Mexico who will eventually suffer health problems because their leaders encourage the importation of hazardous toxic waste to reap the short-term cash rewards?

Second, 'environmental justice' *bases its key arguments on (i) assumptions about power relationships and (ii) group identities, which (iii) reflect the gender, class, and ethnic structures of US society.*

(i) The assumption of the powerless as victim and the powerful as victimizer can lead to a stereotyped view that omits the victimization of those with power and wealth. If wealth and perpetrating environmental crime always go hand-in-hand, how do we conceptualize the Czech industries that polluted rivers then flowing through wealthy Germany, or the threat posed to Norway from Russia's decaying nuclear weapon facilities, or people in Hong Kong and Taiwan who suffer the pollution from mainland China?

(ii) When group identity is the prerequisite of analysis, this can omit the victimization of those scattered within populations who may be vulnerable because, for example, of their clinical status. The link between background radiation from nuclear testing and babies born with Down's Syndrome (Bound et al, 1995: 164–170) involves mothers whose only group identity is that they are over 40, and the true victim group is their unborn children. Class, wealth, race, neighborhood, and gender (of the victims) are irrelevant concepts.

(iii) North American group identities are often not applicable in other settings. For example, the link between minority ethnic groups, poor neighborhoods, and pollution is less strong in regions such as Sweden, China, or the former Soviet Union. Moscow, home to the Russian ethnic power elite, is both one of the wealthiest and one of the most polluted regions in the country. In some settings, standard assumptions about the vulnerability of minority groups seem incorrect. While US research shows that minority ethnic groups suffer more from lead pollution, a study in the UK revealed that Asian children in a London borough suffered less than their white peers (Lansdown and Yule, 1986: 115). Later in this book, Sharon Stephens (1996) argues that the environmental justice frame does not readily embrace a global perspective on children.

Third, because environmental justice usually adopts an activist stance, it often *lacks academic objectivity*. This puts it in a weak position to address conceptual conundra that are familiar to traditional victimology – for example, 'victim participation' in, or 'victim precipitation' of, the circumstances that cause their suffering. Truck drivers who have respiratory ailments because of particulates in exhaust emissions are an obvious case. There are limitations on how activist arguments – often reflecting what the victimologist Ezzat Fattah (1992: 12) has dubbed 'missionary zeal' – will bring about the necessary changes in thinking among hardened politicians for whom self-interest is usually the primary motivation.

Most importantly, the activist position, often manifest as 'nonviolent direct action,' leads to an avoidance of any discussion of violent victim resistance. It may be that most responses in the US have been nonviolent (see Hays et al 1996: 163), but that is not so within a global view. Understanding the violent spirals surrounding environmental victimization is crucial, and, as will be argued later, will probably be the most distinctive feature of a victimology perspective.

ENVIRONMENTAL VICTIMOLOGY

The 'environmental justice' approach has played a vital role in generating an awareness of the human dimensions of environmental change, mobilizing action, and in amassing data. However, its shortcomings propose that other, complementary perspectives now need to be developed. Although currently an unfashionable area of academic study, victimology is the obvious direction to look. The UN Declaration on Victims of...Abuse of Power (1985) provides a starting point, and appears prescient of the likely concerns of an environmental view. It relates specifically to:

> *persons who...have suffered harm...through acts or omissions*
> *that do not yet constitute violations of national criminal laws but*
> *of internationally recognised norms relating to human rights (in*
> *Fattah, 1989).*

An environmental perspective fits within the framework of 'Radical Victimology' (Mawby and Walklate, 1994: 8, 13), which is broadly concerned with human rights, abuses of power, and human suffering irrespective of whether the circumstances are within the ambit of law.

This chapter therefore proposes working definitions, embraces a brief critique of the 'environmental justice' approach, consolidates an emerging epistemology, and outlines issues that could be the concern of an environmental victimology in the future. Finally, it raises the question as to whether, in the context of the scale and nature of environmental victimization, 'justice' or 'security' is the guiding principle.

DEFINITIONS

Who are 'Environmental Victims'?

The notion of victims in relation to the environment has been applied very loosely. The study entitled *Victims of the Environment* (Rossi et al, 1983) only concerns natural disasters such as tornadoes and earthquakes, in which there are no apparent perpetrators. In the headline 'Brain Damage Found in Victims of Bhopal Disaster' (*British Medical Journal*, 1994: 359), meanwhile, the meaning is very different since the environmental factors were not natural and there were clearly culpable entities. Michael Reich adopts the term 'victims,' giving it the same meaning, throughout his book *Toxic Politics: Responding to Chemical Disasters* (1991). In an editorial in *Down to Earth*, India's environmental magazine, Anil Agarwal wrote recently of his experience of cancer: 'I was speaking not just as an environmental activist, but also as an environmental victim' (1995: 4). The term therefore arises naturally in discussion of contemporary environmental problems, but without sufficient precision for academic purposes.

Surprisingly, 'environment' is rarely defined clearly in law or international declarations (Birnie and Boyle, 1992: 2). Through usage, it is now generally taken to comprise four components: chemical, physical, micro-biological, and psychosocial (Lee, in Bullock et al, 1988: 275). The importance of the latter is in relation to corporate abuses of power that manipulate the other three components. An example would be cigarette advertising aimed at children or developing countries.

When formally conceptualizing 'environmental victims,' it is helpful to exclude those more accurately described as 'environmental casualties' – those who suffer as a result of natural disasters. Implicit in the etymology of 'casualties' is the notion of *chance*, while the concept 'victims' embodies the idea of suffering caused by a *deliberate or reckless human act* (including an act of omission). Some circumstances that appear natural may, if analyzed in greater depth, be a consequence of human acts. Those killed by the flooding of the Yangtze River in 1995 may have been victims of deforestation and soil erosion that precipitated the surge (Bird, 1995: 2). Environmental suffering that has affected many generations, such as iodine deficiency, might not be seen as victimization until power relationships are examined. Why are the communities that suffer iodine deficiency forced to live on land that cannot sustain human life properly? Later in this book, Peter Penz (1996) and Meena Singh (1996) further develop the possibilities in relation to transnational victimization and environmental refugees.

Environmental law usually embodies the principle that the outcome of an act must have been 'reasonably foreseeable' for it to constitute an offense. So far, however, most environmental law relates to damage to the physical world, not human injury. If we are considering human injury as a specific outcome, it seems more appropriate to borrow from common law in relation to personal injury offenses, for example assault, where the principle is whether an act is deliberate *or reckless*. Reckless behavior may not embody foreseeing a *specific outcome*, simply that an act could, by its nature, be dangerous to others. The distinction is important. Many claims for compensation for environmentally mediated injury fail because the perpetrator maintains that it was impossible to foresee a specific outcome. For example, the dumping of a particular substance may be excused because it was not known, at the time, to be hazardous (the specific negative outcome was not 'foreseeable'). Yet, in the same circumstances, it might be claimed that to dump the substance was *reckless* because it was not proven safe. In the light of the inability of science to keep up with the problems it causes, this common-sense precautionary principle seems more in accord with human well-being. It is the tradition of common law on personal injury, not environmental protection, that has at its heart the direct well-being of humans.

Intergenerational responsibility must be implicit in any conceptualization because of the time-latent nature of much environmental victimization. The UK *Congenital Disability (Civil Liabilities) Act* 1976, for example, embraces environmentally mediated injury causing 'predisposition (whether or not susceptible to immediate prognosis) to physical or mental defect in the future.' There needs also to be an assumption that both victims and perpetrators might be individuals or groups. Moreover, as will be argued later in relation to causation, it is more appropriate to phrase a definition 'consequence of' rather than 'caused by.'

The outcome of victimization is better described as 'injury' rather than 'suffering.' Injury, as an 'adverse health effect' caused by environmental factors, is neatly defined by Christiani (Chivian et al, 1993: 15): 'any effect that results in altered structure or impaired function, or represents the beginnings of a sequence of events leading to altered structure or function.' Implicit in the term 'injury' is a relationship between two events (cause and effect) that culminate in tangible harm; suffering implies less acute general experiences that might be tolerated without actual injury. This distinction also addresses the debate, common now in poorer countries, that people must endure some environmental suffering for the benefit of economic development, such as dam building. This is an arguable trade-off, but in no justice system is it acceptable to trade off the infliction of human *injury* (or causing death) against economic benefit.

This restriction to 'injury' therefore creates a much narrower frame of reference than that used within the environmental justice debate. Later in this book, Peter Penz argues well for a broadening of the definition when considering transnational dimensions (1996). Pragmatically, if an aim of a victim conceptualization is to change policy, then governments are more likely to respond in relation to tight, manageable definitions, which may be stretched a little, than to 'catch all' concepts that might appear to carry a host of hidden ramifications. As a starting point, 'environmental victims' can therefore be defined as:

> *those of past, present, or future generations who are injured as a consequence of change to the chemical, physical, microbiologi-cal, or psychosocial environment, brought about by deliberate or reckless, individual or collective, human act or act of omission.*

The etymology of 'victim' embodies 'sacrifice,' and this underlying meaning provides a helpful insight. Environmental victims are often, in effect, sacrificed for the benefit of a more powerful entity. It is common for industrial polluters to argue that the environment of a few downstream/downwind individuals must be sacrificed for the greater good of improving national economies or providing employment. It is an interesting coincidence that we find the US government talking formally of toxic no-go areas as 'environmental sacrifice zones' (Walker, 1988: 8). It is even more chilling to find that the local term for children downwind of US nuclear test sites in Nevada, who were born with birth defects, is 'the sacrifice babies' (Gallagher, 1993: 217).

What is an 'Environmental Cause' of Victimization?

Arguing causation is the prerequisite of establishing victim status. Although it is convenient for an activist to talk of problems as 'environmentally caused,' a cause in relation to the definition of 'environmental victim' (above) is human interaction with the environment, not the environment itself – 'environmentally mediated' would be a more apt term, but as yet this has no legal meaning. The understanding of causation requires greater clarity.

Initially, there is a conceptual legacy within law that must be challenged – the requirement that cause and effect must be adjacent. The law is usually framed in terms such as '*proximate* cause,' '*immediate* violence,' or 'a *continuing, operating*, and substantial cause' (Emmet, 1984: 60), reflecting the rule of criminal jurisprudence *cause proxima non remote spectatur*. Existing law has therefore been weak at conceptualizing the indirect nature of environmental victimization. Causal understandings of 'interjacency' are needed – embracing space, time, and multiplicity and interaction of causes and effects – that reflect the 'creeping disasters' or, in the UNICEF term 'slow emergencies,' which now threaten human safety. Court judgments provide one source of evolving concepts, such as that of 'major contributory cause.' *Toxic Torts* (Pugh and Day, 1992) provides a number of examples, which can inform a victimology perspective.

Another approach to the problem can derive from the philosophy of law: the importance of how the causal question is phrased. This is raised by Hart and Honore, in *Causation in the Law* (1985), who cite a judge who considered the form 'Did the injury cause X' inferior to 'Did X result from the injury' (p 87), and argue that their own preferred form is 'Was X the consequence of Y' rather than, 'Was Y the cause of X' (p 135).

This can be exemplified in terms of environmental victimization involving a toxic release that degraded farmland, leading to malnutrition, and then to a high incidence of disability in the local population. In this case, it is easy to argue that the toxic release did not 'cause the disability' – the direct cause was malnutrition. It is less easy to argue that the disability was 'not a consequence' of the release.

How should an 'environmental cause' be defined in legal or quasi-legal terms? One approach is the recognition of environmental causes as the *presence* or *absence* of environmental factors, with each of these embracing the standard distinction in criminal and civil laws defining offenses, and therefore victimization, as stemming from human *acts* or *omissions*. Broadly, 'environmental causes' would then fall into four groups, which are exemplified in Table 1. Specific instances of victimization may well fit within more than one of these four categories, or may fit better in a different category at different periods over a long time scale (ie, in the case of 'creeping disasters').

Table 1 *Defining 'An Environmental Cause of Victimization'*

	Act	*Omission*
Presence of environmental agent	Eg, the *presence* of methyl-isocyanate caused by an act of polluting and poisoning (Union Carbide – Bhopal)	Eg, the *presence* of excess lead in water supplies caused by an *omission* of the duty to provide safe drinking water
Absence of environmental agent	Eg, the *absence* of food and micronutrients leading to malnutrition and brain injury resulting from land degradation caused by the act of dumping toxic waste	Eg, the *absence* of iodine caused by an *omission* of failing to iodize salt in accordance with the law (India)

The model is not hypothetical. Although scattered, laws and judgments already exist that acknowledge these four forms of environmental cause. For example, legislation in some Indian states redresses the *absence* of iodine in the environment by a statutory requirement that iodine is included in salt. Victimization, if iodine is not added to salt, therefore results from an *omission*. A UK Court of Appeal ruling in 1995 found that 'running a sewerage system in an unmaintained state is sufficient to entitle a jury to find the party responsible for the system guilty of causing pollution...failure implied an omission' (Tan, 1995: 11). This provides an instance of *presence/omission*. A definition emerges from this model, that an 'environmental cause' of victimization is 'a presence or absence of chemical, physical, micro-biological, or psycho-social environmental factors, resulting from individual or collective human act or omission, over any time-scale, of which the consequence is human injury.'

9

AN EMERGING EPISTEMOLOGY

'Environmental justice' naturally provides an important contribution to the emerging epistemology of a victim perspective, but mainly from a rich-nation perspective. An issue of *Social Problems* in 1993 (Perrolle) presented key papers concerning class, ethnicity, gender, and race in relation to community and workplace environmental hazards. So, too, do *Toxic Struggles* (Hofrichter, 1993) and *Environmental Justice* (Bryant, 1995). Later in this book, Barten, Fustukian, and de Haan (1996) provide an example, however, of how rich-nation concepts need to be questioned in relation to occupational health.

The links between race and environmental victimization have been well analyzed by Robert Bullard (eg, 1993), but when we look globally, concepts become less easy to generalize. 'Minority groups' can sometimes appear to act against their own interests. In the Solomon Islands, the Western approach of coercive environmental law fails because, although it may seem to be in the best interests of those it relates to, the perceived need for regulation is not shared culturally. A more consensual approach to implementing environmental regulation is required (ELR, 1994: 19).

Cultural perspectives on *determining what constitutes, as distinct from simply stating the experiences of*, environmental victimization are largely missing from the environmental justice debate. An indigenous community may feel little concern over the aesthetics of massive industrial development, but might consider disturbance to a small sacred lake or shrine by minor oil pollution to be extreme eco-vandalism. Alicia Fentiman (1996) provides an example of necessary cultural understanding later in this book.

Specific problems experienced by women, particularly concerning workplace 'fetal protection policies,' are explored in the US and UK contexts in *For Whose Protection* (Kenney, 1992). Feminist concerns are more broadly discussed in relation to North-South divides in *Ecofeminism* (Mies and Shiva, 1992).

However, the feminist contribution to environmental justice has yet to resolve unambiguously a central conflict: that between the rights of women over their bodies and the right to work, and the rights of unborn children not to be exposed to toxic substances. The usual conclusion is that the work environment should be made safe for everyone. Unfortunately, US-oriented discussion does not then go on to consider the dilemma when the work environment is not made safe, which is the case in most poorer countries.

Conflicts between the rights of the mother and the potential unborn victim extend beyond the workplace. In the US, pregnant women who take drugs are being charged with 'distributing' drugs to their babies – a measure that is not accepted by most feminist academics. Should the rights of the unborn victim be subjugated to those of the mother, or is the womb the 'environment' of the fetus and thus subject to the same ethical considerations that we now apply to other human environments? Once born, most nations accept that, in a case of conflict, the best interests of the child take precedence. Why should there be any difference for the unborn child? This takes us back to the need for objective definitions of environmental victimization, and to the first aspect of the emerging epistemology, the status of the unborn victim.

The Unborn Victim

In the light of the copious writings, and common rhetoric, about the need for 'intergenerational justice' over millennia (eg, Laslett and Fishkin, 1992), it is curious that very little has been said about the first stepping stone to this glorious ideal – the immediate next generation – the unborn child. Environmental medicine now provides considerable evidence of the vulnerability of the fetus to environmental toxins and genetic transfer. Yet, in general, this understanding has not been satisfactorily translated into bases for action within either formal or informal justice frames. What is the status of an unborn victim?

One of the few attempts to clarify this question was the UK Law Commission report, *Injuries to Unborn Children* (1973). The authors were of the view that 'where a child is born with a disability which was caused by someone's fault occurring before birth, he [sic] should be entitled to recover damages from that person' (p. 8). In the UK, a recent Court of Appeal ruling concluded that, although under English law an unborn child has no independent legal personality, courts will adopt the civil maxim that 'an unborn child shall be deemed to be born whenever its interests require it' (Tan, 1992: 32). This derived from earlier precedents in Canada and Australia (Law Commission, 1973: 5, i). Without the 'best interests' *caveat*, the ruling would probably have conflicted with lawful abortion in the case of an impaired or unwanted child.

The UK Congenital Disability (Civil Liabilities) Act of 1976 was intended to establish the rights of the unborn victim following confusion surrounding the disabilities caused by the Thalidomide drug, but it is far from ingenuous. Compensation is denied if injury to the parent preceded conception and one or both parents knew of the reproductive risk related to their job. It is unlikely that parents working in, for instance, a nuclear power station could prove that they did not know of the risk factor. In effect, employers can negate their responsibility by telling employees that their work poses a reproductive hazard (see Miller, 1989). Why are the rights of unborn victims diminished by the actions or knowledge of others (their parents) over whom they have no control?

In 1992, a UK woman who kicked a pregnant neighbor in the stomach, causing fatal brain damage to the fetus, was charged with manslaughter. This was the first case of its kind in the UK (*Guardian*, 1992b: 29). A later UK appeal ruling concluded that a man who stabbed his pregnant girlfriend, killing the unborn child, could be convicted of murder or manslaughter (Dyer, 1995: 7).

These cases raise interesting questions. Could a fetus also be a direct victim of a criminal assault? Might injury from an environmental agent constitute an assault, murder, or manslaughter? Could a fetus be awarded compensation for injuries following a conviction for assault against its mother or itself? In the UK, an unborn child *could* be considered eligible for an award from the *Criminal Injuries Compensation Board* (Clark, 1993). A recent decision held: 'We accept that "personal injuries" is a term which can properly be applied to injuries occurring before birth and do not regard the precise stage at which injuries occurred as relevant to our decision' (*R* v. *CICB ex parte* P 1993).

In the US, before 1946, the unborn victim was rarely recognized. Since then, the courts of every North American state have held 'as a development of the common law and despite previous decisions to the contrary,' that a child can recover damages for a prenatal injury (*Guardian*, 1992a). Yet doubt lingers – only a few states will acknowledge injury resulting from events happening *before* conception (eg, high blood lead in a mother, due to employment a year earlier, which later crosses into the fetus). This question might be clarified, however, by applying a 'man-trap' test. If a farmer set a 'man-trap' in 1990, which injured a ten-year-old child in 1995, the farmer would clearly be responsible for the injury. Yet what if the child were only three years old? Again, there seems little doubt that the farmer would be responsible, even though the child had not been conceived at the time of the act that caused the injury.

Many of the concerns of unborn victims are at present outside the remit of law, legislation varies considerably between nations, and cultural dimensions have been ignored. How would victim status for an unborn child be reconciled in some African communities, where babies do not achieve full human status until a naming ceremony at around 18 months of age? It has proved possible to agree on children already born in the *UN Convention on the Rights of the Child*. Is it possible to agree on the rights of the unborn child? Debates to achieve international consistency should establish three points of consensus, which already exist in isolated agreements, that:

- The unborn child has full victim status when this is in its interests, for example, in relation to criminal and civil actions and compensation schemes;
- Acts or omissions, affecting parents before conception, can constitute victimization of an unborn child;
- The rights of the unborn child cannot be diminished by the acts or omissions of others – logically, the concept of contributory negligence cannot be applied to unborn victims.

Avoidance of Liability and Responsibility

Theoretical discussions of causation take us to the practical aspect – deliberate denial of causal links – the avoidance of liability and responsibility by perpetrators. Although a familiar part of mainstream victimology – concerning, for example, children, women (Fattah, 1989), or disabled people (Williams, 1995) – the discussion takes on new dimensions in relation to the environment, for two reasons: the *complexity* of establishing causation creates an easy escape for perpetrators, and the *scale* of remediation is usually immense and so the incentive to avoid liability is great.

At the domestic level, David Dembo, in *Abuse of Power* (1993: 142), provides an excellent synopsis of diversionary tactics employed by industrial and other corporate victimizers to avoid liability:

- Deny the problem;
- Put it in perspective;
- Blame a hysterical public;
- Blame the victim;
- Try to divide the victims; and
- When possible, settle with the government if it will be less costly.

Delaying court hearings so that victims and witnesses die, 'papering out' court proceedings by producing an excess of irrelevant data, and regular press releases providing copious information that is always the same are other common approaches. Another common tactic is for corporate polluters to accuse communities of creating the environmental problems for which they are, in the main, responsible. As discussed below, *Shell* adopted this approach in relation to Ogoniland (Slayter, 1995: 16). An easy excuse for avoiding liability is provided when people migrate to a disaster area and attempt to claim compensation, as at Bhopal. Yet why should there be any surprise at such responses by people in poor communities? They are a natural consequence of the original victimization and, more significantly, of delays in admitting liability and providing redress. Environmental victimology could usefully develop understandings of these social dynamics, because although the corporate polluter may win a court case, it will certainly not win in the eyes of the global community and therefore lose that priceless asset, public trust.

Governments also become conspirators in avoidance. In the Bhopal case, special legislation *diminished* the rights of victims through giving the state absolute control over claims and denying liability for future generations (*Bhopal Gas Leak Disaster [Processing of Claims] Act*, 1985). The US *Radiation Exposure Compensation Act*, 1990, operates similarly through excluding regions in Nevada where fallout from weapons testing was greatest, and again denying liability to future generations (Gallagher, 1993: *xxvii*).

The international context provides even greater possibilities for avoidance. In some situations, time-scales mean that responsible entities will either disappear or change dramatically, and this does not just concern intergenerational responsibility over centuries. Chernobyl provides the obvious example – the responsible nation ceased to exist three years after the nuclear disaster. Russia then claimed control of the nuclear industry, but maintained it had no liability because it too was a victim. (This is akin to 'I am not guilty of assault because I hurt my fist when I hit you!') Guilty individuals were then named by the new state, without any trial; the real culprits became high-ranking officials in the new government. The government controls the courts (Fedorychyk, 1994: 5). South

Africa provides another unique dimension (Singh, 1996). It seems unlikely that black environmental activists would hold the Mandela government accountable for environmental problems created by the former apartheid regime.

How acceptable is the claim that responsibility is annulled by an apparent change of regime? If this question is not addressed, one result might be that in the future, regimes may commonly abdicate power as a means of avoiding responsibility for environmental disasters – the nation-state equivalent of going bankrupt and setting up again under a new name. One answer would be to hold banks and other international funding agencies responsible for the environmental victimization they have financed.

Environmental problems now create land areas that have negative value, and the incentive to cut the line of responsibility is obvious. In recent years, a dilapidated oil refinery was sold for just one dollar because of its toxic legacy, and the US Energy Department 'is now reconciled to writing off some nuclear factory sites as "national sacrifice zones," where a complete cleanup would be prohibitively expensive' (Walker, 1988: 8). Thinking further, might we see large nations *force* independence on environmental disaster regions to avoid responsibility? Will we see future presidents tell local mayors that they can have 'countries' of their own, which happen to come with a decaying nuclear power station? What will be the reaction of potential environmental victims in such circumstances – 'freedom struggles' to fight *against* independence?

Our formal knowledge of corporate avoidance strategies is now quite comprehensive, although much of the work is probably of more help to perpetrators than victims. Less thought has been given to the ultimate form of avoidance – if you create an environmental problem, give it away. The approaches reflect what Michael Reich terms 'a strategy of diversion combined with a strategy of dissociation' (1991: 263). Avoidance will increase until we learn to understand and counter both these strategies *in parallel*.

Victim Syndrome

Avoidance of liability leads to failures to prevent or redress victimization, and a social impact that has been dubbed the 'environmental victim syndrome.' Although considerable attention has been given to clinical or psychological outcomes, for example, cancer or post-traumatic stress (eg, Bass et al, 1993), much less attention has been given to psychosocial outcomes of environmental victimization. David Marples' book, *The Social Impact of the Chernobyl Disaster* (1988), is one of the few examples of a comprehensive case study, and *Who Pays the Price: The Sociocultural Context of Environmental Crisis* (Johnston, 1994) provides a more analytical, anthropological perspective.

It is possible to gain an impression of the more obvious concerns from informal accounts. Rosemarie Gillespie (1994: 13) reports, from firsthand experience, that the results of industrial victimization from an RTZ copper mine in Bougainville include 'a deep sense of social malaise...which expressed itself in clan tensions,

depression, alcohol abuse, rage, traffic accidents, and incidents of violence....'
Green Cross detects in the former Soviet Union 'instability in contaminated regions, caused by the feeling of "being left alone" with the toxic threats' (GC, 1994). More formal typologies arise in relation to experiences in hazardous work environments. Roberts (1993: 74) determines anxiety, fatalism, depression, lowered self-esteem, and anomie and describes exploitation, selfishness, and a loss of confidence in commercial practice, government, science, and organized labor.

Women may suffer particular problems in situations where they are especially valued for their reproductive capabilities. Any perceived threat to reproductive health can lead to alienation. Padma Prakash (1985) describes how women who were conspicuously injured in Bhopal suffered from divorce, abandonment, and violence. Myth can be as potent as fact. Madhursree Mukerjee puts the Bhopal situation bluntly: 'Because reproductive disorders are so commonplace, young women who were exposed to the gas are assumed to be infertile, and no one will marry them' (1995: 16). Children, too, may become marginalized. From Belarus, in a village where Chernobyl victims are receiving medical help, it is reported that 'there is tension between the local children and "these Chernobyl kids" who are bullied and ignored' (Barnett, 1994: 9).

Migration is a common consequence of environmental problems, as Meena Singh discusses in Chapter 7 (see Myers, 1995). The implications for a community can be subtle. Who leaves? In northwest Bohemia, where the burning of lignite coal produces severe air pollution, it is the doctors and other professionals who migrate first. Family life can be disrupted if some members wish to move from an affected region and others want to remain. This was an explanation for increased divorces among Welsh farmers in areas affected by Chernobyl nuclear disaster fallout.

Do specific forms of environmental victimization produce specific outcomes? The problems caused by iodine deficiency are now quite well documented. Researchers from the *Programme Against Micronutrient Malnutrition* describe the situation in the Philippines: 'The result is poor productivity; a nation not up to par economically; a substandard quality of life for its citizens; and a country which cannot compete globally' (PAMM, 1995: 2). From a local perspective, social problems in villages in northern India are described by Hetzel (1989: 92) as 'a major block to human and social development,' including 'a high degree of apathy' (even affecting domestic animals) and 'effects on initiative and decision-making.' In one Chinese village, known locally as 'the village of idiots,' 'the economic development of the village was retarded.... [N]o truck driver or teacher was available. Girls from other villages did not want to marry and live in the village.'

In north Indian villages, in which contaminated drinking water is reportedly causing a 40 percent incidence of intellectual disability (Saxena, 1991: 3), there is an absence of village headmen, the villagers cannot remember the last time they held a village meeting, and they say that statutory health and education services have disappeared, but are not motivated to complain. This appears to be a manifestation of a concern expressed by the UN (1991): 'learning disorders are a particular source of danger because they may affect an entire population and even impair its capacity to resist exploitation.'

Environmental factors that affect the brain and cause intellectual decline have predictable outcomes in terms of the capabilities of a community, but might less obviously affect social order. Needleman et al (in Barten, 1992: 15) found what appears to be an insignificant relationship between lead intake and an IQ deficit of 2 to 5 points. However, the effect trebled the number of children with IQ scores below 80 and there was a threefold reduction in the number with IQ scores above 125. An IQ of around 80 is directly related to increased criminal activity (because those concerned are vulnerable to criminal influence, but are still capable enough to carry out criminal activities). Most industrialized communities already have a skill shortage of technically able labor at around IQ 125, which would be exacerbated by this lead-related IQ deficit.

Another danger is that environmental health problems create 'false norms' within a community. The Programme Against Micronutrient Malnutrition reports that in the Philippines, iodine deficiency disease 'is so commonplace, that many feel it is a normal part of life' (PAMM, 1995: 2). In the 19th century, in regions of Switzerland in which iodine deficiency created large numbers of cretins, families who did not have such a child were considered not to have been blessed by God. Within communities, poor health, low intelligence, and the psychosocial symptoms of victimization become an accepted part of a community's expectation of life.

Studies of communities following the Hiroshima and Nagasaki bombs provide a good basis for understanding the unique outcomes of nuclear contamination. Victims suffered occupational discrimination, marriage opportunities were affected, and any minor illness gave rise to fears about genetic health problems (Lifton, 1967: 106). Lifton coined the term 'nuclear numbing' to describe the form of denial among the post-bombing society in Hiroshima and Nagasaki.

Lifton's work is echoed in analyses of the Chernobyl disaster. Fedorychyk reports a 'syndrome of the victim,' which 'spreads among people and means that people consider themselves doomed':

> they don't want to have long-term plans...[and] their life attitude
> is aggressively parasitical.... [P]eople have lost their confidence
> in the State, because it acted against people; in science, because
> it caused the problems which it could not solve; in medicine,
> because it was used as a political instrument; in world
> community...people in Ukraine try to forget about Chernobyl in
> order not to go mad.... [T]his generation will have serious
> discrimination problems in getting married (1994: 2).

An awareness of 'victim syndrome' can form the basis for specific case studies and, more importantly, for remediation strategies. An affected community seems likely to display the following symptoms: family disruption; alienation, particularly of women and children; reduced marriage and employment prospects –

because of a perceived genetic or health legacy; a perception that life has no future; social apathy; community and personal abandonment; loss of confidence in social institutions; 'denial' of the victimization; false norms; economic dislocation; local and domestic conflict; skills deficit; migration; increased criminality by those of low, but not clinically diagnosed, IQ deficit; exploitation; and a breakdown of traditional structures for community management.

Because it arises from a quasi-clinical patient/victim outlook, the psychosocial evidence usually omits two crucial aspects. First is the *resilience* of victims, natural or assisted. In Chapter 3, Sharon Stephens describes how involvement in activism can change adverse outcomes among children. A similar effect was noted in relation to *Love Canal* (Stone and Levine, 1986). Second, there is the possibility of violent resistance, which will be discussed later.

FUTURE ISSUES

The distinction between 'epistemology' and 'issues' is, to some extent, arbitrary. However, the preceding topics have attracted sufficient attention to argue that there is at least a distinct body of knowledge and formal analysis relating to them. The following three areas of discussion exemplify concerns that are evident from general discourse and the media, but have not yet, it seems, attracted significant attention from the academic community.

Environmental Blackmail

The degree to which the environment will become a vehicle for domestic and international blackmail is difficult to predict and little thought has been given to possible responses. On the domestic level, threats equate with other forms of blackmail. The Mafia has taken an interest in toxic waste in the US and Italy (Block and Scarpitti, 1982; Bond, 1994: 3), which extends to threats to dump waste on private land if landowners do not pay up. (This gives a new meaning to the term 'environmental protection'!). In 1994, most of Lithuania was without electricity for a day because of a Mafia bomb threat at a nuclear power station. It was not reported whether money changed hands, but the incident raises the possible specter of 'double blackmail,' in which a poor state turns to its wealthy neighbors and suggests that they might pay the sum demanded, because they are just as likely to suffer if the threat is carried out.

On an international scale, Martin Woollacott concludes of Ukraine's request that the G-7 nations fund the closure of the still-functioning reactors at Chernobyl and build new plants:

> *A Chernobyl pay-off carries with it serious dangers. One is that it could be a precedent for other such payments to governments elsewhere. The idea that you can pressure the wealthier nations into giving you aid by persisting in running dangerous*

*technologies whose effects, when they go wrong, will not be
confined to your own country, is dangerously close to blackmail
(1994: 22).*

Paul Brown (1994: 37) describes similar circumstances surrounding the funding
by the European Bank of Reconstruction and Development of new reactors at
Mochovce in Slovakia. Mochovce is near the Austrian border, and Brown
concludes, 'there are plenty more unfinished reactors and safety work to do in the
stricken lands of the East – and the prospect of more Chernobyls is a loaded gun
to hold at the head of bankers.' 'Paying up' is not necessarily the answer.
European aid to assist Bulgaria to improve safety at its Kozloduy station was
given on the understanding that the reactor was closed down, but in the winter of
1995 it was brought back into operation. The official EC comment was dry, but
provides an indication of how crudely negotiations of this nature now operate: 'It
seems they've gone back on the agreement. That raises the question of whether
they should get any more funds' (Traynor, 1995: 13).

International blackmail may entail more subtle cross-border implications.
Teichman and Barry reported in 1992: '...financially strapped Khazakhstan is
accepting and burying South Korean nuclear waste at $1,000 per kilo and hoping
to leverage its willingness to accept hazardous waste against the Ukraine for
badly needed food' (Tufts, 1992). Did Khazakhstan learn a trick from the
Ukraine? If you do not have your own nuclear disaster to use as a threat, then
import one.

Threats may well be linked to other conflicts. The firing of oil wells by Iraqi
forces during the Gulf conflict demonstrates that blackmail in the form of eco-
war is no longer science fiction. During the 1994 to 1995 Chechnya–Russia
conflict, the Chechen President Dzhokhar Dudayev threatened terrorist attacks
on nuclear power stations and weapons stores if Russian forces deposed his
government. As a former high-ranking officer in the USSR Air Force, he was
well placed to use such tactics.

Whatever the future scenarios for environmental blackmail, it is certain that
if threats are ever carried out, there will be significant victimization of entirely
innocent third parties, avoidance will be easy, and redress virtually impossible.
As yet, there seem to be no policies to address environmental blackmail, as there
are, for example, in relation to plane hijacks. Perhaps the starting point is for the
global community to use the word 'blackmail' overtly, in response to comments
such as that reported from President Leonid Kuchma of the Ukraine about the
ongoing threat from the Chernobyl reactors: 'If the world, particularly Europe, is
really concerned about safety, then let us look at the financial situation'
(*Independent*, 1995:2).

Violence

There has been growing interest in environmental problems as a source of conflict between nations or regions in relation to scarcity of essential resources such as water (eg, Bächler et al, 1993). However, little academic consideration has been given to the violent spirals deriving from environmental victimization, a circumstance that is distinct from conflicts over natural resources.

In Bougainville (Solomon Islands), indigenous people's resistance to pollution from copper mining by Rio Tinto Zinc (RTZ) included blowing up electricity pylons, which brought about the closure of the mine (Gillespie, 1994). This catalyzed an independence struggle, which has transmuted into an ongoing conflict with blockades and a shoot-to-kill policy involving local people, RTZ, the Papuan militia, and the Australian government (Pacific Research, 1994: 19–30). The outcome is in no one's interests, particularly that of RTZ, which consequently experienced difficulties in attracting financial backing for other projects.

Even nonviolent popular resistance to oil pollution caused by Shell in Ogoniland (Niger Delta) provided the opportunity for widespread violence and human rights abuses by state security forces (Rowell, 1995: 6; Orr, 1995: 15). Environmental activism then embraced broader political aims, principally a fairer distribution of oil revenues in favor of the Delta region. One refinery was forced to close down because (according to Shell) of fears for staff safety. Four traditional chiefs were killed, it was claimed, by activists, which then led to the 'judicial murder' of Ken Saro-Wiwa and other environmental activists following a show trial and international protest in 1995. Shell also admitted importing weapons into Nigeria to help the police protect its oil installations (Duodu, 1996:1).

Shell maintains that environmental damage was not the 'cause' of the spirals of violence – an argument that probably would not hold if we apply the 'consequence' test proposed within the definition of causation outlined above. International protest against Shell suggests that public perception does make the causal link, but we still lack the necessary formal conceptualizations. The starting point is an understanding that environmental victimization can be considered, both informally and legally, as an act of violence (Williams, 1996b). If this is established, it is then not difficult to comprehend that the response to corporate violence may be public violence, provoked by the initial victimization (see Hays et al 1996:163). The prevention of violence should *not*, therefore, be an implicit assumption within environmental victimology. As argued later, if it is the only option to ensure human security, it is morally defensible.

How Do Victim Responses Evolve?

At this point, it should have become clear that an important purpose of environmental victimology will be to understand the spirals of violence associated with victimization. It is therefore important to develop an awareness of how victim responses appear to evolve over time in relation to violence. From a global perspective it is possible to hypothesize a generalized pattern (see Figure 1):

1   *Passive acceptance*, which seems evident in regions where people are faced
    with other more pressing problems, eg, following major political transition
    as in Eastern and Central Europe, where pre-1989 environmental activism
    has nearly disappeared, and in South Africa (see Singh, Chapter 7); then,
2   *Confrontation and litigation*. Bhopal provides a current example. As
    Sarangi records in Chapter 5, there was the potential for violent confronta-
    tion at the mass protests in the first two years following the disaster, but
    activists opted instead to use legal channels for redress. That potential did
    not become actual violence is worthy of analysis. The promise of
    compensation, combined with a tradition of tolerance, may be part of the
    explanation. Then either:
3   *Violence*, which is often linked to other political action, as in Bougainville
    and Ogoniland. The link between environmental and political activism was
    most evident in the Eastern bloc before 1989, and was demonstrated more
    recently in the response of people in Tahiti to the French nuclear tests in the
    South Pacific (Williams, 1996b); or:
4   *Nonviolent community conflict resolution*, as exemplified by the US Good
    Neighbor Agreements (Lewis and Henkels, Chapter 8).

The latter is obviously a desirable goal and the key to achieving this end is a
public right of access to environmental information. In the US, where recent
freedom of information legislation has led to local monitoring and publication of
industrial discharges, solution-oriented community action with (rather than
against) industrial polluters is emerging in the form of 'Good Neighbor
Agreements' (GNP, 1994). Pollution statistics and worst-case scenarios are
appearing in local papers, and software for domestic PCs is becoming available
to help with local analysis. One result is that some polluters have realized how
much money they are losing through their factory chimneys in the form of expensive, retrievable substances. Lewis and Henkels (1996) in Chapter 8 further
explain both the broad principles and the details of Good Neighbor Agreements.
The question raised by this approach is: How applicable is it in a poor-nation
setting where community resources do not match those in the US? Might Good
Neighbor Agreements have prevented the violence in Bougainville or Ogoni?

CONCLUSION – JUSTICE OR SECURITY?

Environmentally mediated injury is now a significant aspect of personal victimization, resulting from both conspicuous and 'creeping' disasters. Environmental
law has a restricted potential to address this threat; thus the need for parallel social
justice perspectives. The 'environmental justice movement' has been the most
prominent alternative so far, but it is limited because of its subjective definitions,
assumptions about power relationships and group identities, and an activist stance.
    Traditional victimology is the obvious source of inspiration for a comple-
mentary approach but, surprisingly, it has not yet embraced an environmental

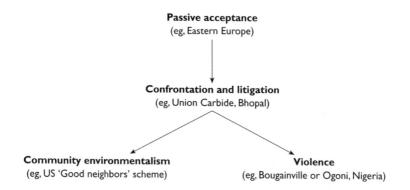

Figure 1 *Evolution of Victim Responses (in Relation to Current Situations)*

perspective. The *UN Declaration on Victims of...Abuse of Power* (1985) provides a clear starting point, from which definitions of 'environmental victims' and 'environmental cause' can be developed.

From diverse sources it is possible to construct an emerging epistemology in relation to environmental victims. It addresses concerns such as the status of the unborn victim, avoidance of liability and responsibility, and a 'victim syndrome.' Possible future issues, as yet largely ignored by academics, are likely to include environmental blackmail, spirals of violence, and the ways in which victim responses evolve. Other areas of concern, not discussed within this article, are cultural dimensions (eg, Fentiman, 1996), the cost consequences of victimization (eg, Williams, 1996c), theories of innovation and change (eg, Hetzel, 1989: 148; Lansdown and Yule, 1986: 271), educational implications, case studies of specific outcomes (eg, Williams, 1996a), and how to conceptualize disparate victimizer groups, for example, car drivers.

Justice or Security?

The takeoff point for this view of an environmental victimology was a brief, functional critique of the environmental justice approach. Yet the scale and nature of contemporary environmental victimization prompt a deeper question: Is 'justice' in any form always an adequate reference point?

Common ethics accept that individual conscience can and should, in certain circumstances, be put above the law. How else do we sanction the actions of those who fight against 'lawful,' but unjust regimes such as apartheid in South Africa, or find guilty those who commit atrocities, through following 'lawful' orders, at trials such as Nuremberg? Similarly, there is a circumstance in which the day-to-day principles of justice can be suspended for a greater good – that of *security*. The taking of human life, enforced labor in the form of military service, and the appropriation of privately owned resources are examples of justice norms that can be set aside in the interests of (usually national) military security. There is also one significant example of a shift from justice to security ethics in an environmental context: China's one-child policy. Injustice at the family level is 'accepted' (by the state, most educated Chinese, and more recently the international community) to ensure the security of a whole population through preventing ecological overload.

At what point does environmental victimization start to represent a threat to human survival sufficient to permit us to shift from the ethics of justice to those of security? In Chapter 2, Peter Penz (1996) hints that cross-border victimization, such as pollution, may sanction military actions against another nation. This would represent a shift from a principle of international justice as the guiding ethic – the autonomy of nation-states over their territory – to the ethics of national security. How long before we see the security forces of a wealthy nation 'take out,' by force, an upstream/upwind polluting factory in a neighboring state, which has been the basis for environmental blackmail?

The 1995 Commission on Global Governance seems prescient of this scenario, proposing (albeit in another context) that:

> ...in certain severe circumstances [fundamental human rights]
> must prevail over the ordinary rights of individual states...where
> people are subjected to massive suffering and distress.... [T]here
> is a need to weigh a state's right to autonomy against its
> people's right to security (CGG, 1995: 68,71).

Note the compatibility between this assertion and the UN Declaration on Victims, quoted earlier. Within this new framework, security needs might prevail over justice not only between nations, but also between a state and its citizens. There are three possibilities:

1   *when a state fails to protect its citizens from domestic threats*, as in Bougainville (Australia had trusteeship) and Ogoniland – and remember that in these examples victims did in fact 'take out' the industries that threatened their security, through actual or fear of violence;
2   *when the state diminishes the rights of its victim-citizens through legislation*, as in relation to the Union Carbide (Bhopal) disaster and US weapons testing; and
3   *when the state is victimizer*, such as in the case of Iraq's deliberate poisoning of the waters that sustain the life of the Marsh Arabs.

This line of thinking generates an obvious question. If, between states and between state and citizen, the need to ensure human security 'must prevail' over justice norms as reflected in international or domestic law, and we accept the inference that military force may then legitimately be used against the entity posing the threat to human security, do we then accept that the principle extends to violence by community activists against the threat posed by the lead smelter down the road? From the common law perspective on personal injury, we hardly need the Commission's sanction. Morally, the notion of self-defense could appear sufficient.

To illustrate the need to rethink our response to the new environmental security threats of the post-Cold War era, Gwyn Prins remarks, 'You can't shoot an ozone hole' (1991: 12). The illustration is thought-provoking, but just one end of a spectrum – you *can* bomb a filthy factory. Understanding the spirals of violence, which appear inevitable when our ethical basis is forced to shift from justice to security, is the broader purpose of an environmental victimology, and is distinct from the remit that the environmental justice movement currently sets itself. We need urgently to develop better *and broader* understandings of environmental victimization, and through these to develop a consensus on the relationships between justice norms and the sometimes conflicting demands of human security.

REFERENCES

Agarwal, Anil (1995) 'Editorial.' *Down to Earth* December 31.

Bächler, G, V Böge, S Klötzli, and S Libiszweski (1993) *The Destruction of Nature as a Cause of Conflict.* Münster: Agenda-Verlag.

Barnett, Lynn (1994) 'Coping with the Psychological Aftermath of Chernobyl.' *Global Security* (Winter).

Barten, Françoise (1992) *Environmental Lead Exposure of Children in Managua, Nicaragua.* Den Haag: CIP-Gegevens Koninlijke Bibliotheek.

Barten, Françoise, Suzanne Fustukian, and Sylvia de Haan (1996) 'The Occupational Health Needs of Workers: The Need for a New International Approach.' *Social Justice* 23,4 (Winter).

Bass, Corin and Janet Kenny (1993) *Beyond Chernobyl: Women Respond.* London: Envirobook.

BGIA (1992) *Compensation Disbursement: Problems and Possibilities.* Bhopal: Bhopal Group for Information and Action.

Bird, Matyann (1995) 'Yangtze Death Toll on Rise.' *Independent on Sunday* (July 9).

Birnie, Patricia W and Alan E Boyle (1992) *International Law and the Environment.* Oxford: Clarendon Press.

Block, Alan and Frank Scarpitti (1982) *Poisoning for Profit: The Mafia and Toxic Waste in America.* New York: William Morrow.

Bond, Michael (1994) 'Poisonous Trail of the Toxic Cowboys.' *The European* (May 27).

Bound, John, Brian Francis, and Peter Harvey (1995) 'Down's Syndrome: Prevalence and Ionising Radiation in an Area of North West England, 1957–1991.' *Journal of Epidemiology and Community Health* 49.

British Medical Journal (1994) 'Brain Damage Found in Victims of Bhopal Disaster.' *British Medical Journal* 309.

Brown, Paul (1994) 'Slovak Debate Sums Up Nuclear Power Struggle.' *The Guardian* (December 31).

Bryant, Bunyan (1995) *Environmental Justice.* Boston: Island Press.

Bullard, Robert D1 (1993) *Confronting Environmental Racism: Voices from the*

Grassroots. Massachusetts: South End Press.

Bullock, Alan, Oliver Stallybrass, and Stephen Trombley (1988) *Dictionary of Modern Thought*. London: Fontana Press.

Capek, Stella M (1993) 'The "Environmental Justice" Frame: A Conceptual Discussion and an Application.' *Social Problems* 40,1: 5–24.

CGG (1995) *Our Global Neighbourhood – The Report of the Commission on Global Governance*. Oxford: Oxford University Press.

Chivian, E, M McCally, H Hu, and A Haines (1993) *Critical Condition: Human Health and the Environment*. Cambridge, Mass: MIT Press.

Clark, J (1993) Private Correspondence from the Criminal Injuries Compensation Board (UK).

Dembo, David, Ward Morehouse, and Lucinda Wykle (1993) *Abuse of Power – Social Performance of Multinational Corporations: The Case of Union Carbide*. New York: New Horizons Press.

Duodu, Cameron (1996) 'Shell Admits Importing Guns for Nigerian Police.' *The Observer* (January 28).

Dyer, Clare (1995) 'Judge Wrong over "Killing" of Baby.' *The Guardian* (November 25).

ELR (1994) 'Pacific Legal Developments.' *New Zealand Environmental Law Reporter* 1.

Emmet, Dorothy (1984) *The Effectiveness of Causes*. London: Macmillan.

Fattah, Ezzat A. (1992) *Towards a Critical Victimology*. London: Macmillan. (1989) 'On Some Neglected Types of Victimisation – Victims of Abuse of Power.' E Fattah (ed) *The Plight of Victims in Modern Society*. London: Macmillan.

Fedorychyk, Serghiy (1994) 'Experiences of Chernobyl.' Unpublished paper presented to the Permanent Peoples' Tribunal, London.

Fentiman, Alicia (1996) 'The Anthropology of Oil: The Impact of the Oil Industry on the Fishing Communities in the Niger Delta.' *Social Justice* 23,4 (Winter).

Gallagher, Carole (1993) *American Ground Zero: The Secret Nuclear War*. Massachusetts: The MIT Press.

GC (Green Cross) (1994) *Green Cross – The Legacy Programme*. Geneva: Green Cross.

Gillespie, Rosemarie (1994) 'The Case of Bougainville.' Unpublished paper presented to the Permanent Peoples' Tribunal, London.

GNP (Good Neighbor Project) (1994) The Good Neighbor Handbook: A Community-Based Strategy for Sustainable Industry. Waverly: Good Neighbor Project.

Guardian (1992a) 'A Child Disabled by Pre-Natal Injury Can Sue for Damages.' *The Guardian* (May 20).

Guardian (1992b) 'Woman Killed Unborn Baby by Kicking Neighbour in Stomach.' *The Guardian* (May 15).

Hart, H L A and A M Honore (1985) *Causation in the Law*. Oxford: Oxford University Press.

Hays, Scott, Michael Ester and Carol Hays (1996) 'Radical Environmentalism and Crime' in Edwards, Sally, Terry Edwards and Charles Fields, *Environmental Crime and Criminality: Theoretical and Practical Issues*. New York: Garland Publishing.

Hetzel, Basil S (1989) *The Story of Iodine Deficiency*. New York: Oxford University Press.

Hofrichter, Richard (ed) (1993) *Toxic Struggles: The Theory and Practice of Environmental Justice*. Philadelphia: New Society Publishers.

Independent (1995) 'Chernobyl May Not Be Shut Down.' *The Independent* (November 12).

Johnston, Barbara R (1994) Who Pays the Price? *The Sociocultural Context of Environmental Crisis. London:* Island Press.

Kenney, Sally J (1992) *For Whose Protection? Reproductive Hazards and Exclusionary Policies in the US and Britain.* Michigan: University of Michigan Press.

Lansdown, Richard and William Yule (1986) *Lead Toxicity: History and Environmental Impact.* Baltimore: Johns Hopkins University Press.

Laslett, Peter and James S Fishkin (eds) (1992) *Justice Between Age Groups and Generations.* New Haven: Yale University Press.

Law Commission (1973) *Injuries to Unborn Children – Working Paper No 47.* London: The Law Commission.

Lewis, Sanford and Diane Henkels (1996) 'Good Neighbor Agreements.' *Social Justice* 23,4 (Winter).

Lifton, Robert Jay (1967) *Death in Life: The Survivors of Hiroshima.* London: Weidenfeld and Nicolson.

Marples, David R (1988) *The Social Impact of the Chernobyl Disaster.* New York: St Martin's Press.

Mawby, R I and S Walklate (1994) *Critical Victimology: International Perspectives.* London: Sage.

Mies, Maria and Vandana Shiva (1992) *Ecofeminism: Reconnecting a Divided World.* New Delhi: Kali for Women.

Miller, Christopher E (1989) 'Radiological Risks and Civil Liability.' *Journal of Environmental Law* 1.

Mukerjee, Madhursree (1995) 'Persistently Toxic: The Union Carbide Accident in Bhopal Continues to Harm.' *Scientific American* (June).

Myers, Norman and Jennifer Kent (1995) *Environmental Exodus: An Emergent Crisis in the Global Arena.* Washington: Climate Institute.

Orr, David (1995) 'Ogoni Spirits Unbroken by New Repression.' *The Independent* (November 30).

Pacific Research (1994) 'The Failure of the Bougainville Peace Talks.' *Pacific Research* (November).

PAMM (1995) 'Misconception of IDD Prevalence Obstacle to Strong Legislation.' *PAMM News* (January).

Penz, Peter (1996) 'Environmental Victims and State Sovereignty: A Normative Analysis.' *Social Justice* 23,4 (Winter).

Perrolle, Judith A (1993) *Social Problems – Special Issue on Environmental Justice.* Lafayette: Society for the Study of Social Problems.

PPT (Permanent Peoples' Tribunal) (1992) *Findings and Judgments.* London: Permanent Peoples' Tribunal.

Prakesh, Padma (1985) 'Neglect of Women's Health Issues.' *Delhi Economic and Political Weekly* (December 14).

Prins, Gwyn and Robbie Stamp (1991) *Top Guns and Toxic Whales: The Environment and Global Security.* London: Earthscan.

Pugh, C and M Day (1992) *Toxic Torts.* London: Cameron May.

Reich, Michael R (1991) *Toxic Politics: Responding to Chemical Disasters.* Ithaca: Cornell University Press.

Roberts, J Timmons (1993) 'Psychosocial Effects of Workplace Hazardous Exposures: Theoretical Synthesis and Preliminary Findings.' *Social Problems* 40.

Rossi, Peter H, James D Wright, Eleanor Weber-Burdin, and Joseph Pereira (1983) *Victims of the Environment: Loss from Natural Hazards in the United States*. New York: Plenum Press.

Rowell, Andy (1995) 'Trouble Flares in the Delta of Death.' *The Guardian* (November 8).

Sarangi, Satinath (1996) 'The Movement in Bhopal and Its Lessons.' *Social Justice* 23,4 (Winter).

Saxena, Rajiv (1991) 'Excess Fluoride Leaves in Its Wake a Village of Cretins.' *Sunday Observer* (India, December 15).

Singh, Meena (1996) 'Environmental Security and Displaced People in Southern Africa.' *Social Justice* 23,4 (Winter).

Slayter, Adrian (1995) 'Why the Nigerian People Can Be Sure of Shell (letter).' *The Guardian* (November 15).

Stephens, Sharon (1996) 'Environmental Justice: The Case of Children.' *Social Justice* 23,4 (Winter).

Stone, Russell A and Adeline G Levine (1986) 'Reactions to Collective Stress: Correlates of Active Citizen Participation at Love Canal.' *Prevention in Human Services* 4.

Tan, Ying Hui (1995) 'Unmaintained Sewage System Caused Pollution.' *The Independent* (January 31).

Tan, Ying Hui (1992) 'Children Have Right to Sue for Pre-Natal Injuries.' *The Independent* (April 8).

Traynor, Ian (1995) 'Europe Faces Nuclear Nightmare.' *The Guardian* (October 26).

Tufts (1992) *International Security – The Environmental Dimension (Tufts International Symposium)*. Massachusetts: Tufts University.

UN (1991) Document E/CN Sub 2/1991/31. New York: United Nations.

Walker, Martin (1988) 'Ageing Atom Industry in Cash Crisis.' *The Guardian* (December 12).

Williams, Christopher (1996a) 'The Environmental Causes of Intellectual Injury – A Victim Perspective.' *International Review of Victimology* (forthcoming).

Williams, Christopher (1996b) 'Environmental Victimization and Violence.' *Aggression and Violent Behaviour* (forthcoming).

Williams, Christopher (1996c) 'Environmental Victims – Arguing the Costs.' Environmental Values (forthcoming). (1995) *Invisible Victims: Crime and Abuse Against People with Learning Difficulties*. London: Jessica Kingsley.

Williams, Christopher (1997) *Terminus Brain: The Environmental Threats to Human Intelligence*. London: Cassell.

Woollacott, Martin (1994) 'Nuclear Accidents Waiting to Happen.' *The Guardian* (July 6).

Yeager, Peter C. (1991) *The Limits of Law: The Public Regulation of Private Pollution*. Cambridge: Cambridge University Press.

Chapter 2

Environmental Victims and State Sovereignty: A Normative Analysis

Peter Penz

INTRODUCTION

Today's world is characterized by dramatic instances of people being poisoned by radiation (Chernobyl in the Ukraine), deadly industrial gases (Bhopal in India), industrial pollution of water (Minamata Bay in Japan), and toxic land-dumps (Love Canal in the United States). Less dramatic but more pervasive are the persistent forms of poisoning by industrial pollution (industrial cities in Eastern Europe, the cotton fields of Central Asia, the 'petrochemical corridor' along the Mississippi in Louisiana in the United States) and disease caused by untreated sewage. More than one million people are displaced every year from their environment by development projects that put these environments to new uses, such as valleys flooded by dams and forests exclusively reserved for commercial logging (Cernea and Guggenheim, 1993: 2). Slower, but at least as extensive in impact, are environmental processes that are undermining the livelihood of people and displacing them: desertification (as in the Sahel), appropriation of land for commercial uses, forcing subsistence farmers on fragile soil to reduce the fallow periods and thus impair the soil's fertility, and flooding caused by upstream erosion (as in the Brahmaputra Delta due to Himalayan deforestation). In the future, there is the prospect of upstream states diverting water for irrigation and depriving downstream users (eg, on the Tigris and Euphrates), of some countries (eg, Libya) overusing regional aquifers and creating shortages for neighboring populations, and, most serious of all, of regional declines in agricultural productivity and coastal and delta inundation due to global warming. All

The author wishes to thank Melissa Thomson for her research assistance.

these processes, which represent a pandemic pattern, involve environmental victims. (For one survey, although now a little dated, see Jacobson, 1989.)

Protecting people against becoming environmental victims is clearly a task of the first order of importance in the world today. Is this compatible with the centrality of the principle of state sovereignty in international relations? This is the question that this article addresses. First, the case for state sovereignty will be considered from an environmental angle, with particular concern for environmental victims. This is followed by a critique of state sovereignty. It is an immanent critique in that it begins within a perspective that emphasizes the strengths of state sovereignty. In the end, however, it is rejected in favor of a federal system of divided authority, extended down to the local level, and up to the global level.

Some might argue that a normative critique of state sovereignty has little real-world significance, since capitalist globalization (as well as the politics of environmental interdependence and universal human rights) is in any case eroding state sovereignty. In defense of this analysis, first note that increasing economic interdependence may be as much a matter of state choices as is the erosion of state power and, second, that erosion does not mean disappearance. Keohane and his collaborators have argued that 'neither sovereignty nor interdependence' is about to disappear (Levy, Keohane, and Haas, 1993: 417). The tension between the processes of erosion and the determination of power holders to assert sovereignty suggests that it may be timely to review state sovereignty as a contribution to the question of whether, for example, environmental and international justice activists should work to shore it up or, alternatively, to transform it into something new.

The acceptance or rejection of state sovereignty, also with reference specifically to the environment, has been the subject of controversy. On the one hand, there are those who argue for working with state sovereignty to develop environmental protection regimes and even for strengthening state sovereignty (eg, Piddington, 1989; Keohane, Haas, and Levy, 1993: 4; Commission on Global Governance, 1995: 68–72). Others have argued that ecological processes do not respect state borders and that state sovereignty hinders the effective environmental protection that the scope of the ecological processes requires (eg, Mische, 1989; Camilleri and J. Falk, 1992: 179). Although this article does not deal with the political process by which an ideal or better way of organizing international environmental relations could be reached, it does deal with the question of what the possibilities and weaknesses of a sovereignty-based approach are and what basic qualifications or alterations to it are required to improve it. It thus represents an argument concerning a worthwhile ideal to strive for; it does not go so far as to develop a strategy to attain it, nor even present an argument that it is an ideal attainable from the status quo. The latter are questions that require separate treatment.

As a normative analysis, its emphasis will be on ethical justification.[1] Although the discussion of environmental victims, state sovereignty, and international relations is quite general and theoretical, with respect to ethics the analysis is relatively applied, in that it does not focus on the various foundational debates.

Instead, I am adopting a particular ethical position, but one that can rest on alternative theoretical foundations. The position is that of cosmopolitanism, ie, the notion that at least in certain arenas of public policy, universal standards of political ethics are applicable. In this chapter I only claim that this applies to the issue of environmental victims. The alternative theoretical foundations upon which cosmopolitanism can rest are those of utilitarianism, contractarianism, libertarianism, and even communitarianism. A brief point might be made regarding the last of these foundations, partly because cosmopolitanism and communitarianism are typically treated as opposed and partly as a defense against the currently popular criticism of ethical universalism. (For an elaborate defense against a range of such attacks, see Doyal and Gough, 1991: 9–45.) Ethical universalism can be based on the observation that we have a developing global political system – a global community – and that this system has generated universally applicable norms of governmental behavior and is continuing to do so. There is therefore no need to refer to culture-transcending ethical principles, other than those that have become the ethical resources of the global community. It is in the context of the political culture of our global political system and its norms that the following discussion is conducted. Despite the focus on ethical justification, the analysis of this article does not assume power politics away. Instead, it locates the analysis in the field of tension between ethics and self-interested, or at least nationalistic, politics.[2]

ENVIRONMENTAL VICTIMS AND THE RESPONSIBILITIES OF STATES

To make my discussion more systematic, I will use a formal definition of environmental victims. I will take that term to refer to people who are or have been harmed by processes that emanate from the natural environment, are mediated by it, or impair access to it, without being fully compensated for such harm. This definition deviates from that found in Chapter 1 (Williams, 1996) in two ways. First, it allows that the concept of 'victim' does not necessarily imply human agency and that earthquake or flood victims are environmental victims, without requiring human action or responsibility to have been implicated. The reason for this is not only that, in ordinary language, we recognize as 'victims' those who have been harmed by natural disasters; it is also to provide scope for an obligation of states to assist this category of victims. Second, I interpret harm more broadly than 'a negative mental or physical health outcome' and include injury to livelihood and environmental displacement without adequate compensation. The latter can be more serious than the former, as when people impoverished by such a process are worse off than people suffering temporary illness. The significance of this definitional difference is that in this article environmental victims are interpreted more broadly and this leads to a somewhat wider range of state responsibilities. However, the narrower definition would not greatly alter the argument regarding the merits of state sovereignty and the need for its alteration or replacement.

The focus in this article is on social responsibility in relation to such environmental victims. More specifically, it is on the responsibility of states. As indicated above, I am adopting a certain cosmopolitan approach, one that derives from the emergence of a common political culture concerning ideas about the responsibilities of states. The right of states to territorial sovereignty implies certain responsibilities in relation to their citizens. This includes responsibilities with respect to potential or actual environmental victims. To detail these responsibilities in a systematic way, they will be identified in relation to different kinds of environmental victims. A basic distinction to be made in the contemporary state system is that between (a) the victims of *inter*national environmental harm, and (b) those of *intra*-national environmental harm.

The first category parallels the concern of traditional international relations thinking with aggression. It consists of the victims of environmental harm across territorial boundaries. In particular, three kinds of transboundary harm are possible. (1) A population can be harmed by being deprived of access to its environment through invasion and either expulsion from its historical habitat or the imposition of a new population with which the original population now must share the environment. Settler colonialism, such as in North America, Australia, and New Zealand, is a clear case in point. (2) A natural resource may be depleted by another state or its population when the resource is an international commons, as in the case of coastal fishing or transboundary aquifers. (A more complex case is that of shared rivers, where an upstream country controls the flow in a way that harms the downstream country.) (3) Finally, people can be harmed by transboundary pollution, carried by water or air (eg, acid rain or nuclear radiation), or even by transportation as in the case of the toxic waste trade. The effects of transboundary pollution can be global, as in the cases of climate change and a sea level rise due to global warming. While harm type (1) consists of aggression, harm types (2) and (3) represent injurious selfishness. In all these cases, the responsibility of states is for the security of their citizens against transboundary harm.

The other kind of environmental harm occurs within the territories of states. I will distinguish between four kinds of environmental victims and the corresponding responsibilities of states. (1) One category of environmental victims are those who are environmentally harmed by state action directly, such as valley dwellers displaced by state-built dams as well as forest dwellers (eg, indigenous people) evicted from forests or restricted in their traditional use of forests so that these can be reserved for commercial logging. The responsibility of states here is for the socio-environmental effects of their own projects. (2) Then there are those who are harmed by the environmental effects of the actions of individuals and organizations within a state's territory. Examples are toxic pollution, overuse of common-property resources such as underground water, and flooding caused by deforestation. The corresponding responsibility of states is for justice in environmentally mediated social relations within their territories, such as preventing environmental harm to one group by another or at least assuring adequate compensation for such harm. (3) Next there are those who are harmed by natural disasters. Even if it would be unreasonable to consider state action (or inaction) or the actions of individuals or organizations within state territory as having exacerbated the consequences for the victims (eg, through the export of food during a drought), states are responsible for assisting victims of natural disasters to survive and regain their livelihood. (4) A final category of environmental victims consists of those who degrade their own natural environment as a result of some kind of helplessness and this threatens their environmentally dependent livelihood and health. This helplessness can take the form of severe deprivation that forces people to put short-term survival ahead of long-term sustainability.[3] Another form of helplessness is the destruction by economic modernization of traditional cultures that have provided for environmentally protective practices. The socio-environmental responsibility of states in these cases is for environmental sustainability (quite apart from their socioeconomic and sociocultural ones).

There are corresponding obligations for action by states. Again, we can distinguish between external and internal ones. With respect to external relations, the state has an obligation to defend its population from external harm, whether in the form of the appropriation of territory, the overuse of an international commons, or transboundary pollution. A military threat may need to be met in kind. Environmental harm through injurious national egoism may call for measures other than military ones, such as diplomatic pressure and economic threats, but if survival is at stake, perhaps even military intervention to counter the environmental intervention may be required in the absence of protection by the community of states.

Intranationally, five kinds of state obligations for action can be distinguished. (1) In order not to create environmental victims by its own projects, the state has an obligation of self-restraint. (2) To make sure that environmental injustices are not committed among its citizens or by commercial (or other) organizations, it has an obligation to regulate actions with socio-environmental consequences. This applies also to ensuring environmental sustainability. (3) Where the state has failed to prevent environmental victimization, either due to a failure in public responsibility or because of other state responsibilities that required public actions that then environmentally victimized some people, there is an obligation for adequate restitution. Full restitution, when that is possible, ends victimization.[4] (This is morally called for even where the environmental victimization occurred in previous generations, if contemporaries still suffer from the consequences. In that case, however, the nature of the restitution may need to be different.) (4) Where environmental victimization is due to natural causes or to interactive social processes, often mediated by complex natural processes so that culpability cannot be readily assigned, at least public *assistance* (if not collective restitution) is owed to those who are harmed by such processes. Such assistance is also called for where desperate circumstances or cultural destruction push people into using their own environment unsustainably. (5) Finally, just as the state has a negative obligation to refrain from environmentally victimizing projects, so it also has a positive responsibility to engage in preventive and rehabilitative projects, ie, projects that prevent or minimize the destructive consequences of natural processes for people and to reverse environmental destruction that the state has not been able to prevent in the past.

To what extent will these obligations be met by a political organization based on the principle of state sovereignty? I will first explore the capabilities of sovereign states to perform these functions, before making a critique of sovereignty in terms of the actual propensities of states.

STATE SOVEREIGNTY AND ENVIRONMENTAL HARM

First of all, the notion of state sovereignty needs to be clarified. It refers to supreme political authority, where political authority in turn refers to the legitimate exercise of coercive power. State sovereignty thus refers to a state's capacity and right to exercise supreme coercive power within its territory.[5] This, too, has both internal and external implications. Internally, there are no other sources of authority to constrain those of the state; the state reigns supreme. Externally, there is no supervening authority, but there are other states with the same right. Given that they have the same right, a general principle of state sovereignty requires the obligation of noninterference in the affairs of other states.[6] The absence of a supervening authority means that states have a right to self-defense against outside interference. This principle of international relations came to be articulated by the Treaty of Westphalia of 1648, reflecting an abandonment of the medieval ideal of imperial authority as the means to maintain order and peace among the states of Europe (Miller, 1990: Chapter 2). Its application worldwide, however, occurred only with the historically recent era of decolonization.

Given this definition, strict state sovereignty rules out, on the one hand, world government, which constrains the external autonomy of states, and, on the other, anarchism, which precludes coercive state power internally.[7] Between these ideal-type polar cases there are others that do not fit at least the strict formulation of state sovereignty. Externally, international law, or at least certain forms of it, constrains state sovereignty. This certainly holds for *jus cogens*, 'peremptory norms of general international law,' which take precedence over treaties, eg, prohibitions against genocide and slave trading (Shaw, 1991: 98–99, 593–594). Even treaties that a state has signed can be deemed to limit its sovereignty, at least if it cannot unilaterally abrogate them. Internally, polities with 'divided sovereignty,' such as federal systems, are really not sovereign states, since there is no one power center that is supreme. Divided sovereignty or divided supremacy is a contradiction in terms. Undivided supreme authority may be held by an absolute monarch, ie, 'the sovereign,' but also by representative systems of government, as in a unitary democracy.[8]

Two further clarifications are needed with respect to this principle. The first concerns the nature of the principle. It is not a justificatory principle, since it is still in need of justification itself. It is more in the nature of an institutional principle that guides the design of institutions and the instrumental norms that support them. Second, as an institutional principle, my articulation of it is in a particularly stark form.[9] It has, in fact, been interpreted in many different ways. My approach is not to look at how the principle has revealed itself in the real world.

The real world is to a considerable extent 'unprincipled'; it is shaped by a variety of principles, considerations, and forces. Instead of trying to generalize about how state sovereignty has been adapted over time and geographic space to meet various historical contingencies, I have taken the essence of the concept to present it as an ideal type.

The approach is to identify those qualifications to this essential formulation of the concept for which the consideration of environmental victimization calls. The ideal-typing of state sovereignty is thus merely a starting point. In the end, this ideal-type formulation of state sovereignty turns out to be too rigid and brittle to be normatively sustainable and an approach of conditional and divided authority is advocated. Others, who have not been troubled by what I see as a contradiction in terms in the notion of divided sovereignty, view sovereignty as a much more protean notion that can survive crucial qualifications and constraints. Thus, some of the differences between a normative rejection of sovereignty and its retention may be no more than conceptual. However, the focus on the environmental dimension and the extension of the federal principle to both the local and global levels is what substantively distinguishes the approach in this article. I will begin, however, by offering a rationale for state sovereignty and specifically one in terms of the previously listed responsibilities of states in relation to environmental victims. In the process I will articulate a conception of 'environmental state sovereignty.'

With respect to external relations, sovereignty is the right of states to noninterference. It creates the corresponding obligation not to interfere in the territory and affairs of other states.[10] With respect to environmental processes, that means that states and agents under their authority (businesses, citizens) have an obligation not to harm other states and their territories and populations environmentally, whether through deprivation of the exclusive access to their legitimate land or water domains (ie, conventional invasion or other territorial transgression) or through degradation of their terrestrial, aquatic, or atmospheric environments by pollution, the control of river flows, or the excessive (unsustainable or inequitable) tapping of common aquifers. Environmental state sovereignty, then, refers in its external aspect to the right not to be harmed environmentally by other states.

Noninterference is not only the external, but also the negative aspect of sovereignty; it refers to what is not to be done. The positive aspect is conventionally taken to be self-determination. 'Self-determination is one of the most important [but also] most obscure principles of contemporary international law and practice' (Beitz, 1979: 93). Rather than enter the labyrinth of all the ambiguities that this concept involves, I will confine myself to the environmental aspects and again refer to environmental state sovereignty. In this framework, the internal or positive aspect of sovereignty is the capacity and right of the state to meet its obligations to protect its citizens against environmental harm. This capacity requires it to have legitimate power that can prevail over all those within its jurisdiction who engage in environmentally injurious activities. In other words, the state must be sovereign to prevent environmental victimization. This is the positive and internal aspect of environmental state sovereignty.[11]

Although state sovereignty is the central principle of the contemporary state system, in practice it does not include environmental sovereignty. It focuses heavily on security with respect to territorial political control. Interventions that threaten such control (eg, invasion, spying, assassinations on foreign soil, financing subversive groups) are clearly recognized as violations of state sovereignty and are therefore carried out either in brazen defiance of the norms of the international order, or surreptitiously, or in a thick fog of rationalizing propaganda. By contrast, other forms of interference, such as environmental transboundary damage, are typically not viewed as similarly constituting violations of sovereignty. Only where environmental sovereignty and political sovereignty coincide, as in the case of security of territorial political control, are such violations recognized in this way.[12] To the extent that environmental sovereignty is desirable, it has yet to be achieved. It would require that cross-border pollution, for example, is not merely a problem to be solved, but represents a breach of the central principle of the international system of states.[13]

However, to justify advocating and implementing environmental sovereignty, as part of the stark form of state sovereignty that has been articulated here, requires closer analysis. The critical assessment of state sovereignty, to which I will now turn, will consist of two questions: Do sovereign states in a state system have the capacity to protect their citizens against environmental harm? Second, do sovereign states have the motivation to protect their citizens against such harm? Each question, I will argue, leads to qualifications to the principle of state sovereignty.

EXTERNAL ENVIRONMENTAL SOVEREIGNTY AND THE CAPABILITIES OF STATES

Let us assume (for now) that states are fully committed to preventing environmental harm to their citizens. Are they *able* to do so? Would they be able to protect themselves against international environmental harm by agreeing to cooperate to institute an international regime of environmental state sovereignty? This would mean that any form of environmental harm across borders would be in violation of this principle.

However, only states with the most limited and unrealistic conception of their interests would agree to such a principle. It would require that states have only negative environmental interests, ie, that they are concerned only with preventing harm to the environment and not harm by limiting the productive use of their natural environment. In that case, it is possible that a regime of environmental state sovereignty would be instituted. In such a wonderland scenario, it would even be the case that the odd wayward state that perpetrates international environmental harm (or allowed it to be done by its subjects) could be deterred by a collective commitment to punishing perpetrators through collective action that could include military intervention with the aim of replacing an environmental outlaw regime with an internationally law-abiding one.

Even if states were only concerned with environmental sovereignty, their interest in environmental autonomy must be expected to encompass the economic aspect of that interest, namely the interest in using the environment for production and consumption. Harm implies damaging something from which people have been benefiting. Environmental harm means a loss of certain benefits from the environment. Some of these benefits are in the form of production and consumption. Thus, one form of environmental harm is to deprive people of access to the environment such that they can no longer use it for production and consumption; another is to degrade their environment so as to make it less productive. Environmental sustainability is to a considerable degree the maintenance of the productivity of the environment. Preventing environmental harm, therefore, also means preventing harm to the economic productivity of the environment. This, however, opens a gate to major conflicts of interest. To the extent that banning all environmental damage – even when it benefits human health, aesthetic enjoyment, and the overall interests of future generations (not to mention considerations of ecocentric ethics) – restricts current production and consumption, states must deem it to be in their interest to allow at least some environmental damage. That includes transboundary damage. An agreement to ban all environmental international harm will therefore be resisted. In fact, states that aggressively defend themselves against all forms of environmental harm are a threat to peace; they treat as provocation, and thus as a call to self-defense, processes that are everyday occurrences in today's world. Such a development is precisely what the principle of state sovereignty has been designed to avoid.

Yet this conclusion does not necessarily mean either that states are unable to protect their citizens against environmental victimization, or that the principle of environmental state sovereignty is inapplicable. It is conceivable that states suffer environmental damage, but nonetheless have processes of adjustment and compensation that avert environmental victimization. It requires, however, that environmental harm between states is limited to forms that are reparable as far as people are concerned. When airborne radiation from a Chernobyl-like incident shortens people's life spans and leads to suffering from illness, it is doubtful that it is possible to make full restitution – in the sense that, if given a choice, people would not mind accepting the illness and shortened life in return for the compensation. Compensation can thus reverse environmental harm only when it is reparable.

Even though states will not agree to the banning of all international environmental damage, the notion that such damage must be compensated for is something that might well be acceptable to states. In other words, while they would not want all polluting economic uses of the environment blocked, they might agree to limit such uses to activities whose benefits are large enough that compensation for damage to other countries could be paid and still leave net benefits. In this way, the principle of environmental state sovereignty would be workable and could be instituted.

There is, however, one qualification. The principle of environmental sovereignty leaves certain questions of just compensation unresolved. These arise as a result of two features typical of pollution. There is often more than one producer of pollution and some level of pollution is often absorbed by the environment without harm to human beings. This has meant that certain uses of the environment, whose pollution effects are below the threshold of harm, may be deemed harmless and therefore do not require compensation. Thus, if rice fields were the only source of anthropogenic greenhouse gases, they would probably not cause global warming and no compensation would be owed. The question then becomes: Which uses of the environment that do have pollution effects would be deemed harmless for purposes of assessing compensation? Are these the historically oldest uses? Are they the uses by the neediest? Are such entitlements simply to be distributed on a per capita basis, regardless of the affluence or poverty of the countries involved?[14] A principle of justice must be imported; it is not generated by the principle of environmental sovereignty. The principle of environmental sovereignty is insufficient and has to be supplemented by an independent principle of international justice.[15]

Whatever complications supplementary notions of justice might involve, agreement of states on such notions, together with a principle of environmental sovereignty that does not ban environmental harm but requires full compensation for it, is in principle possible, assuming that states have an actual propensity to cooperate. In other words, the capability exists; the question is that of state interests and structural incentives.

INTERNAL ENVIRONMENTAL SOVEREIGNTY AND STATE LEGITIMATION

At this point the definition of sovereignty bears reiterating. It is the supreme coercive power of the state. The focus so far has been on the external aspect of sovereignty, namely state autonomy. It is the negative norm of noninterference. The definition of sovereignty, however, brings out the internal (and positive) aspect of sovereignty. The rationale for this internal aspect is the capacity of the state to protect and advance the interests of its citizens. That involves not merely preventing harm from outside the territorial boundaries, but also by preventing mutually predatory behavior (and behavior that is preemptively aggressive or retaliatory) among its citizenry, leading to violence and disorder – the Hobbesian 'war of each against all.' More positively, exclusive state control makes it possible to institute a legal system of rules that, apart from making social peace possible, promotes social justice and the common good, such as economic prosperity. It allows states to raise taxes to create widely beneficial infrastructure and provides assistance and restitution to those who are harmed by social change or are left behind by it. With respect to the environment specifically, it enables the state to take action to promote environmental sustainability and to prevent environmental harm within its jurisdiction or pay compensation for such harm.

This rationale, however, is confined entirely to enabling states to fulfill these responsibilities. Like the discussion in the previous section, it is articulated wholly with respect to the capacities of states. It does not address the question of whether a system based on sovereignty will induce states to fulfill these responsibilities. This is the question of propensity to which I now turn.

Whether states will fulfill their responsibilities depends in large part on their particular system of governance. Authoritarian states, for example, surprise us if they do so because the structural pressures to attend to the needs and concerns of the citizenry are relatively weak.[16] Democratic systems, on the other hand, force governments to respond to the demands of the electorate. One of these demands presumably will be protection against environmental harm and victimization.

Is the right to sovereignty dependent on the form of governance? The answer to this question has varied. One position has been that, to protect international peace, state regimes are entitled to noninterference as long as they meet two conditions: they do not commit aggression against other states and they have proven themselves to be in control of their particular state. Minimizing war requires minimizing the reasons for going to war. Therefore, authoritarian regimes must not be interfered with, even if they are not held in high regard.[17] The opposing position is that the right to supreme coercive power requires some basic form of consent by the people being governed and not merely the exercise of control; it must be politically legitimated.[18] Holding to this formulation requires the treatment of authoritarian governments as outlaw regimes that are not entitled to the protection of the injunction against external interference. Although the prevailing behavior of states in the recent past has varied between amoral realism (interfering or not interfering simply according to the national interest)[19] and the first version of state sovereignty (sovereignty regardless of the form of government), I will briefly explore the second version, where sovereignty depends on internal legitimation. The reason is that, in states without such legitimation, the chances that state responsibilities will be fulfilled, including that of protecting their citizens against environmental harm, are very low.

DEMOCRACY AND ENVIRONMENTAL FEDERALISM

Given the better prospects under democracy, will that system prevent environmental victimization? The actual record suggests not. Are there structural reasons for that? These reasons are manifold. In this kind of capsule treatment, all I can do is briefly refer to five. (In the following section on international relations, further reasons will be offered.)

(1) Most obviously, democracy generally operates on the majority principle and majority decisions can readily lead to people being made worse off, including through the various forms of environmental victimization identified at the beginning. To the extent that the gains for the majority involve costs for minorities and to the extent that notions of social justice do not inhibit such majoritarian moves, majority decisions can create environmental victims. The construction of dams for hydroelectricity frequently benefits many people while only a limited number are displaced. Token efforts to compensate the 'oustees' (a term used in India) are typical in developing countries.

(2) The state needs revenues to sustain its activities. Generally, it is the use of the environment, not its protection, that generates state revenues, whether through natural resource royalties, the profits of state corporations, or taxes on productive activities. Although from this perspective protecting the environment is a way of protecting the future revenue base, state regimes are not necessarily all that concerned with the revenue base in future generations. Consequently, they will bring a bias toward use of the environment and against its protection to both their domestic policies and their international relations. This can explain, in part, the indulgent approach of Third World governments toward transnational corporations. This tendency is intensified where state elites use their position to enrich themselves, since it is the use of the environment, rather than its protection, that provides the source for such enrichment.

(3) States are concerned not only with their revenue base, but also with the maintenance of their authority. This involves both the authority of the state as an institution and the power of a particular elite occupying it. That means that where there is a conflict between environmental protection and the prevention of environmental victimization, on the one hand, and the protection of central authority, on the other, the latter will generally prevail, although democratic processes may limit that. Thus, even if centralized decision-making may be less efficacious with respect to certain forms of environmental protection, particularly those that have predominantly local impacts, centralization may be preferred to ensure that rival centers of power do not emerge.

(4) State activities are shaped to a greater or lesser extent by the interests of the dominant class. In capitalist polities, that is in the first instance the class that deploys capital for the productive activities that both the population and the state depend on. Protecting the environment generally is not very conducive to profit-making. Here, then, is another source of a bias in favor of the use of the environment and against the protection of the environment.

(5) Capitalist dominance can operate in ideological terms. Although this will generally support more direct capitalist power over the state, it can operate instead as a more indirect exercise of power. When the citizenry accepts the private sector with minimal government restraints as the foundation of society's well-being, environmental harm will be accepted as the price that has to be paid. This holds even when the majority experiences environmental harm.

For these and other reasons, people experience environmental harm as a result of state priorities. The distance of state officials from the impacts of environmental effects, which are often quite local, intensifies this insensitivity to environmental harm. Ultimate decision-making power rests at the level of sovereign states, rather than at that level in society where accountability is most effective, which is where the decision-makers are also those who experience the effects of the decisions. Decision-making regarding the use of the local environment is experienced primarily by the local population. It is therefore now widely argued that such decision-making should be local.

> [S]ustainable development is the result of a political order in
> which society is capable of learning from and responding to

> *mistakes in the use of natural resources. Experience suggests*
> *that both the potential and the incentive for learning are greatest*
> *when those making resource-management decisions are the ones*
> *directly experiencing the results of those decisions. Thus, within*
> *a framework of condemning harm to the environment of other*
> *communities [and making it illegal or subject to reparations],*
> *empowering local people to control and manage their resources*
> *is generally the best guarantee of sustainable environmental*
> *management (Commission on Developing Countries and Global*
> *Change, 1992: 45).*[20]

It is true that sovereign, unitary states delegate much decision-making to more local levels and are typically organized into regional, district, and local governments. It is also true that coordination between levels of government and between governments at the same level is necessary and that such coordination often has to be authoritative. Yet unitary states have the power to create the decision-making frameworks. State regimes will be concerned to maintain the power of the state to assert itself, and that will be given priority over assuring environmental sustainability, promoting environmental productivity, and protecting against environmental harm. Beyond that, state regimes can be expected to pursue their own interests, whether this is simply to stay in power or to enrich themselves and the elites of which they are part. Although democratic structures (and cultures) can put restraints on such behavior, the opacity of democracy – ie, the inability of citizens to know and understand all that is going on in government and to connect it with their interests and with norms of the public interest and of social justice – will generally give state regimes much latitude to pursue these concerns and interests. This then is likely to militate against local autonomy, which could breed new and potentially competing centers of power.

To put this into a theoretical context, there is a basic divergence between the theory of sovereignty and the theory of federalism. The theory of sovereignty argues that most governmental matters within a particular territory, preferably one inhabited by people with a sense of affinity with each other, have to be managed by one overwhelmingly powerful authority, while the affairs between them can be managed by voluntary cooperation, based on the principle of noninterference. Federalism rejects both the idea of exclusive jurisdiction and the idea that lateral coordination does not require a supervening authority. Instead, governing authority is divided.[21] It is divided vertically into two levels of government. There is a federal or central government that has a certain range of responsibilities, including responsibility for international relations, as well as the authority necessary for them; then there is another, 'lower' level of government (that of cantons, provinces, lands, or 'states') that has a different range of such responsibilities and the corresponding authority. At this 'lower' level of government, authority is also divided territorially, in that the authority of this level of government is spatially assigned to particular cantons, 'provinces,' 'lands,' or 'states.' There are rights to noninterference, but these involve territorial exclusivity only in the horizontal, inter-cantonal relations, not in the vertical relations between cantons and the federal government. The latter consist of jurisdictional exclusivity. Moreover, even jurisdictions may be shared, eg, the authority to tax. However it is organized, authority is divided and overlapping both with respect to territory and to jurisdiction.

This suggests the idea of environmental federalism in lieu of environmental sovereignty. Rather than depend on state regimes to decentralize authority appropriately to enhance the capacity and incentives to prevent environmental victimization, limited exclusive authority can be vested in local communities or 'bioregions' (those in which environmental interdependence is particularly pronounced), so that they can manage them in such a way that their people do not suffer harm. Other communities are protected by intercommunity liability. Interests and norms that transcend local communities are either left to negotiation, as they currently are in the realm of international relations, or appropriate and limited authority is vested in a higher level of government in order to carry out the necessary responsibilities.

STATES, ENVIRONMENTAL VICTIMS, AND GLOBAL GOVERNANCE

It is a noteworthy paradox of the existing state system that there is distrust and rejection of anarchic solutions (ie, solutions based on voluntary cooperation) within territories generally inhabited by people who perceive some degree of linguistic, cultural, historical, or other affinity, ie, 'nations,' while the anarchic approach is somehow deemed appropriate for the management of international problems occurring between peoples with different identities and cultures. However, I concluded the section on internal sovereignty with the claim that states have the capability to manage global processes through voluntary agreements. Paradox or not, does this not mean that, even if the concept of sovereignty should be rejected internally, its external aspect, that of mutual noninterference, is still applicable between states? It is important to recall that I analyzed the state system strictly in terms of the capabilities of states, not in terms of their actual propensities. In the next two sections, I introduced actual state regimes and their propensity to act in ways that do not protect people against environmental harm. Similarly, it is now necessary to revisit states regarding their actual behavior patterns in international relations. Although states committed to preventing environmental harm, at least by assuring full compensation for such harm, could arrive at international regimes of environmental management that are effective in accomplishing this end, it is unlikely that they would.

The reasons given earlier for the failure of democratic states to prevent environmental victimization internally will also generally weaken any commitment to preventing environmental harm from outside the state's borders. I will merely add two considerations that apply particularly to international relations. Both stem from the earlier distinction between interests in protecting the environment and interests in using the environment.

(1) The first reason involves international power. Even though relying on a right to restitution for environmental harm, rather than an across-the-board ban on such harm, can leave the door open to uses of the environment whose benefits outweigh the costs, powerful states that generate more international pollution than they suffer are likely to block such a principle, either in its adoption or in its implementation. Since political power comes with economic development, powerful states will typically produce a much larger share of global pollution than their share of world population. The result is that, rather than the adoption of a general principle to deal with international environmental harm, we get selective environmental treaties dealing with particular problems where a sufficient coincidence of interests has emerged.

(2) State elites expect to be rewarded. Although notions of clean government generally require that salaries out of state revenues serve this purpose and that this process be democratically controlled, corruption cannot be ruled out. Just as in the case of state revenues, it is the uses of the environment, rather than environmental protection, that generate the wherewithal for payoffs. Reward, however, need not be strictly material. Simply being accepted as part of the global elite leads state elites into behavior that is likely to be biased in favor of global capitalism at the expense of environmental protection.[22]

Within the anarchic organization of international relations, the interests of state elites are thus generally best served by dragging their heels in approaching international environmental protection. Here again, the alternative of environmental federalism commends itself. Instead of relying on the voluntary agreement of states to establish international environmental law and to rely either on voluntary compliance or on voluntary enforcement, a global jurisdiction and authority would be established to prevent international environmental harm. (This would be an environmentalist version of world federalism.) Such an authority could be legitimated by democratic representation rather than state representation as is currently the case in the administration of international treaties and the United Nations, our current global confederation (as distinct from federal authority). Moreover, a system of democratic representation at the global level is more likely to contribute to the current emergence of a global morality than is a system representing states. A global environmental protection authority (whether as a freestanding functional institution or as part of a fully developed world-federal government)[23] would not be globally sovereign. It would merely be part of an extensive system of divided authority, with the distribution of authority going all the way from the local to the global level.

A global environmental protection authority could have, as part of its jurisdiction, the prevention of the more egregious forms of environmental victimization occurring in lower jurisdictions, including those of states. Protection against environmental harm is becoming part of the conception of human rights, and human rights are being accepted as part of international law. Even within the existing state system, extreme violations of human rights are becoming justifications for 'humanitarian intervention,' that is, the prevention of massive human suffering by the use of force by other states. This, however, is always a worrisome approach to solving such problems, since intervening states generally are not free of national interest agendas in the process. A global environmental protection authority that is adequately empowered and democratically governed would be much more trustworthy in dealing with states that commit or allow extreme cases of environmental injury to their own citizens.

CONCLUSION

This chapter has explored the normative implications of a commitment to protecting people from becoming environmental victims for the principle of state sovereignty. Environmental victims are those who are harmed by natural environmental processes, by anthropogenic processes mediated by the natural environment, and by restrictions in access to the environment. Protecting against such victimization is one of the obligations of states. Internally, it requires states to appropriately manage their own infrastructural and productive projects, regulate uses of the environment, and ensure restitution, assistance, and rehabilitation where harm has not been prevented initially. Externally, states are obliged not only to defend their territory for their citizens, but also to protect it from environmentally transmitted harm from outside their borders. Sovereignty provides states with the authority necessary to carry out these obligations. Internally, it gives them the supreme coercive authority to manage social relations; externally, it prohibits interference and harm by other states and their subjects. However, current practice does not give the right to noninterference an environmental interpretation and thus does not embrace what here is called environmental state sovereignty. A major reason is that using the environment for production is at least as much of an interest as protecting it. Restitution for international environmental harm would, however, make this compatible with preventing or eliminating environmental harm.

Although sovereignty enables states to prevent environmental victimization, there are structural reasons, essentially involving power and self-interest, why they will often not do so, even when governance is formally democratic. This applies both internally and externally. A more promising institutional principle is environmental federalism, ie, an extension of federalism down to the local level, for decision-making regarding the local environment, and up to the global level, for authoritative coordination and adjudication regarding transboundary processes. Federalism, however, is not consistent with strict sovereignty; it represents divided authority instead. The conclusion, then, is that environmental federalism offers better protection against environmental victimization than does environmental sovereignty.

The point of this discussion is not that activists and social movements committed to preventing environmental victimization should make state sovereignty their primary target. First of all, where states are weak, state authority needs to be strengthened in various respects in order to improve the capacity of responsible states to protect their environment and the people dependent on it.

Second, even while pressing for a new division of governance authority, for purposes of political discourse it might be best not to reject the notion of sovereignty. Sovereignty has acquired a sacrosanct quality. My strict definition of this principle was designed for analytical clarity. In real-world struggles, treating sovereignty as more protean and accepting notions such as divided or shared sovereignty may smooth the road for institutional change. Not only should cases of environmental victimization, whether strictly internal or the result of transboundary processes, be a concern for the global community, but governance authority must also be distributed in new ways.

NOTES

1   I use 'ethics' broadly and not, as Brilmayer (1989: 27) does, in distinction to political theory and considerations of justifications of state authority, ie, as concerning only the relations between individuals.

2   However, power and politics must not be seen as categorically antithetical to ethics. Political power needs to be legitimated and ethics is one basis for legitimation. Moreover, ethically motivated activists mobilize moral judgments and feelings in the electorate and put pressure on governments and thus insert ethical considerations into politics. This is not to deny that ethics has an uphill struggle in the realm of politics, but merely to reject that there is no room whatsoever for ethics in politics, including international politics.

3   The notion of victim generally implies that the harm comes from a source other than the victim herself or himself. Tracing harm to the deprivation of victims implies that the harm is due to causes that the victims did not control. That is certainly problematic. For example, shifting cultivators might be deemed to be responsible for soil depletion when they reduce the swidden cycle from a sustainable 15-year period to five years or less. On the other hand, if this is due to land having been taken from them and therefore leaving them with no option other than to accelerate the swidden cycle on the land left to them, then they cannot be held responsible. Yet they are responsible for their insistence on retaining their swidden culture. This means that the notion of responsibility hinges on an a prior notion of justice, namely, whether it is just to appropriate land traditionally used by swidden cultivators and to leave them so little as to force them indirectly to abandon their way of life. (For a discussion of the case of the Chittagong Hill Tracts in Bangladesh, see Penz, 1993.)

4   If full restitution is not possible, is environmental harm necessarily unjustifiable? I can think of at least two exceptions:

(1) It is possible to imagine environmental harm resulting from strictly defensive action. If coastal dikes are built to protect inland areas against sea level rise, this may require the sacrifice of coastal land. Compensation may still be required to the owners of that land, but in this case it is a fair distribution of net sacrifices that is at stake, rather than full restitution for losses. Less than full compensation may be entirely just, given that others also have to sacrifice, at least in the form of providing for the compensation. However, this raises the question of international justice, whether in the form of restitution for harm or global distributive justice. (In the specific case of a sea level rise, if attributable to anthropogenic greenhouse gases, there is a wider human collectivity that has benefited, through production and

consumption; in that case, the issue of compensation arises at the international level.) *(2)* Another instance of environmental victimization that may not constitute an injustice is where certain agreed-upon environmental risks cause injuries that cannot be compensated. Environmental risks may be like the risks involved in militarily defending one's community; victims of death cannot be compensated (although the surviving family members can). Take the historical case of terrace agriculture. If a community decides (consensually and not oligarchically) to incur the risk of earth slides by proceeding to develop this technology before the technology of such cultivation is fully mastered, because the benefits are deemed to be worth the risk, then environmental fatalities may not constitute an injustice, but merely a tragedy. (A more contemporary example is that of tiger reserves in India, which are deemed to serve species preservation, but expose villagers to the risk of being killed by wayward tigers. This is not to argue in favor of the tiger-reserve policy, but merely to make the case that such a policy is not *obviously* unjust. In other words, the question of justice is contentious.) However, the environmental risks that some communities are willing to take reflect their general living conditions; a willingness to take high risks (such as to collect honey in a jungle area containing man-eating tigers) often indicates economic relations of disadvantage with other communities. In that case, environmental victimization again implies injustice.

5   State sovereignty is a quite distinct notion from popular sovereignty, although the latter is often used to qualify the acceptability of the former. Democratic constraints on state sovereignty are discussed later in this article. Popular sovereignty is conceptually more akin to consumer sovereignty, a concept that I have explored in depth in Penz (1986).

6   The standard term in international relations is 'nonintervention.' However, in explaining nonintervention, as careful a theorist as Beitz (1979: 71–92) has used 'intervention' and 'interference' interchangeably, indicating that these two terms are not seen to be different in a way that matters in this context. Further, the Charter of the Organization of American States contains the following declaration:

Article 18. No State or group of States has the right to intervene, directly or indirectly, for any reason whatever, in the internal or external affairs of any other State. The foregoing principle prohibits not only armed force, but *also any other form of interference* or attempted threat against the personality of the State or against its political, economic, and cultural elements (emphasis added; cited in Brilmayer, 1989: 105).

7   Watson (1992: 311–318) has argued that, on a spectrum ranging from independence to empire, state sovereignty represents the rhetorical ideal of the extreme independence end. Yet this framework is strongly statist and is therefore not as comprehensive as one that includes the anarchist option.

8   Whether systems with checks and balances between the different branches of government should be treated as systems of divided authority or not is a conceptual issue that I will not pursue here. The question is whether it is merely the state, with whatever division of authority there is among its various institutions, that is to be sovereign or a particular institution within the state structure, such as parliament. Checks and balances within a unitary state are not a problem for the former interpretation, but they are for the latter.

9   Despite the juridical starkness of the conception employed here, it does not go as far as Maritain's position, drawing on Bodin, the original author of the concept of sovereignty, that sovereignty is equivalent to absolutism and rules out popular government (Stankiewicz, 1969: 7–10).

10 In the absence of a supranational authority, sovereignty also involves the right to self-defense when the right to noninterference is being violated. This is sometimes referred to as the laissez-faire feature of the state system (Miller, 1990: 29–32).

11 'Environmental sovereignty' has also been used by Piddington (1989: 39), but only in the sense of the entitlement of the state to manage to its own territorial environment, not in the sense of a right to noninterference in the form of environmental harm.

12 In this article, I am bypassing the very complex issue of economic sovereignty. However, a certain intersection between economic and environmental aspects of state sovereignty needs to be mentioned. In reaction to demands by sections of the North in the Uruguay Round of GATT negotiations, a particular claim to sovereignty has been made by sectors of the Third World, namely the assertion of sovereignty specifically with respect to the natural resources within states' territories (eg, Commission on Developing Countries and Global Change, 1992: 68). Only to the extent that it involves international environmental harm is this issue a concern in this article. As such, it is discussed later in terms of the conflict between the use and the protection of the environment. Otherwise, the basic right of states to control their natural resources has not, to the best of my knowledge, been challenged in international negotiations, with one exception. Constraints on sovereignty have been proposed where threats to global commerce have been claimed. This concerns economic sovereignty, which I do not address here.

13 This lack of recognition of environmental interdependence in relation to sovereignty is reflected in the following statement by Brilmayer (1989: 106): 'This norm of nonintervention or self-determination stands as protection not only against territorial occupation, but also against colonialism, political subversion, and (when interpreted broadly) economic pressure.' Subsequently, however, she used the examples of acid rain and oceanic testing of nuclear weapons as possible and controversial instances of sovereignty-relevant forms of international harm (1989: 108).

14 These issues apply not only to the pollution threshold, but also to the phenomena of synergistic and cumulative effects, so that the damage that a unit of a particular pollutant causes depends on what other pollution is occurring or has already occurred. The economist's notion of marginal cost can be applied, but that would mean that necessity uses, like growing rice, which in the past have been harmless, may now be assessed as having a substantial marginal external cost, making them liable for reparations.

15 Such a principle is, of course, needed also for distributive justice in access to and use of the global commons, apart from feedback effects to state territories. Examples are oceans (excepting coastal areas), Antarctica, outer space, and the radio wave spectrum. Both the ambiguities in the notion of just compensation and distributive justice regarding the global commons represent a moral opening for supplementing environmental sovereignty with a principle of equality in access to the global commons. That, in turn, can lead to a much more far-reaching global egalitarianism. However, such an argument will not be pursued here.

16 Pressures to satisfy the public are by no means completely absent under authoritarianism, because, even though authoritarian regimes can to a considerable extent dispense with public support by relying on coercion, there are limits to this approach, since large-scale coercion is difficult to organize and costly to maintain.

17 It should not be forgotten that 'the European concept of sovereignty...was an aim of rulers and princes, who wanted to be masters over all their subjects but to acknowledge no master over themselves' (Watson, 1992: 316).

18 This position combines the doctrine of state sovereignty with the doctrine of popular sovereignty.

19 To be accurate, this should refer to 'internationally amoral' realism, since certain forms of realism make one of two moral claims. One is that state officials have no right to compromise their population's security and that the nature of international relations is such that attention to moral considerations concerning other countries will necessarily involve such compromises. The other is that the moral obligation of state officials is to maximally advance their people's interests more generally, which again leaves no room for moral considerations concerning other states or peoples.

20 This should not be taken to mean that antidemocratic power is not exercised at the local level. The expectation, however, is that people are more easily mobilized to protect their environment at the local level.

21 It is conventional to refer to 'divided sovereignty,' but that is a contradiction in terms if sovereignty still means supreme coercive authority.

22 The assumption here is that the electoral process of democracies works imperfectly. The opacity of governmental processes, barriers to electoral competition and communication, and the inevitably limited understanding of the citizenry give state elites considerable autonomy from electorates. This is particularly so where the democratic structures are so new that they have not been reinforced by democratic cultures.

23 Deudney (1993: 286–289) has argued that functional transnational institutions have a better chance of being accepted into the existing system than does full-fledged world government. That has also been the pattern of the emergence of European federalism.

REFERENCES

Beitz, Charles R (1979) *Political Theory and International Relations*. Princeton: Princeton University Press.

Brilmayer, Lea (1989) *Justifying International Acts*. Ithaca: Cornell University Press.

Camilleri, Joseph A and Jim Falk (1992) *The End of Sovereignty? The Politics of a Shrinking and Fragmenting World*. Great Britain: Edward Elgar.

Cernea, Michael M and Scott E Guggenheim (eds) (1993) *'Introduction' to Anthropological Approaches to Resettlement*. Boulder: Westview Press.

Commission on Developing Countries and Global Change (1992) *For Earth's Sake*. Ottawa: International Development Research Centre.

Commission on Global Governance (1995) *Our Global Neighbourhood*. Oxford: Oxford University Press.

Deudney, Daniel (1993) 'Global Environmental Rescue and the Emergence of World Domestic Politics.' In Ronnie D. Lipschutz and Ken Conca (eds) *The State and Social Power in Global Environmental Politics*. New York: Columbia University Press: 280–305.

Doyal, Len and Ian Gough (1991) *A Theory of Human Need*. New York: The Guilford Press.

Haas, Peter M, Robert O Keohane, and Marc A Levy (eds) (1993) *Institutions for the Earth: Sources of Effective International Environmental Protection*. Cambridge, Mass.: MIT Press.

Jacobson, Jodi L (1989) 'Abandoning Homelands.' Lester R Brown et al, *State of the World 1989*. New York: Norton.

Keohane, Robert O, Peter M Haas, and Marc A Levy (1993) 'The Effectiveness of International Environmental Institutions.' In Haas, Keohane, and Levy (eds), 1993: 3–42.

Levy, Marc A, Robert O Keohane, and Peter M Haas (1993) 'Improving the Effectiveness of International Environmental Institutions.' In Haas, Keohane, and Levy (eds) *Institutions for the Earth: Sources of Effective International Environmental Protection*. Cambridge, Mass.: MIT Press: 397–426.

Miller, Lynn H (1990) *Global Order: Values and Power in International Politics*. Second Edition. Boulder: Westview Press.

Mische, Patricia M (1989) 'Ecological Security and the Need to Reconceptualize Sovereignty.' *Alternatives* 14: 389–427.

Penz, G Peter (1993) 'Colonization of Tribal Lands in Bangladesh and Indonesia: State Rationales, Rights to Land, and Environmental Justice.' Michael C Howard (ed) *Asia's Environmental Crisis*. Boulder: Westview Press: 37–72.

Penz, G Peter (1986) *Consumer Sovereignty and Human Interests*. Cambridge, UK: Cambridge University Press.

Piddington, Kenneth W (1989) 'Sovereignty and the Environment.' *Environment* 31,7: 18–20, 35–39.

Shaw, Malcolm N (1991) *International Law. Third Edition*. Cambridge, UK: Cambridge University Press.

Stankiewicz, W J (1969) 'In Defense of Sovereignty: A Critique and an Interpretation.' W J Stankiewicz (ed) *In Defense of Sovereignty*. New York: Oxford University Press: 3–38.

Watson, Adam (1992) *The Evolution of International Society: A Comparative Historical Analysis*. London: Routledge.

Chapter 3

Reflections on Environmental Justice: Children as Victims and Actors

Sharon Stephens

In *Radical Ecology*, Carolyn Merchant (1992) argues forcefully that the modern world's dominant norms of production, social relations, and ideology are resulting in an accumulation of ecological stresses on the air, water, soil, and diverse life forms, as well as on the capacity of human societies to maintain and reproduce themselves over time. Although these ecological stresses are a result of globally articulated processes, she notes, they are 'experienced differently in the First, Second, and Third Worlds and by people of different races, classes, and sexes' (*Ibid*: 10). This is also true, she might have added – but tellingly did not – of people of different ages.

Merchant's important insights – that environmental risks are experienced differently by different groups and, moreover, that they are borne disproportionately by those groups that are already the most socially, politically, and economically vulnerable – are core concepts in the rapidly proliferating literature on 'environmental justice.' (See, for example, Bryant, 1995; Bullard, 1994; and Hofrichter, 1993b.) The concept has been developed during the last decade by theorists and activists, largely in the US, to describe what many regard as a qualitatively new sort of grass-roots environmental movement, linking concerns with social justice to concerns about environmental quality. This linkage has important implications for how people perceive environmental problems and for the practical responses they develop to address these problems. Here I wish to argue that the term 'environmental justice' has been developed in distinctive ways in the context of US culture and politics, and that this context has significantly affected the nature of environmental justice theory and its usefulness in other contexts.

Since 1992, I have been involved in the development of an international, interdisciplinary 'Children and Environment' research program and network, based at the Norwegian Centre for Child Research in Trondheim, Norway. (See Stephens, 1994.) Because of the magnitude and seriousness of environmental risks to children in Eastern Europe and the former USSR, the Centre has been particularly concerned with developing a network of relations with researchers and activists in these regions. When I first encountered the notion of environmental justice, I felt there was great potential here for providing powerful theoretical and practical tools to address the special environmental vulnerability of children and to illuminate distinctive constellations of risks in particular world regions. Significantly, however, references to children of the former USSR are almost entirely absent from the existing environmental justice literature. I suggest that the neglect of these topics can be linked to a particular construction of 'community' – one that is in some respects distinctively American and is dominant within the environmental justice movement. This is a view of community that tends to make children invisible, as a special class of victims and especially as actors. It is also a view of community that poses formidable obstacles to international coalition building.

This chapter begins with a brief discussion of the history of the environmental justice movement and of the reasons why race, ethnicity, class, and occupation (and, to lesser and problematic extents, geopolitical location and gender) are theorized in the literature, while age is ignored as a significant dimension of environmental justice thinking. (My focus here is on children, but this discussion could be productively extended to include the special environmental vulnerabilities of the elderly as well.) I then discuss ways in which perspectives on children as a distinctive environmental 'special interest group' offer important possibilities for developing a more inclusive and effective environmental justice movement, both within the United States and internationally.

ENVIRONMENTAL JUSTICE THEORY: THE US CONTEXT

Historians of the environmental justice movement (for example, Bullard, 1993a, 1993b; Di Chiro, 1995) argue that there is a broad-based, culturally diverse grassroots environmental movement in the US today that differs in important ways from the essentially white, middle-class environmental movement they call 'mainstream environmentalism.' This mainstream movement grew out of the late 19th- and early 20th-century conservationist movement, which is mainly concerned with protecting endangered species and natural wonders from destruction and commodification in the frenetic process of US industrialization and urbanization.

After World War II, the environmental movement in the US became somewhat broader based. There was continuing concern with species and wilderness preservation, but there was also increasing concern with such urban issues as pollution, traffic, and density of population. Nevertheless, the main actors in the postwar environmental movement remained middle-class whites. This affected the way they viewed environmental problems and possible solutions. They tended to emphasize the importance of scientific and technical evaluations, legislative approaches, and political lobbying at the national level. Most of the important mainstream environmental groups, eg, the Audubon Society, the National Resources Defense Council, and Friends of the Earth, have a lobbying center in Washington, DC, aimed at influencing national regulations and policies.

During the 1970s and 1980s, however, an increasing number of grass-roots environmental groups began to form at the local community level, initially in response to specific environmental risks, such as the siting of waste disposal areas or incinerators, the building of lead smelters, the heavy use of pesticides in local agriculture, and nuclear weapons testing. Activists in these local groups tended *not* to be typical 'mainstream environmental activists.' They were generally *not* white, middle class, or well educated (in terms of 'mainstream' educational standards).

They represented instead those groups most at risk from corporate and military development: people of color, the poor, and working-class populations. As Bullard (1993b: 17) notes: 'The most polluted urban communities are those with crumbling infrastructure, ongoing economic disinvestment, deteriorating housing, inadequate schools, chronic unemployment, a high poverty rate, and an overloaded healthcare system.' Because of the legacy of racism in the US, people of color (particularly African Americans and Latino Americans) are disproportionately represented in these troubled communities. At the heart of the environmental justice movement is the claim that certain groups have borne the greatest burden of 'development,' without proportionate access to the benefits or a chance to question the language of cost/benefit balancing itself.

Di Chiro (1995: 299) recounts the illuminating story of a 1993 encounter between mainstream environmental groups (including the Sierra Club and the Environmental Defense Fund) and the group called Concerned Citizens of South Central Los Angeles, based in a predominantly African American, low-income community that was concerned about plans to build a 1,600 ton per day solid waste incinerator in the center of their neighborhood. Members of Concerned Citizens were informed that potential contamination of an urban community by highly toxic dioxins, fluorons, and other chemicals likely to be released by the incineration facility was a 'community health issue,' not an environmental one.

Environmental justice advocates claim that grass-roots environmental groups in the US are redefining the scope of the environmental movement by showing that environmental problems are inseparable from other social injustices. The quest for environmental justice thus becomes an extension of the quest for basic civil rights. Indeed, the strategies that characterize many of the new grass-roots groups show historical continuities with the Civil Rights Movement of the 1960s and 1970s. Having little access to formal structures of power, civil rights groups were dependent on mass direct actions, such as protests, street demonstrations, and grass-roots voting registration programs. Similarly, grass-roots environmental groups often employ confrontational direct action strategies, such as public demonstrations, petitions, community education hearings, and debates. Some grass-roots leaders have become adept at using the public media to help publicize what often seem to be David and Goliath struggles of disenfranchised groups against powerful corporate polluters and state and federal governments.

However, to do so more effectively, many are arguing, it is necessary to move beyond single-issue protests based in particular communities to form multi-issue, multicultural coalitions. Much of the writing on these coalitions tends, in my opinion, to be rather utopian in celebrating the potential for a national network of community activists to transform and revitalize American democracy, 'from the bottom up.' Lois Gibbs, head of the nationwide Citizens' Clearinghouse for Toxic Hazards, asserts (1993: x): 'A major goal of the grass-roots movement for environmental justice is to rebuild the United States, community by community.' Such statements seem at times to be motivated by nostalgia for the community-based 'yeoman democracy' celebrated in some versions of early American history, in contrast to the overdeveloped bureaucracies and out-of-human-scale political institutions that appear to characterize the present.

However, with an estimated 5,000 local, community-based antitoxic groups in the US today, there is a real danger that community-based activism will merely shift problems around, without getting at the structural roots of the problems themselves. For example, a successful protest against high levels of lead contamination in the soil of a poor, largely Latino community in West Dallas led to a cleanup project, which resulted in the redeposition of lead-contaminated soil in a landfill in Louisiana – perhaps not surprisingly located in a predominantly African American community (Bullard, 1993a: 28).

The dangers of uncoordinated community-based activism have become even more pronounced in the present era of 'flexible capital accumulation.' (See Field, 1994, for discussion of distinctively 'post-Fordist' environmental problems in the US) The economic recession in the last decade in the US has led to concerted corporate attacks against the environmental movement and to increasing attempts to cut production costs and increase profits by paying less for labor and circumventing environmental regulations. In the name of flexibility, the state is allowing corporations to buy and sell 'pollution credits,' which means that some factories can legally exceed federal limitations on the amounts of pollutants they emit. An example is the Tennessee Valley Authority, which greatly exceeds federal limitations on sulfur dioxide emissions. Again, it should come as no surprise to learn that this is an area populated largely by African Americans. The expectation has been that this is a population not likely to be able to mount effective, sustained protests.

The hope among advocates of the environmental justice movement is that diverse groups can organize around interlinked concerns for environmental quality and social equity, with the aim of effecting significant social and institutional changes, rather than merely relocating problems from one area to another. Environmental justice advocates are calling for greater citizen participation in basic social planning for economic development, land use, and zoning. Eventually, advocates claim, the movement could lead to radically transformed relations among local citizens, corporations, and government, to the point that concerns about the quality of everyday life and sustainable communities could begin to hold their own against powerful corporate and political interests.

Evaluation of such claims is beyond the scope of this article. What I wish to argue here is that the implementation of such a radical democratic agenda would require comprehensive structural-historical understandings of integral links among the organization of capital, patterns of social inequality, and the distribution of environmental risks, not only in the US, but also internationally. Such a radical political program would also require developing new and innovative approaches to community mobilization and coalition building. As I argue below, recognition of children – as both environmental victims and actors – represents an important, largely untapped, resource for mobilization in the environmental justice movement. Why then, have perspectives on children's situations and possibilities and on the international dimensions of environmental justice remained so undeveloped within this movement?

Part of the answer is that environmental justice theory was articulated initially in connection with analysis of environmental risks and activism within 'communities of color' within the US. The considerable strengths – and limitations – of the movement need to be assessed in this light.

ENVIRONMENTAL RACISM

A case of large-scale civil disobedience that occurred in Warren County, North Carolina, in 1982 has been identified by some movement historians as the first active demonstration of an emerging environmental justice movement.

> *At this demonstration, hundreds of predominantly African American women and children, but also local white residents, used their bodies to block trucks from dumping poisonous PCB-laced dirt into a landfill near their community. The mainly African American, working class, rural communities of Warren County had been targeted as the dumping site for a toxic waste landfill that would serve industries throughout North Carolina…. Unlike social activism against toxic contamination that predated this event, such as the struggle against Hooker Chemical Company at Love Canal, New York, in the late 1970s, this action began to forge the connections between race, poverty, and the environmental consequences of the production of industrial waste. The Warren County episode succeeded in racializing the antitoxics agenda and catalyzed a number of studies that would document the historical pattern of disproportionately targeting racial minority communities for toxic waste contamination (Di Chiro, 1995: 303).*

One such study was the influential report sponsored by the Commission for Racial Justice (1987), which showed race to be the leading factor in the location of commercial hazardous waste facilities in the US Sixty percent of African Americans and Latino Americans and over 50 percent of Asian/Pacific Islanders and Native Americans live in areas with one or more toxic waste sites.

It is not just that politically underrepresented and economically marginalized communities are more likely to be polluted than others, but that environmental regulations are also less likely to be enforced in these areas. According to a *National Law Journal* study of civil court cases in 1991 (reported in Hofrichter, 1993a: 2–3), 'penalties under hazardous waste law at sites having the greatest white population were about 500 percent higher than penalties at sites with the greatest minority population.'

The term 'environmental racism' was coined in 1987 by the Reverend Benjamin Chavis, executive director of the Commission for Racial Justice. Chavis (quoted in Di Chiro, 1995: 304) defines environmental racism as:

> *racial discrimination in environmental policy making and the*
> *enforcement of regulations and laws, the deliberate targeting of*
> *people of color communities for toxic waste facilities, the official*
> *sanctioning of the life-threatening presence of poisons and*
> *pollutants in our communities, and a history of excluding people*
> *of color from leadership in the environmental movement.*

The term 'environmental racism' allowed people to identify and name conjoined environmental/social forces affecting communities of color across the country and provided a conceptual foundation for uniting communities with very different cultures and histories. In 1991, the First National People of Color Environmental Leadership Summit in Washington, DC, brought together African, Native, Latino, and Asian American delegates from the US, as well as a number of delegates from Canada, Central and South America, Puerto Rico, and the Marshall Islands. The aim of the conference was to develop a 'multiracial movement for change,' based on a commitment to working out from the realities of discrimination in people's everyday lives and environments to a principled critique of the power structures that were responsible for these inequalities – and that had historically kept diverse communities of color largely unaware of their common interests.

Thus, migrant farmworkers in the US (of whom 95 percent are Latino, African American, Afro-Caribbean, and Asian) began to link their concerns about pesticide exposure and unhealthy field and living conditions to Native American concerns about the environmental and health consequences of uranium mining and nuclear waste disposal sites on reservation lands. These largely rural populations have begun to find common cause with urban communities of color. Because of the history of institutionalized racism in the US, linked to discriminatory practices in housing, health care, education, and employment, African Americans are seriously – and disproportionately – affected by industrial toxins, contaminated air and drinking water, and the location of hazardous waste treatment and storage facilities. Research shows that even when social class is held constant, African Americans are at significantly greater risk than whites of exposure to a wide range of toxic materials. Lead poisoning is a classic example, affecting approximately four million children in the US today. Across the spectrum of income levels, African American children are two to three times more likely than white children to suffer from lead poisoning (Bullard, 1993a: 26). This is largely because people of color do not have the same opportunities as whites to 'vote with their feet' – to escape unhealthy physical environments by moving.

The racialization of the grass-roots antitoxics movement in the US has sparked important studies, galvanized local communities to action, provided a powerful foundation for regional and national coalition building, and at least partly succeeded in transforming mainstream environmentalism. Some organizations – for example, Greenpeace – have responded to challenges from the environmental justice movement by incorporating social justice issues into their discussions and including more people of color on their governing boards and general staff. Members of mainstream organizations have also provided expert testimony about environmental risk exposures in court cases and have provided technical assistance in monitoring exposure levels in communities of color.

We may also ask how the emphasis on race as a factor of environmental discrimination might limit the usefulness of environmental justice theory in other regions of the world, where the dominant axes of discrimination are linked to a history of colonialist relations, or to religious or ethnic affiliation. It is important to remember that American constructions of 'race' as a category of identity and a basis for political activism are far from universal. As noted above, the theory and practice of the environmental justice movement in the US have been strongly influenced by its roots in the Civil Rights Movement of the 1960s. This movement was developed in opposition to US structures of racial discrimination and was grounded in notions of human rights and democratic participation that are extended only with difficulty to the situations of other groups – for example, to Ukrainian and Belorussian populations in the vicinity of Chernobyl, or even to women and children in the US. (The question of universal human rights in relation to the special rights of particular groups is discussed more fully below.)

OTHER DIMENSIONS OF ENVIRONMENTAL JUSTICE: CLASS, OCCUPATION, AND GEOPOLITICAL LOCATION

The contemporary literature on the theory and practice of environmental justice is marked by attempts to expand the range of groups considered to be at special risk. Some groups become particularly vulnerable because of occupation – for example, workers in hazardous oil, petrochemical, and nuclear industries, and rural farmworkers, particularly those in large 'agribusiness' regions (Noble, 1993; Chavez, 1993). Given the structure of American race relations, there are, of course, integral links between patterns of environmental racism and occupation and class-based environmental inequities.

Some of these links are discussed in the environmental justice literature. Yet there is little discussion of how constellations of race, class, and occupation might be very differently structured outside the US, making coalition building along lines of 'environmental racism' extremely difficult. This may be one reason why, despite frequent arguments for the importance of connecting grass-roots groups at national and international levels, there are very few examples of the latter.

Bullard (1993b: 19) provides a striking example of what he calls 'toxic colonialism,' whereby the First World exports its most profitable and dangerous production methods, goods, and waste disposal strategies to the Third World. Bullard refers to an internal memorandum written in 1991 by Laurence Summers, chief economist at the World Bank. This memorandum caused a minor international scandal after it was leaked to the press. Summers lists a number of reasons why the World Bank should be encouraging, rather than discouraging, the movement of dirty industries to the less-developed countries. These reasons include lower health costs and less likelihood of public opposition. Summers (quoted in Bullard, 1993b: 19) observes: 'I've always thought that under-polluted areas in Africa are vastly *under* polluted: their air quality is probably vastly inefficiently low compared to Los Angeles or Mexico City.' He goes on to speak of 'world welfare enhancing trade in air pollution and waste' to the Third World. We are certainly justified in asking more specific questions about *whose* welfare is actually being enhanced here, and in what ways.

The environmental justice literature includes important discussions of the export of industrial and military wastes to the Third World (Greenpeace, 1992), the relation between nuclear weapons states and indigenous peoples (Nietschmann and Le Bon, 1987), and some of the difficulties and challenges of forging a truly international environmental justice movement (Kiefer and Benjamin, 1993; Peng, 1993; and Buttel, 1995). What is generally lacking, however, is systematic discussion of the ways in which globally significant changes in politics, economy, and culture in recent decades have affected the environmental experiences of local communities in the United States. Although there is a growing body of historical studies of the environmental justice movement in the US, there is little reflection about *why* this movement appeared when it did – in the mid-1970s. This was a period when notions of 'everyday life' and 'community' were becoming problematic in new ways, when the economic, political, and environmental situations of the poor were steadily deteriorating at the local level, and when skepticism about the efficacy of mainstream political parties and strategies was increasing.

The mid-1970s has been characterized as a transition period in the movement to 'late' or 'advanced capitalism' and a 'global regime of flexible accumulation.' (See Harvey, 1989.) This shift involved changes in the international structuring of capital and finance institutions, including new and expanded roles for the World Bank, International Monetary Fund, and multinational corporations. These globally significant developments have challenged the capacities of nation-states to regulate and control their domestic economies, resulted in cutbacks and 'downsizing' of social welfare programs and institutions around the world, and rendered increasingly problematic attempts at economic and political 'renewal' and 'revitalization' that are framed primarily in local or even national terms. Since the 1970s, 'flexibility' has become a sort of corporate and fiscal mantra, leading to attacks on nationally organized labor unions and federally mandated environmental regulations, as well as to greater economic and political disenfranchisement of already marginalized communities (Harvey, 1989; Martin, 1994).

Chawla (1995: 71) outlines four dimensions in which global capital is currently being restructured for flexibility in order to raise industry profits:

> *First, flexibility in labor processes through new technologies and forms of organization intensifies work itself, increasing its pace, the length of the work day, and supervisory control, and decreasing social relations among workers. Second, capital achieves flexibility in labor markets by subcontracting, part-time employment, and other means by which work can be quickly reallocated from one group of people to another. Third, flexible state policies allow capital to shed its social responsibilities to workers and to the communities in which it operates. Finally, computers and telecommunications enable flexible geographic mobility, fragmenting production and administration, and giving capital the ability to effectively 'deterritorialize' itself, freeing its operations from local and national controls.*

This restructuring has profound consequences for individuals, families, and communities around the world. 'It results in unemployment or job insecurity, declining wages, long work days, the privatization or loss of social services, high stress, and unraveling social networks,' as well as 'alienated and dangerous communities' (*Ibid*). It also results in environmental pollution, particularly in areas where it is believed that residents lack the education and political leverage for effective protest. In the face of such assaults on the integrity of local communities, it becomes increasingly problematic to rely uncritically on notions of local community action as the primary springboard to a revitalized democracy and transformed corporate/political agenda.

Of course, it also becomes increasingly important to think about the importance of community for human growth and development, life quality, and identity, and about the many different visions of community we might draw upon in strengthening, rebuilding, and, to some extent, constructing anew the communal frameworks of our daily lives.

ECOFEMINISM

Recent environmental justice writings have attempted to theorize not only race, class, and occupational correlates of environmental risk, but also gender dimensions (Epstein, 1991; Kraus, 1993a, 1993b, and 1994; and Rosenberg, 1995). It has been estimated that over 80 percent of the leaders of grass-roots protests in the US are women, from predominantly blue-collar and minority backgrounds. Pardo (1990) describes, for example, the Mothers of East Los Angeles, a group of Latino American women who successfully opposed the building of a hazardous waste incinerator in East Los Angeles and went on to work for improved housing, schools, and neighborhood safety – all issues they saw as being equally 'environmental.'

In *Love Canal: My Story*, Lois Gibbs (leader of the national organization Citizens' Clearinghouse for Hazardous Waste) describes her entry into political life, motivated by a wife's and mother's concerns about her family's health. When her daughter developed a rare blood disease and her son was diagnosed with epilepsy, Gibbs began to speak with other parents, who were increasingly concerned about their own children's health. Little by little, they pieced together an understanding of how local chemical contamination in their neighborhood might be linked to health problems in their families. Gibbs describes her increasing politicization, as she took a leading role in community efforts to gain access to information, acknowledgment of local concerns from authorities and corporate representatives, and compensation for damaged health and local environments. In the course of negotiating with predominantly white, male, middle-class business people and policymakers, she began to develop broader understandings of social inequities that determine which communities are subject to the greatest environmental risks and which groups have the power to set political agendas.

It is interesting, however, that race and class tend to be more prominent than is gender, both in the environmental justice theoretical literature and in the autobiographical accounts of women activists. One reason is the uneasy relation between the American feminist movement and the perspectives of activist women, who see concerns about children, motherhood, families, and communities as the primary motivations for their political involvement. Another reason is that grass-roots environmental campaigns grow out of local, geographically identifiable communities. Given patterns of residential segregation in the US, spatially identifiable communities can often be correlated with race and class, but obviously not with gender.

Capek (1993: 5) observes that the interpretive frame of 'environmental justice' was 'fashioned simultaneously from the bottom up (local grass-roots groups discovering a pattern to their grievances) and from the top down (national organizations conveying the term to local groups)' and depending upon them for their political legitimacy and momentum. This integral relation between theory and practice was much less the case with grass-roots activism and 'ecofeminism,' an intellectual development beginning in the late 1970s that attempted to bring together insights from the feminist, environmental, and peace movements (Seager, 1993a, 1993b; Mies and Shiva, 1993; Shiva, 1994; Diamond and Orenstein, 1989). The ecofeminist literature often tends to be framed in abstract language from feminist theory that working-class women find distant from their own concerns. This, together with the 'new age' spiritual bent of some prominent ecofeminist authors, tends to diminish the potential relevance of ecofeminist theories for local activists.

57

In my opinion, however, ecofeminism has much to offer to the environmental justice movement. This literature is particularly strong in tracing links between militarism – a project heavily infused with structurally 'male' imagery and motivations – and serious environmental problems that often put women (and children) at special risk. A UN report from Iraq after the Gulf War (reported in Seager, 1993b: 63) notes that one important consequence of war-related environmental destruction in the area is that women and children are spending increasingly large parts of their days searching for food, fuel, and water. Many toxic agents in wide use by military forces have particularly damaging effects on the sensitive reproductive systems of women. For example, the 25 million gallons of defoliants, herbicides, and other chemicals used by the US military services in Vietnam have been linked to studies indicating that Vietnamese women have the highest rate of spontaneous abortions in the world, as well as high incidences of vaginal infections, cervical cancers, and occurrences of birth defects in their offspring (*Ibid*: 64). Gallagher (1993) documents some of the human costs, particularly in terms of reproductive abnormalities and childhood illnesses, of populations living downwind of US nuclear weapons tests in the deserts of Nevada.

Despite such compelling evidence, however, the links between gender and environmental risk still remain only partially developed in the environmental justice literature. The situation is even more problematic when we turn our attention to children and the variable of age.

CHILDREN AS A SPECIAL ENVIRONMENTAL INTEREST GROUP

It is extraordinary how little attention has been given in the environmental justice literature to the special vulnerabilities of children (with the exception of lead poisoning in children, often cited in connection with pronounced environmental risks to African American populations). The neglect of children is especially striking, when we consider that concerns about child health and welfare figure prominently among the reasons given by grass-roots activists – a majority of them women – for their own political activism. Lois Gibbs (quoted in Kraus, 1993a: 113) emphasizes how action aimed at the protection of children 'brings a concrete moral dimension to our experience – they are not an abstract statistic.' At a recent conference in Ann Arbor, Michigan (December 1995), on 'The Environmental Connection: Rising Rates of Breast Cancer, Reproductive Disorders, and Children's Disease,' I was struck by how many of the talks by grass-roots activists began with personal tales of the suffering of children – their own or others'. 'Statistics,' many repeated, 'are human beings with the tears removed.' Activists resolutely defend a view of the grass-roots movement that remains close enough to people's everyday lives and experiences to keep the tears in view.

Yet even though concerns about children are clearly central to the engagement of grass-roots activists themselves, the social dimension of age remains outside the boundaries of theoretical discussion. The following statement by Mary Mellor (1993: 37) is typical of the environmental justice literature: 'Ecological fault lines follow structures of economic power: from whites to people of color, men to women, rich to poor, North to South.' She *might* also have added, 'from adults to children' – but, significantly, she did not.

We have ample evidence that the developing bodies of children are characterized by biological processes and interactive relations with the physical world that are in many respects very different from those of adults (Ebrahim, 1982; World Health Organization, 1986; Stephens, 1994). Children have been identified as the 'canaries in the mines,' insofar as their bodies are particularly vulnerable to deteriorating environmental conditions. (This phrase refers to mining practices in the last century aimed at monitoring the quality of underground air. When canaries brought down into the mines became sick and stopped singing, it was an early warning sign that the air had become dangerous for miners as well.)

Children are also vulnerable to environmental risks because of their distinctive pathways of exposure. A dramatic example of this point may be the marked increase in childhood cancers and mysterious swollen abdomens among Iraqi children after the Gulf War (Hoskins, 1993). Some scientists have argued that these health problems may be due in part to children playing with empty artillery shells made from 'depleted uranium,' a byproduct of the nuclear industry that is desirable in weapons production because it is so hard. Although the Pentagon insists that the shells are only 'very, very mildly radioactive' – not enough to be classified as 'radiological weapons' – it is unlikely that Pentagon scientists ever considered the possible consequences of children playing with the empty shells. A doctor who was part of an international medical team evaluating the postwar situation of Iraqi children reported seeing children in Basra putting empty artillery shells over their hands and using them as hand puppets.

Di Chiro (1995: 303) notes that environmental justice activists are attempting to redefine 'the environment,' away from notions of a pristine, natural environment untouched and uncontaminated by human actions and toward a community-based vision of the environment as 'the place you work, the place you live, the place you play.' In fact, there is little play going on in the environmental justice field.

We know that children do an increasingly large share of subsistence work, both in the Third World and elsewhere (Ennew and Milne, 1989; Niewenhuys, 1994). Children are also increasingly drawn into the wage-labor market in conditions that are often dangerous to their physical and social development. However, children not only work, they also *play*, and these activities constitute special forms of 'the environment' that are not apprehensible from an adult-centered perspective. A focus on children's experiences of environmental risks calls our attention in the most demanding ways to the micro-processes of human/environment relations. What consequences do environmental changes and regulations have for children's everyday lives, for the nature of their social interactions, for the spaces they occupy in work and play, for the very composition of the air they breathe, the food they eat, and the dirt under their nails?

Children around the world are increasingly bearing the burdens of 'development.' This may be most starkly apparent in the ways that global restructuring and increasing disparities between the 'haves' and 'have nots' are played out in the lives of poor children. As Chawla (1995: 71) notes, these processes frequently translate into 'diminished nutrition and health care, substandard schools, or schools that become inaccessible when attendance fees are imposed, alienated and dangerous communities, street work or other child labor to supplement inadequate family incomes.' They also frequently translate into deteriorating environments with particularly serious consequences for children in urban slum and squatter areas. Blanc (1994: 21–22) observes:

> children can be seen playing, washing themselves, and drinking
> the polluted waters of Bangkok's canals, or roaming through the
> uncollected garbage in Nairobi.... The shortage of water,
> sewage, and sanitation forces parents and their children to use
> particularly polluted outlets. Overcrowding increases the
> possibility of the spread of infections and contagious diseases.

Infants and children in developing countries are several hundred times more likely to die from diarrhea, pneumonia, and measles than are children in Europe and North America (Hardoy et al, 1990).

Children's environmentally related health problems are strikingly evident in the former USSR. A recent UNICEF study on conditions in Central and Eastern Europe – entitled 'Crisis in Mortality, Health, and Nutrition' – notes that 17 percent of the former USSR has been declared an ecological crisis area (UNICEF, 1994: 29). Children's respiratory diseases (chronic bronchitis and asthmatic diseases), allergies, retarded intellectual development, and anemia have been linked to high levels of environmental contamination (including pesticides and toxic metals in groundwater and soil, as well as sulfur dioxide, nitrogen oxides, and lead pollution in the air). There has been a striking increase in thyroid cancer among children in Belarus, Ukraine, and the Russian Federation following the Chernobyl accident (World Health Organization, 1995). These environmental problems are compounded by social problems in a 'political economy of transition': 'cracks in the system' – in the form of decreasing availability of social services, increasing unemployment, family tensions, and urban violence – are widening and children are often the first to suffer the consequences (UNICEF, 1994: 10).

We might ask about the consequences of global development and restructuring for the environments, health, and psychological and social welfare of more materially privileged children as well. Increasing numbers of children in the industrialized world suffer from environmentally related allergies, respiratory ailments, and immune system disturbances, linked to chemical burdens in food, air, clothing, and the indoor environments of homes and schools (Rapp, 1991: 262–317). These problems are not correlated with class, ethnicity, or race in any simple way.

While acknowledging that childhoods around the world are very different and that children do not comprise a self-evidently unitary group (any more than do 'women' or 'people of color'), we can still see ways in which the special characteristics of children's biology and development represent a foundation for regarding children as a special category of environmental victims. This point has significant implications for national and international environmental policy formation. Consider, for example, children's special vulnerability to radiation risks, which are greatest to rapidly dividing cells and developing organs. It is noteworthy that powerful international organizations (such as the ICRP, International Commission for Radiological Protection) concerned with setting 'safe' or 'acceptable' levels of radiation exposure base these standards on risk assessments done with respect to 'normal' populations. Many of these studies are occupational studies of workers in nuclear plants. The 'normal' population thus turns out to be largely white, male, healthy Euro-Americans of working age.

'Ecofeminist' perspectives would appear to be relevant here in explaining the lack of attention to children's special vulnerabilities. The 13-member, self-appointing executive committee of the ICRP consists exclusively of male representatives from the 'hard' sciences – primarily physicists and radiation biologists. There has never been a public or community health specialist on the governing committee, or a social scientist, or a woman. Study after study shows a significant gender gap in the ways people think about radiation risks, and this gap persists even among radiation scientists themselves (Slovic, 1991). This finding makes it difficult to argue, as some have tried to do, that the gap can be attributed to women's relative lack of knowledge and reliance on feelings. There are probably multiple overdetermined reasons – inflected by race and class, as well as gender – why the ICRP's executive committee has not registered significant concern with children or grass-roots public concerns about radiation safety.

Such perspectives are also potentially relevant for explaining the marked neglect of children as a special environmental interest group in the environmental justice literature. In part, this may reflect the general neglect of children in the 'macro' disciplines of sociology, economics, and political science. Despite important developments in recent years in the sociology of childhood (see James and Prout, 1990), research on children, particularly in the US, still tends to be 'ghettoized' in the fields of child development, education, and the child welfare branch of social work.

A low priority is also given to children in American political life, despite their current ubiquity in discussions of the need for welfare reform. The 'needs of children and future generations' are cited, repeatedly, as reasons for getting tougher with unwed welfare mothers, for streamlining and 'downsizing' the welfare system, and for calling on states and local communities to take over services no longer guaranteed at the federal level. Children in these debates seem to be a sort of 'empty sign,' brought in to sweeten the bitter pill of drastic welfare cuts that are likely to have very damaging consequences for the health and well-being of real children, as the Children's Defense Fund and other child advocacy organizations frequently assert.

I believe, however, that the most important reason for children's neglect in the environmental justice literature is the widespread assumption that although children may be *objects* of environmental inequalities, they cannot be *actors* and *participants* in grass-roots activism.

CHILDREN AS ENVIRONMENTAL ACTORS

The environmental justice movement puts a high priority on the potential for political mobilization of groups at special risk. Children have not traditionally been seen as political actors. In this connection, it is of interest that the Warren County, South Carolina, demonstration regarded by many as the founding act of the environmental justice movement, involved 'hundreds of predominantly African American women and children' who 'used their bodies to block trucks from dumping poisonous PCB-laced dirt into a landfill near their community' (Di Chiro, 1995: 303). Yet the participation of children quickly and characteristically disappears from the discussion, in favor of issues of race, class, and gender.

There is a tendency in American culture to naturalize and essentialize children as passive victims or beneficiaries of adult actions. 'They are innocent, vulnerable, and dependent, and therefore society's primary responsibility is to protect them from adult experiences, like war and work, so that they can develop in their separate spheres of school and play' (Chawla, 1995: 73). We have seen, however, that the boundaries of these separate spheres of childhood worlds (which certainly never existed in the idealized ways in which they are now often nostalgically conceived) are increasingly transgressed. The everyday lives of children are increasingly subject to forces that are currently restructuring families, communities, classes, racial and ethnic groups, nations, and world regions. (See Stephens, 1995, for a discussion of children's changing life conditions in 'late capitalism.')

Di Chiro (1995: 310) develops a perspective on the environmental justice movement as a 'political culture based on community-organized and network-oriented social organization.... Community becomes at once the idea, the place, and the relations and practices that generate what these activists consider more socially just and ecologically sound human/environment configurations.' The emphasis on community has allowed movement activists to argue for integral connections between ostensibly separate realms of environmental quality and social justice. Pam Tau Lee, a board member of the National Toxics Campaign Fund, observes:

> *[Environmental justice is] able to bring together different issues that used to be separate. If you're talking about lead and where people live, it used to be a housing struggle; if you're talking about poisoning on the job, it used to be a labor struggle; people being sick from TB or occupational exposures used to be separate health issues, so environmental justice is able to bring*

> *together all of these different issues to create one movement that*
> *can really address what actually causes all of these phenomena*
> *to happen and gets to the root of the problems (quoted in Di*
> *Chiro, 1995: 301).*

Yet insofar as the core notion of community draws on conventional ways of thinking about children's situations and interests as reflections of the situations and interests of adults, children become merely background to and passive recipients of adult actions on their behalf. It is interesting that historians of the environmental justice movement represent one of the decisive outcomes of the First National People of Color Environmental Leadership Summit in 1991 as a rejection of the old 'partnership based on paternalism' with mainstream environmentalists (Di Chiro, 1995: 303). People of color, the argument goes, are taking a collective stand against being treated like children and denied participation in decision-making processes that profoundly shape their daily lives. However, we might also begin to question why children themselves continue to be 'treated like children.'

There is evidence from around the world that children are playing increasingly important roles in 'investigating, planning, monitoring, and managing the environments of their own communities' (Hart, 1994: 92). (See also Bajracharya, 1994; and Miljeteig, 1994.) A fascinating and illuminating case in point appears to be the involvement of children and youth in grass-roots environmental activism in the former USSR.

There is growing evidence that women in the former USSR – as in the US, and in many other regions of the world – are taking central roles in the grass-roots environmental movement. (See, for example, Feshbach and Friendly, 1992.) We have as yet only suggestive, anecdotal information about children's involvement. Zhirina (1994) describes the participation of children in environmental activities in the Bryansk region of southwestern Russia. This area suffers from considerable fallout from Chernobyl, as well as from toxic industrial chemicals. Concerned about these problems, Viola, a local environmental group, carried out studies to measure levels of radiation in the soil and in local vegetation and amounts of heavy metals and organic compounds in river and local drinking water. The group then embarked on public information programs aimed at politicians and business people. Viola found that even when local authorities were well informed about pollution levels and health risks, there was little practical response. The political and business communities appeared to be more concerned about immediate economic problems than about environmental and health problems.

The group then turned their attentions to 'ordinary people' – factory workers and residents of polluted towns and villages in the region. Again, there was little response. Many people found it difficult to challenge polluting industries they depended on for employment. The weight of knowledge about extensive radioactive and chemical pollution in their communities and, more generally, in the former USSR resulted in a kind of 'psychic numbing,' making people unwilling or unable to acknowledge personal dangers, either to themselves or their families.

Finally, as a last resort, Viola began working with children. The group started environmental education programs, both within the schools and local communities. In the period 1986 to 1990, parents and teachers had noticed a sharp increase in depression, passivity, and aggression among young people. This situation improved markedly as children (some as young as 10 years old) became involved in monitoring local pollution – drawing up maps of the effects of acid rain and measuring levels of chemical and radioactive contamination.

One group of children found high levels of mercury in ponds and ditches where they played. They traced the chemical to a local factory producing mercury vapor lamps for the military. The children, together with 'Viola' members and some parents and teachers, then made formal protests to local authorities and factory officials. This resulted in the factory installing cleanup equipment that eliminated the runoff of mercury into local water supplies. Another group of children located radioactive hot spots on local playgrounds. Sand on the playgrounds was removed and the play area paved over with asphalt, minimizing dangers from direct contact with radioactive soil.

Admittedly, these are small actions within a very seriously contaminated area. Yet Viola members also reported that mobilization of children had significant effects on adults as well as children. Children's engagement with environmental concerns helped to break through the adults' 'psychic numbing,' so that parents, teachers, and administrators became more openly concerned about environmental problems and more willing to consider environmental cleanup programs and health rehabilitation programs that do not have immediate economic payoffs.

The Norwegian Centre for Child Research and the Moscow-based Center for Independent Ecological Programs (a research branch of the Socio-Ecological Union) developed plans for a jointly sponsored workshop, held outside Moscow in June 1996 on the topic of 'Children's Participation in Community-Based Environmental Care.' Aims of the meeting were to develop plans for studying the nature and dimensions of children's participation in grass-roots environmental activism in the former USSR, to compare these activities with various sorts of children's environmental participation in the West, and to explore possibilities for international network building.

To my knowledge, no studies have yet been done of children's participation in grass-roots environmental activism in the US. This, it seems, is a crucial area for future research. How do concerns about children's health and well-being figure in people's motivations for involvement? How do children understand adult concerns, debates, and actions, and to what extent are children themselves actively involved in the 'new environmentalism'? How might serious considerations of children as both environmental victims and actors change the ways we envision environmental justice theory and practice? Opening up this area of research requires a reconceptualization not only of children and childhoods, but also of community, democratic participation, and human rights.

CHILDREN AS RIGHT HOLDERS

The fact that the United States was one of the last countries to sign the United Nations *Convention on the Rights of the Child* (adopted by the UN in 1989 and signed by the US in 1995) suggests deeply entrenched – and divided – thinking about the appropriate role of children in society. Opposition to US ratification has come from two sources: conservative 'family values' groups, concerned about the ways that children's rights claims might undermine parental rights over children, and women's rights advocates, concerned that an emphasis on children's rights might deflect attention and resources away from adult women, who are more able to analyze various forms of discrimination against them and to carry out concerted political actions.

The UN *Convention on the Rights of the Child* is in many respects an unprecedented document in the international human rights arena (Alston et al, 1992; Freeman and Veerman, 1992; Stephens, 1995). Earlier UN Conventions, such as the UN *Convention on the Elimination of All Forms of Discrimination Against Women* (1979), were based on claims that particular collectivities have special rights because of a history of discrimination that had denied them the full range of internationally recognized human rights. The Women's Convention stresses that it is the duty of ratifying states to modify or abolish all social imped-iments to the formal equality of individuals – male *and* female – before the law. In contrast, the children's convention (defining the 'child' as a person up to the age of 18) puts forth a notion of children as rights holders, associated with differ-ent sorts of rights at different stages of development and with respect to the child's evolving capacities for rational consideration and moral judgment.

The UN *Convention on the Rights of the Child* has been characterized by the Three P's: Protection, Provision, and Participation. Children have the right to be protected from harm, to be provided with services necessary for their healthy growth and development, and to participate in decisions that affect them accord-ing to their evolving capacities. An argument can be made that the child's rights to protection and care should be foregrounded in connection with very young children, while rights to self-expression and meaningful social participation become more important in connection with older children.

One of the qualitatively new aspects of the Convention is its emphasis on the capacity of children to act at least partially independently of adults. Thus, the Convention lays down rights, such as children's rights to freedom of expression (Article 13), association (Article 15), and participation (Article 12) that are not just protective, but also enabling. The contentious 'participation clause' (Article 12) – asserting that the child shall have a right to express his or her own views 'in all matters affecting the child, the views of the child being given due weight in accordance with the age and maturity of the child' – has sometimes been narrowly interpreted to refer to parental custody cases, but is increasingly construed much more broadly (Miljeteig, 1994).

There is no general consensus in international law on either the right to a decent environment as an individual human right or environmental rights as collective human rights. Nevertheless, some legal scholars (for example, Pevato, 1994) have argued that a child's right to a decent environment may be found by implication through other human rights recognized in various conventions – in particular, the UN *Convention on the Rights of the Child*. Note, for example, articles 6 (right to life), 24 (right of the child to the enjoyment of the highest attainable standard of health), 27 (right of every child to a standard of living adequate for the child's development), and 31 (right of the child to rest and leisure and to engage in play and recreational activities). Pevato (*Ibid*: 178) argues that the convention 'stresses that children need special safeguards, including "appropriate legal protection" and children living in "exceptionally difficult conditions" need special considerations. Such circumstances would no doubt include environmentally disastrous locations where children struggle to survive.'

Although plausible and compelling arguments may be made for arguing that ratifying states are obliged to work toward providing the quality environments children require to enjoy their convention-guaranteed rights, much work still must be done in exploring the implications of the 'participation clause' and the levels and kinds of children's environmental participation that might be regarded as being in 'children's best interests.' (Obviously, children's age, cultural backgrounds, social situations, and specific concerns are of central relevance here.) There is a growing body of literature (for example, Chawla and Kjoerholt, 1996; Edwards, 1996; Miljeteig, 1994; Hart, 1992; King, 1995; and Stephens, 1994) concerned with complexities of 'children's participation' and the social possibilities – and dangers – associated with this notion. I have argued elsewhere (Stephens, 1994: 14) that:

> *the expectation that children have special responsibilities to identify, articulate, and propose solutions for adult-created environmental problems parallels the notion that it is the Third World poor, in many respects the victims of international development policies of previous decades, who are responsible for turning the tide of global processes of environmental degradation and for initiating a new era of sustainable global development.*

There is a danger of asking children to become 'small adults' and take on enormous burdens before they are ready (Elshtain, 1996). Yet, in the case of the children of Bryansk, the environmental participation of even fairly young children seems to have resulted in real improvements – material, psychological, and social – in children's lives and in the community as a whole.

Debates about the desirability and consequentiality of different sorts of children's participation, and about children's rights more generally, point to changes in children's life conditions and changing social constructions of childhood that have not yet had an impact on the environmental justice literature. Capek (1993: 8) observes that 'environmental justice is premised on the notion that the rights of toxic contamination victims have been systematically usurped by more powerful social actors, and that "justice" resides in the return of these rights.' As I have argued above, the US Civil Rights Movement has provided the master frame validating the struggle for environmental justice by other disenfranchised groups. We might ask how other sorts of internationally significant rights claims – such as the claims for special women's and children's rights – might challenge theorists of the environmental justice movement to reframe their discussions, and might even provide important new concepts and languages for people 'on the ground' to recognize and name injustices in their everyday lives and to forge new connections across social and geographical boundaries. The social category of children is unique in crosscutting all others (race, class, gender, ethnicity, religion, and nationality). It thus holds out the possibility for coalition building that unites special interest groups grounded in more narrowly defined localities or social conditions.

CONCLUSION

There are important practical arguments for including children in the environmental justice movement. As noted above, much of the literature in this area tends to rely on somewhat romantic, or at least uncritical, assumptions about the powers of citizen democracy. Yet where do adult citizens develop these strengths? It is not enough just to hold a town meeting. It is also necessary to have people attend these meetings who have the skills and knowledge to participate in democratic institutions. We need to know much more about the ways that children are already involved in grass-roots environmental activism, both in the US and elsewhere; about the possibilities and consequences for children of different types and levels of involvement in different social and cultural contexts; and about the ways in which children's participation can affect the adults around them, as well as contribute to the development of concerns and capacities with important implications for their future actions as adult citizens.

The virtual absence of discussion of children in the environmental justice literature – either as victims or actors – suggests that there may be inequities within the movement itself (as well as constraining assumptions about children and childhood on the part of people who study and write about this movement). However, opening up this field to serious considerations of children's experiences, understandings, concerns, and potentials for action is not just a matter of social equity. It also raises important theoretical issues for discussion and new possibilities for practical engagement at the community, national, and international levels.

REFERENCES

Alston, Philip, Stephen Parker, and John Seymour (eds) (1992) *Children, Rights, and the Law*. Oxford: Clarendon Press.

Bajracharya, Deepak (1994) 'Primary Environmental Care for Sustainable Livelihood: A UNICEF Perspective.' *Childhood* 2,1–2 (February-May): 41–56.

Blanc, Cristina Szanton (1994) *Urban Children in Distress: Global Predicaments and Innovative Strategies*. New York: Gordon and Breach.

Bryant, Bunyan (ed) (1995) *Environmental Justice: Issues, Policies, and Solutions*. Washington, DC/Covelo, Cal.: Island Press.

Bullard, Robert D. (1993a) 'Anatomy of Environmental Racism.' Richard Hofrichter (ed) *Toxic Struggles: The Theory and Practice of Environmental Justice*. Philadelphia, Penn./Gabriola Island, BC: New Society Publishers: 25–36.

Bullard, Robert D. (1993b) 'Anatomy of Environmental Racism and the Environmental Justice Movement.' Robert D. Bullard (ed) *Confronting Environmental Racism: Voices from the Grass-roots*. Boston: South End Press: 15–41.

Bullard, Robert D. (ed). (1994) *Unequal Protection: Environmental Justice and Communities of Color*. San Francisco: Sierra Club Books.

Buttel, Frederick H. (1995) 'Rethinking International Environmental Policy in the Late Twentieth Century.' Bunyan Bryant (ed) *Environmental Justice: Issues, Policies, and Solutions*. Washington, DC/Covelo, Cal.: Island Press: 187–208.

Capek, Stella M. (1993) 'The Environmental Justice Frame: A Conceptual Discussion and an Application.' *Social Problems* 40,1 (February): 5–25.

Chavez, Cesar (1993) 'Farm Workers at Risk.' Richard Hofrichter (ed) *Toxic Struggles: The Theory and Practice of Environmental Justice*. Philadelphia, Penn./Gabriola Island, BC: New Society Publishers: 163–171.

Chawla, Louise (1995) 'The World Summit for Social Development: Issues for Children.' Barn/Childhood, Norwegian Centre for Child Research No 2: 65–80.

Chawla, Louise and Anne Trine Kjoerholt (1996) 'Children as Special Citizens.' PLA Notes 25 (Notes on Participatory Learning and Action) (February): 43–46.

Commission for Racial Justice (1987) *Toxic Waste and Race in the United States: A National Report on the Racial and Socioeconomic Characteristics of Communities with Hazardous Waste Sites*. New York: United Church of Christ.

Diamond, Irene and Gloria Orenstein (1989) *Reweaving the World: The Emergence of Ecofeminism*. San Francisco: Sierra Club Books.

Di Chiro, Giovanna (1995) 'Nature as Community: The Convergence of Environment and Social Justice.' William Cronon (ed) *Uncommon Ground: Toward Reinventing Nature*. New York: W.W. Norton and Co.: 298–531.

Ebrahim, G.J. (1982) *Child Health in a Changing Environment*. London: Macmillan.

Edwards, Michael (1996) 'Institutionalizing Children's Participation in Development.' PLA Notes 25 (Notes on Participatory Learning and Action) (February): 47–51.

Elshtain, Jean Bethke (1996) 'Political Children.' *Childhood: A Global Journal of Child Research* 3,1 (February 1): 1–28.

Ennew, Judith and Brian Milne (1989) *The Next Generation: The Lives of Third World Children*. London: Zed Press.

Epstein, Barbara (1991) 'Ecofeminism and Grass-roots Environmentalism in the United States.' Richard Hofrichter (ed) *Toxic Struggles: The Theory and Practice of Environmental Justice*. Philadelphia, Penn./Gabriola Island, BC: New Society Publishers: 144–153.

Feshbach, Murray and Alfred Friendly, Jr. (1992) *Ecocide in the USSR: Health and Nature Under Siege*. New York: Basic Books.

Field, Rodger (1994) 'Children, Community, and Pollution Control: Toward a Community-Oriented Environmentalism.' *Childhood* 2,1–2 (February/May): 28–41.

Freeman, Michael and Philip Veerman (eds) (1992) *The Ideologies of Children's Rights.* Dordrecht/Boston/London: Martinus Nijhoff Publishers.

Gallagher, Carol (1993) *American Ground Zero: The Secret Nuclear War.* Cambridge, Mass.: MIT Press.

Gibbs, Lois (1993) 'Foreword.' Richard Hofrichter (ed) *Toxic Struggles: The Theory and Practice of Environmental Justice.* Philadelphia, Penn./Gabriola Island, BC: New Society Publishers: ix-xi.

Gibbs, Lois (1982) *Love Canal: My Story.* Albany: State University of New York Press.

Greenpeace (1992) 'The 'Logic' Behind Hazardous Waste Export.' *Greenpeace Waste Trade Update.* First Quarter: 1–2.

Hardoy, J.E., S. Cairncross, and D. Satterthwaite (eds) (1990) *The Poor Die Young: Housing and Health in Third World Cities.* London: Earthscan Publications.

Hart, Roger (1994) 'Children's Role in Primary Environmental Care.' *Childhood* 2,1–2 (February/May): 103–110.

Hart, Roger (1992) 'Children's Participation: From Tokenism to Citizenship.' UN Children's Fund, *Innocenti Essays* No 4.

Harvey, David (1989) *The Condition of Postmodernity: An Inquiry into the Conditions of Cultural Change.* Oxford: Basil Blackwell.

Hofrichter, Richard (1993a) 'Introduction.' Richard Hofrichter, *Toxic Struggles: The Theory and Practice of Environmental Justice.* Philadelphia, Penn./Gabriola Island, BC: New Society Publishers: 1–12.

Hofrichter, Richard (1993b) *Toxic Struggles: The Theory and Practice of Environmental Justice.* Philadelphia, Penn./Gabriola Island, BC: New Society Publishers.

Hoskins, E. (1993) 'With Its Uranium Shells, Desert Storm May Have Sown Death.' *International Herald Tribune* (January 22): 4.

James, Allison and Alan Prout (eds) (1990) *Constructing and Reconstructing Childhood: Contemporary Issues in the Sociological Study of Childhood.* London: The Falmer Press.

Kiefer, Chris and Medea Benjamin (1993) 'Solidarity with the Third World: Building an International Environmental Justice Movement.' Richard Hofrichter (ed) *Toxic Struggles: The Theory and Practice of Environmental Justice.* Philadelphia, Penn./Gabriola Island, BC: New Society Publishers: 226–237.

King, Donna (1995) *Doing Their Share to Save the Planet: Children and the Environmental Crisis.* New Brunswick: Rutgers.

Kraus, Celene (1994) 'Women of Color on the Front Line.' Robert Bullard (ed) *Unequal Protection: Environmental Justice and Communities of Color.* San Francisco: Sierra Club Books: 256–271.

Kraus, Celene (1993a) 'Blue-Collar Women and Toxic-Waste Protests: The Process of Politicization.' Richard Hofrichter (ed) *Toxic Struggles: The Theory and Practice of Environmental Justice.* Philadelphia, Penn./Gabriola Island, BC: New Society Publishers: 107–118.

Kraus, Celene (1993b) 'Women and Toxic Waste Protests: Race, Class, and Gender as Resources of Resistance.' Robert D. Bullard (ed) *Environmental Justice and Communities of Color.* San Francisco: Sierra Club Books.

Martin, Emily (1994) 'Post-Darwinism.' Emily Martin, *Flexible Bodies: Tracking Immunity in American Culture from the Days of Polio to the Age of AIDS*. Boston: Beacon Press: 227–251.

Mellor, Mary (1993) 'Building a New Vision: Feminist, Green Socialism.' Richard Hofrichter (ed) *Toxic Struggles: The Theory and Practice of Environmental Justice*. Philadelphia, Penn./Gabriola Island, BC: New Society Publishers: 36–47.

Merchant, Carolyn (1992) *Radical Ecology: The Search for a Livable World*. London: Routledge.

Mies, Maria and Vandana Shiva (1993) *Ecofeminism*. London: Zed Books.

Miljeteig, Per (1994) 'Children's Involvement in the Implementation of Their Own Rights – Present and Future Perspectives.' Paper presented at the International Society for the Study of Behavioral Development, Amsterdam (June 28-July 22).

Nietschmann, Bernard and William Le Bon (1987) 'Nuclear Weapons States and Fourth World Nation.' *Cultural Survival Quarterly* 11: 5–7.

Niewenhuys, Olga (1994) *Children's Lifeworlds: Gender, Welfare, and Labour in the Developing World*. London and New York: Routledge.

Noble, Charles (1993) 'Work: The Most Dangerous Environment.' Richard Hofrichter (ed) *Toxic Struggles: The Theory and Practice of Environmental Justice*. Philadelphia, Penn./Gabriola Island, BC: New Society Publishers: 171–179.

Pardo, Mary (1990) 'Mexican-American Women Grass-Roots Community Activists: Mothers of East Los Angeles.' *Frontiers: A Journal of Women Studies* 1: 1–6.

Peng, Martin Khor Kok (1993) 'Economic and Environmental Justice: Rethinking North-South Relations.' In Hofrichter (ed): 219–226.

Pevato, Paula M. (1994) 'Do Children Have a Role to Play in Environmental Protection?' *The International Journal of Children's Rights* 2: 169–190.

Rapp, Doris (1991) *Is This Your Child? Discovering and Treating Unrecognized Allergies in Children and Adults*. New York: Quill/William Morrow.

Rosenberg, Harriet G. (1995) "From Trash to Treasure': Housewife Activists and the Environmental Justice Movement.' Jane Schneider and Rayna Rapp (eds) *Articulating Hidden Histories: Exploring the Influence of Eric R. Wolf*. Berkeley: University of California Press: 191–203.

Seager, Joni (1993a) *Earth Follies: Coming to Feminist Terms with the Global Environmental Crisis*. London: Routledge.

Seager, Joni (1993b) 'Creating a Culture of Destruction: Gender, Militarism, and the Environment.' Richard Hofrichter (ed) *Toxic Struggles: The Theory and Practice of Environmental Justice*. Philadelphia, Penn./Gabriola Island, BC: New Society Publishers: 58–67.

Shiva, Vandana (ed) (1994) *Close to Home: Women Reconnect Ecology, Health, and Development Worldwide*. Philadelphia: New Society.

Slovic, Paul (1991) 'Perceived Risk, Trust, and the Politics of Nuclear Waste.' *Science* 254: 1603–1607.

Stephens, Sharon (1995) 'Children and the Politics of Culture in Late Capitalism.' Sharon Stephens (ed) *Children and the Politics of Culture*. Princeton, N.J.: Princeton University Press.

Stephens, Sharon (1994) 'Children and Environment: Local Worlds and Global Connections.' *Childhood* 2,1–2 (February/May): 1–22.

UNICEF (1994) 'Crisis in Mortality, Health, and Nutrition: Central and Eastern Europe in Transition.' *Economies in Transition Studies, Regional Monitoring Report* No 2 (August). Florence, Italy: United Nations Children's Fund.

WHO (World Health Organization) (1995) 'Post-Chernobyl: Work Cut Out for Decades to Come.' World Health Organization Press Office, *Press Release WHO* 84,24 (November).

WHO (World Health Organization) (1986) *Environmental Health Criteria 59. Principles for Evaluating Health Risks from Chemicals During Infancy and Childhood: The Need for a Special Approach*. Geneva: WHO.

Zhirina, Lyudmilla (1994) 'Viola' Helps Teachers and Children Combat Pollution in Bryansk.' *Surviving Together* (Summer): 34–36.

Part Two

Case Studies

Chapter 4

The Anthropology of Oil: The Impact of the Oil Industry on a Fishing Community in the Niger Delta

Alicia Fentiman

INTRODUCTION

The aim of this chapter is to examine, with some particularity, the impact of oil upon the lives of people in a small fishing community in the Niger Delta.[1] It is hoped that this data will contribute to the scarce literature available on the Niger Delta and help shed light on the various ways in which oil has affected the institutions of at least one ethnic group. Although it is a detailed descriptive study of one community, the basic problems and tensions discernible in the case study apply to much of the Niger Delta.

ETHNOGRAPHIC BACKGROUND

My focus is on the village of Oloma, a rural fishing community on the Island of Bonny in the Eastern Niger Delta. Ethnically, the village's population consists almost entirely of the Ibani-Ijo. The population of Bonny Island is centered in Bonny Town with a number of satellite villages, of which Oloma is one, and several fishing ports dispersed throughout the meandering creeks and waterways. The island is situated within the tidal mangrove swamps of the Eastern Niger Delta. It is bounded by other Ijaw communities, such as those of the Elem Kalabari to the west, the Okrikans to the north, and the Andoni, Opobo, and Ogoni to the east. Bonny is located approximately 50 kilometers southeast of the industrial and commercial center of Port Harcourt. Tributaries of the Bonny River dissect the flat surface of the island, creating swamps and creeks that are bordered by mangrove trees. Much of the land is uninhabitable; fresh water resources are scarce.

HISTORICAL OVERVIEW

Traditionally, the Ibani were fisherfolk dependent on the creeks, waterways, and swamps of the Niger Delta for their livelihood. Fish were found in abundance, and salt was evaporated from the sea water trapped in the roots of the mangrove tree. The Ibani traded their fish and salt to the Ibo hinterland in exchange for agricultural produce. This interzonal dependency created the initial trade routes between the Ijo fisherfolk and the hinterland agriculturists. This internal trade network was well established before European contact and provided the mercantile infrastructure on which the success of Bonny's European trade was founded.

Bonny's coastal location certainly contributed to her involvement in the burgeoning trade[2] that followed the advent of European adventurers in Bonny as early as the 15th century. Bonny had a pivotal role as the fulcrum of a two-way trade between the Ibo hinterland and the Ibani, on the one hand, and the Ibani and the European traders on the other. Food, livestock, and, most importantly, slaves that came from the hinterland markets were brought to Bonny to be traded. The growing European demand for slaves assured the role of Bonny traders as middlemen in the West African-European trade. This lasted until the 19th century.

In the 19th century, the slave trade was abolished and during this period Bonny's merchants turned their attention from slaves to palm oil. The palm oil trade particularly flourished because this new commodity was easily traded along the old channels involving the same personnel. Fortuitously, palm oil became at the same time an important export item because of the Industrial Revolution in Europe. Palm oil was in great demand as a lubricant for machinery as well as for making soap and candles. Bonny prospered during the palm oil trade. Such was its success that the Bonny and Kalabari areas became known as the 'Oil Rivers.'

However, in the 20th century, the prosperity of Bonny began to decline.[3] The major factor was the discovery of coal in commercially viable quantities further inland. A new mainland port was built by the British colonial administration, to exploit better the new coal fields. In 1913, a new industrial city, Port Harcourt, located 50 kilometers up Bonny River, was opened. Bonny's pivotal trading role was bypassed. 'Business gradually moved away from Bonny and Bonny only saw ships passing their way up river. In 1916, there was a great exodus and Bonny faded away to join the ranks of other ports of the past' (Earl, 1962: 31). Bonny also lost its leading position with the colonial government as the center for the administrative, commercial, and religious headquarters of the Niger Delta. By 1930, Bonny was observed to be in a 'state of decay and utter stagnation' (Webber, 1931: 52) and in 1938 moves were made to abolish the third-class township that was accorded to Bonny.

Bonny became an economically depressed area and its isolation from the mainland further contributed to her decline. The creation of Port Harcourt provided the Ibani with two alternatives; one was to remain in Bonny and return to the subsistence economy of fishing; the second option was to migrate to Port Harcourt and compete for jobs in the urban sector.

REVIVAL OF BONNY: DISCOVERY OF OIL

Although Bonny declined as a port in the first half of the century, the discovery of crude oil in commercial quantities led to Bonny's revival. Evacuation and production facilities to process the crude oil and move it to world markets were needed. At first, a temporary export station was built at Port Harcourt; however, it proved unsatisfactory because only small tankers could visit Port Harcourt and even then they could load only half their capacity. Bonny became the ideal alternative because of its strategic location and its ability to cater to both inshore and offshore loading facilities. By 1961, the Shell Petroleum Development Company completed the first phase of the Bonny Terminal. Further terminals were added throughout the 1960s.

The establishment of the oil terminal in Bonny had a tremendous impact on the infrastructure of Bonny Town. There was an influx of people who migrated there, and by 1963 the population had risen to 7,740 people. Skilled jobs, however, were given predominantly to Europeans, whereas the unskilled jobs were given to Nigerians. A study conducted in Bonny on the spatial organization of the oil terminal revealed that most migrants to Bonny were from Rivers State, but were not necessarily Ibani indigenes.[4] A large proportion of Bonny people works outside Bonny due to the lack of employment opportunities within the town and environs (Green, 1982: 11).

The educational system in Bonny Town was revived. In 1966, Shell helped to fund new departments in the Bonny secondary school. In 1977, the Finima Girls' Secondary School was opened, which provided further education for females. In addition, a teacher training college was reestablished, and it once again became an important educational center.

Money generated from the oil industry contributed to new commercial developments in Bonny. New buildings were constructed, such as a post office, a divisional office, Pan African Bank, a police station, and maritime clearing and forwarding houses. In addition, a new hospital was built. Transportation from Bonny Town to Port Harcourt was improved, thus ensuring better communication between Bonny and the mainland. An intermittent supply of electricity was provided by Shell to the main town, but the peripheral Bonny villages still went without. Indeed, the surrounding fishing villages did not enjoy the benefits that the inhabitants of Bonny Town experienced.

Although it may appear that Bonny Town improved with the new opportunities that were a result of the oil industry, there were many detrimental aspects associated with the establishment of the oil industry in Bonny, which often go unrecorded. The lives of the average Bonny person, especially those residing in the fishing villages, have deteriorated because of the impact of oil.

CASE STUDY OLOMA, BONNY: THE SEEN AND UNSEEN EFFECTS OF OIL

What of the effect of such changes on a fishing community? The environmental impact of oil in and around Oloma is clearly visible. Throughout the surrounding creeks and waterways, the intrusion of oil and oil excavation are markedly evident. The canalization and dredging of creeks by oil companies have significantly altered the landscape. A flow station is located at the end of the creek. Sea trucks pass daily to and from the flow station; the gas flares emit light 24 hours per day. Pipes meander throughout the swamps, and signboards scattered throughout the area alert the villagers of 'danger.' These are the visible effects of oil. The presence of oil is all pervading.

However there is another aspect of the impact of oil that often goes unrecorded. This is the way in which the culture of the people has been affected. The institutions, central to the identity of the Ibani fishing community, need to be discussed to understand the overall effect of oil. The community has experienced both environmental and cultural degradation. The former is seen, the latter unseen.

In the course of my research, I frequently asked: How has Oloma changed? Each respondent mentioned that the oil industry has affected their economic livelihood and that oil has interfered with many aspects of their lives. The following interview with a senior male elder vividly portrays the various ways oil has affected the lives of the people of Oloma. He was asked what impact oil has had on the inhabitants of Oloma.

> It wasn't until Shell started dredging the creek that everything
> started to go badly. For example, erosion of land. Before, there
> was a beautiful sandy beach; but look, it no longer exists. In the
> back of my house there was a big playground called ogbo-
> ngelege, but that land has eroded, and now our houses are
> eroding. Our traditional livelihood is fishing, but there are no
> more fish. We now buy tinned fish or stock fish. The chemicals
> from oil spillage have ruined the fish as well as the esem
> (periwinkles) and mgbe (mangrove oysters). We receive nothing
> from Shell. For example, no electricity, no piped water, no
> health facilities, nothing to make us happy. They were supposed
> to build a fish pond, but look around you, there is nothing. They
> destroyed our land and dredged our creek. Behind Ayaminima,
> the neighboring village, there used to be a small creek that was
> used when there was a storm and during the rainy season when
> the Bonny River was rough. But now Shell has closed it; they

dredged it and filled it up with all their oil pipes. They put up a sign and did not think that many of our people are illiterate. Even if they could read English, the paint has worn off and the message alerting people of danger is no longer visible. Our people are told not to go there, so now we have to go to the main creek every time to get to Bonny. This has caused great problems because the sea becomes very rough and dangerous during the rains, and we no longer have an alternative route. Shell promised to fill in our embankment; they came this year and look what the rains have done. It is already washing away. They put a sign on our soil saying that Oloma is part of their development project; but we have suffered. This is not development, but underdevelopment. They don't care about us. Some of the mangrove trees used for firewood spark and blow up. It used to be the village's major energy source; now women are scared and are going into the bush to find fuel; this is not traditional, and it takes so long.

Land where we have our shrines to the gods has been taken away. Parasu, a sacred area near Oloma where we performed Owu (masquerades and sacrifices), has been lost. We were forced to give the government our sacred land and our farmland. Economic trees such as mango, coconut, banana, plantain, paw-paw, and palm fruit have been taken away by the government for the oil industry. At the end of our creek there is a houseboat and flow station; the gas flares scare our fish and the noise of the sea trucks scares our gods and our fish. Sometimes we fish at night depending on the tide, and the sea trucks travel very fast up and down our creek, causing many of us to capsize in our canoes and lose our gear. Those of us who fish often find our nets destroyed and our traps broken; it is so hard to find fish. What are we to do?

Such a view highlights many issues that are associated with the impact of oil on the community. Every aspect of people's lives has been influenced by oil – their economic, political, social, and ritual institutions have all been affected. Indeed, the very institutions that make them culturally unique are eroding at an alarming pace.

CHANGES IN THE FISHING ECONOMY

A model of the economy of the past would show that the major economic activity of the inhabitants of the Eastern Niger Delta was fishing. In Oloma, there was very little farming because the soil was poor and inadequate. Although most families farmed small plots of land, they did not yield enough for subsistence. However, fish were plentiful and salt was abundant. As a result, the Ibani fishermen and women were able to barter their fish and salt with the hinterland markets in exchange for agricultural produce.

The fishing economy was unique in many ways and was structured very differently from any agricultural economy. Most obviously, the private ownership of land was unimportant for the village's prosperity. Instead, the Oloma villagers' economic livelihood was dependent on common assets: on the creeks, water-ways, and fishing ports that were owned by the village as a whole rather than by individuals. Therefore, there was communal ownership of the productive resources. The village claimed exclusive rights of access to certain waterways and creeks. This system united village members across lineage boundaries. It was thus important for it to remain a united community in order to protect its holdings from competing neighboring villages. The fishing grounds were not susceptible to demarcation as farmlands were; they were used by all members of the village without reference to lineage differentiation (see Alagoa, 1970; Horton, 1969).

However, the fishing economy in Oloma has dramatically changed. There are two prime reasons for this: one has been outward migration to urban areas in search of education and wage labor and the other is oil. It was reported:

> [In the past] it was not unusual to see young and old beaming
> with smiles as they return home with canoe load of fishes of
> various description. That was the days of yore when fishing was
> really a worthwhile venture in this part of the country (Niger
> Delta).... Fishing has become a very poor economic activity due
> mainly to rural-urban migration of able-bodied youths and oil
> pollution (Tide, February 27, 1982).

Migration from Oloma to Port Harcourt and other urban centers is frequent. The lack of young men in the community was observed while conducting fieldwork. A census survey revealed that the composition of the village consisted primarily of women, children, and the elderly. Men often migrated to Port Harcourt and other mainland towns in search of wage labor. The men who resided in the village commented that they can no longer rely solely on fishing as an economically viable occupation as they had done in the past. They therefore must leave the village. Those who remain behind encounter many obstacles, often attributable to the oil industry. Fishing as a way of life is becoming more and more difficult. Some of the problems they encounter are described below.

Damage by Sea Trucks: One of the major obstacles to traditional fishing methods in the creeks and waterways is a result of the constant movement of the sea trucks traveling to and from the flow station located at the end of the creek. Fishing lines, nets, and traps are often torn; the sea trucks continually destroy property despite protests from the community. The operators of the sea trucks appear to have very little concern or compassion for the fishermen, fisherwomen, and children. Although there are speed restrictions, it appears that they are often not enforced. Canoes are often capsized as a result of the waves from the sea trucks. The noise generated by the sea trucks is attributed by the local community as a prime reason for scaring away the fish, which is evidenced by low fish yields.

Oil Pollution: Spillage: Despite arguments that over-fishing and overpopulation are responsible for low fish yields, the community believes oil pollution has affected their fishing economy. In Oloma, fewer people reside in the community than in the past and fewer people are fishing. As mentioned above, migration to urban areas has become the sought-after choice and necessity by many. This is consistent with remarks made in the local Bonny magazine, *Ogolo*.

> *Bonny people like other rivering people depend mainly on their*
> *water resources for their livelihood. But in the operation of the*
> *oil companies, all waste products are dumped into the rivers.*
> *The water is thus polluted, fishes are killed, and the fishermen*
> *are forced to find alternative sources of livelihood – which in*
> *Bonny is very difficult. Gradually people migrate out of the*
> *community to other areas to seek beneficial employment, which*
> *has led to increasing depopulation of Bonny (Green, 1982:*
> *10–11).*

However, those who are left behind in the communities try to survive by fishing; there are no alternatives. They are responsible for feeding their households, but are finding it increasingly difficult to make ends meet. The catches are low, and more and more time is spent gathering shellfish. A greater burden has been placed upon the women because of the massive outward migration of men. Each day, women spend hours in the mangrove swamps gathering shellfish such as winkles and mangrove oysters. As one fisherwoman remarked, 'My life is my paddle; without my paddle we do not eat.' It is, however, becoming increasingly difficult to find enough food. The community feels that chemicals and oil are affecting the fish production.

Oil spillage is a frequent occurrence in the Niger Delta, and many communities, in addition to Oloma, in the oil-producing areas have provided descriptive accounts of the impact of oil spillage on their fishing economy. However, scientific data examining the impact of oil pollution on the aquatic life is scarce. A symposium, *The Mangrove Ecosystem of the Niger Delta*, held in Port Harcourt in 1980, gathered scholars in different disciplines to discuss and share information on the changes in the environment; oil was shown to be a major factor contributing to the destruction of marine life. It was shown that crude oil contains compounds that are toxic to marine organisms and contribute to extensive mortality in finfish, shellfish, oysters, and birds. This was observed in the Apoi and Ojobo areas.

A study in Bonny River examined oil pollution and the brackish environment. An experiment that examined the effect of crude petroleum oil and refined oils on aquatic organisms confirmed that crude oil and refined petroleum products in high concentrations were toxic to marine life. By comparing different types of fish and shellfish, it showed that some species were more resilient than others. Data revealed that shrimps were more susceptible to pollutants, followed by oysters and fish. Periwinkles were the most tolerant. Tainting of the flesh

confirmed that the effect of oil spillage was lingering. Even small, though continual, spills affected the productivity of the water. It also showed that pollutants
had a pronounced effect on the growth and reproductive capacity of organisms
(Onuoba, 1985: 131).

A recent spillage in Nembe in 1995 illustrates the problems with which oil
producing communities must contend when there is a spillage. It was reported
that,

> *An oil spill had occurred from an Agip oil pipeline. For several*
> *days, the oil flowed freely into the creeks and mangrove forest.*
> *The area went up in flames one night when a woman on a late-*
> *night fishing trip mistakenly set off the fire with her lantern. The*
> *fire destroyed much of the aquatic life in the area. In addition,*
> *farm crops were destroyed* (Newswatch, *December 18, 1995: 12*).

A problem that many communities face during oil spillages is that many of the
oil companies are unwilling to pay compensation during spillages because they
believe that they are caused by sabotage. The communities, however, stress that
many of the spillages are 'legitimate' – not caused by sabotage, but instead by
poorly maintained and faulty equipment. It is therefore necessary to monitor the
areas regularly and to act immediately during spillages.

The mangrove fauna and flora are also affected by oil spillages; it was shown
that there can be short- and long-term effects to the mangrove from offshore
spillage (Odu and Imevbore, 1985: 133). Mangrove is an essential part of the
Oloma people's economy. Mangrove wood has many uses; it is used for fuel and
for making various items such as fish traps, trays, and hats. In Oloma, women
complained that chemicals from the oil have absorbed into the mangrove wood,
which they use for fuel, and that once ignited, it explodes and causes serious burns.

Gas Flaring and Pollution: Large quantities of methane gas are associated
with oil. During oil production, this gas is burned off at flow stations above the
oil wells. This introduces sulfur dioxide and oxides of carbon and nitrogen into
the atmosphere. The impact of this on the environment has not been substanti-
ated. However, it is said that this could contribute to global warming.

Land Filling: Another factor responsible for disturbing the way of life in
Oloma is land filling. Nearby creeks and waterways have been filled in because
of oil operations. This has affected the accessibility to surrounding villages and
has taken from the Oloma villagers an alternative route to reach Bonny Town.
The Oloma community complained about the landfill because they relied on a
specific water route to reach Bonny Town during the rainy season, which has
subsequently been filled in. The alternative route was preferred during the rainy
season because the Bonny River becomes very rough and dangerous.

Canalization also damages the environment. Oil companies create canals to
either drain out an area for drilling and pipe laying or create channels to transport
drilling and other oil production equipment to the site. The channels alter the
ecology of the area; they can also alter the flood pattern of the delta by resulting

in perennial flooding of the otherwise well-drained plains as was observed in many areas in the Niger Delta (Ekoriko, 1996: 31).

Erosion: The community believes that the continual movement of sea trucks up and down the creek and the dredging of the land and waterways have significantly contributed to the erosion of the land. In Oloma, several households lost their property due to erosion. Recollections by villagers mention the sandy beach area that used to be in front of the village; it has eroded away, and a sand-bank was designed to prevent further erosion. The embankment was promised for several years; finally, in 1984 a contractor constructed an embankment, but it did not last. It quickly washed away during the rainy season. The community feels this was done in a substandard way. Interviews with the contractor at the time of the job revealed that his company had won the contract with the cheapest bid, and he admitted that the job was not going to be sufficient to endure the rainy season. As he rightfully predicted, the embankment gave way, and it became a hazard to the community. Instead of benefiting and improving the situation, it worsened the situation. Gaps in the embankment became dangerous for children and adults walking on the sandbags. One child fell in the gap and broke his leg.

Dredging: Indigenous fishing methods such as dragging a net along the creek bottom are very difficult to perform because the creeks have been dredged during oil exploration, and the water is now too deep to stand in, making this form of fishing obsolete. Dredging also destroys valuable freshwater and mangrove vegetation, which can cause an imbalance in the ecosystem because aquatic organisms depend on them for food and shelter during part or all of their life cycles (Wilcox and Powell, 1985). In addition, during the dredging process, oil is spilled into the water and the burning of fuel releases carbon, sulfur, and nitrogen oxides into the aquatic environment (Odu and Imevbore, 1985: 142).

Oloma and Social Change: Under the Land Decree Act of 1978, many communities throughout the Niger Delta lost valuable farmland. In addition, oil production contributed to the contamination of the land. Although Oloma suffered in many ways when parts of their land were taken away, they have suffered more by losing the access and rights of way to their creeks and waterways. Further, the destruction and contamination of their productive resources have contributed to vast changes within the economic, political, and social structure of the community. As members of the community are forced to migrate because their resources are destroyed, various changes are taking place within these institutions.

RITUAL, BELIEF, AND OIL

Another institution affected by oil in Oloma is the villager's belief system. The stability and continuity of village life are maintained by participation in a series of ritual practices. These ritual activities are a means by which the community retains their social identity and social stability in times of radical changes. Both rural villagers and urban migrants have in common a shared adherence to such practices and the beliefs associated with them. The principal type of ritual activity is the masquerades of the *owu-ogbo* society, which displays elaborate masquerades in honor of the water spirits. The *owu-ogbo* society is central to the social cohesion of the Oloma people. It is a time-honored institution and the practice of the masquerade was brought to Bonny by the Oloma descendants. The Oloma people are known throughout the Delta for their expertise in the *owu-ogbo* plays. Traditionally, when the Ibani engaged predominantly in fishing, the fishermen would return to Oloma during a period called *Fongu-Mini*, the break in the rains in August, to be reunited with their families. The masquerade serves two essential purposes. First, it honors the water spirits, upon whom the fishing economy is thought to be dependent. It is believed that by performing masquerades, the fisherfolk will be rewarded with a successful fishing season. Second, the masquerades are used as a means to unite all village members no matter where they may be.

The rationale of the masquerades is derived from the belief that they represent the imitation of the movements of the water spirits. It is believed that fishermen would spy on the spirits in the water and then return to the village and imitate the dances and songs learned from them. There are several types of masquerades performed in Oloma. Each masquerade headpiece is different, and each represents a specific spirit. The person who plays the part of the masquerade is possessed by the spirit he is imitating. The masquerade society is strictly male. Although the *owu-ogbo* society has undergone many changes due to the impact of Christianity and migration, community members still return to Oloma every holiday season to participate in the masquerades. The masquerades provide a means of social cohesion and reunification of dispersed kin members.

Despite the stability and continuity of the masquerade society, it is clear that some rituals can no longer be performed because sacred shrines used for sacrifices can no longer be accessed. They have been taken over by the government under the Land Decree Act of 1978. The fishermen and women in Oloma are also concerned about the constant flare in the creek; they believe it causes great distress to the water spirits. This is an important consideration because the water spirits are an essential aspect to their belief system.

Little is known about the impact of oil on indigenous ritual beliefs. It is not only the physical destruction of oil, but also the metaphysical aspect that equally needs to be acknowledged.

OIL AND HEALTH

One aspect of the impact of oil upon the inhabitants of the Niger Delta that has received little attention is whether there are any health risks directly associated with oil. Data are scarce and research needs to be done to see whether there is any significant long-term impact. The villagers complain about rashes and other skin ailments, but very little is known as to whether this is attributable to oil.

While conducting field research, it was observed that women and children suffered from skin problems as a result of oil and chemicals in the water. The women who spend several hours in the water are engaged in the labor-intensive gathering activities of collecting shellfish. Most fisherwomen rub their bodies with palm oil before they fish in order to prevent rashes and other skin ailments. Elderly women mentioned that this is a recent precaution because they did not suffer from these skin conditions in the past. It has been written that a variety of skin conditions might be attributed to contact or exposure to oil. Acne, warts, boils, skin cancer, and photosensitization dermatitis have all been cited (Afiesiama, 1985: 169).

It has been reported that those living close to gas flaring sites may be at risk from respiratory illnesses (*Newswatch*, December 18, 1995: 15). In addition, it was reported that there are complaints of sterility by persons living near the flares (Ekoriko, 1996: 31).

Contamination of drinking water because of oil spillage or oil production activities is of great concern. It is feared that oil from spillage can seep into the freshwater drinking supplies. Procedures such as canalization or dredging can affect the freshwater drinking supplies by draining the water in the area that can then alter the ecosystem.

Some questions need to be considered: What are the health risks to the people who eat fish and shellfish contaminated with oil? Can swimming and bathing in the polluted creeks be dangerous to the health of the people? Can living near a gas flaring area be dangerous? Can the freshwater contaminated by toxic waste be hazardous? Research needs to be done to find out precisely what the dangers are to communities. It is also important that consistent guidelines be established and monitored to examine the impact of oil on the health of the local inhabitants.

CONCLUSION

There exists widespread concern with the unfairness of the Nigerian political system towards Rivers State and other states in which the oil wealth of the nation is derived. And within such states, the communities in whose home areas oil is mined suffer neglect from federal and state governments, and the oil companies. Their environment is damaged, and their sources of livelihood destroyed through oil pollution. The oil boom which has done so much for and to the Nigerian economy has, therefore, been little short of a disaster for oil producing states, and even worse for oil producing communities (Alagoa and Tamuno, 1989: 220–221).

This case study of Oloma shows how one community has been affected by oil; this community is not unique. The problems encountered there are shared by other communities throughout the oil-producing area and are representative for the whole Niger Delta. The inhabitants feel that they have not benefited from the oil industry. Although oil is extracted from their areas, causing environmental degradation and disrupting their way of life, they have not been compensated. They are environmental victims.

It is paradoxical that in the past the communities within the Niger Delta who wielded great power, authority, and wealth are now labeled as 'minorities' struggling to survive in Nigeria. The Nigeria they helped to create, it appears, is currently destroying them. The minority groups in the Niger Delta are, as a result, seeking fair representation and compensation from the government as the Ogoni experience has so aptly symbolized. Ken Saro-Wiwa fought for the rights of his people. With the establishment of MOSOP (Movement for the Survival of Ogoni People), he attracted international awareness to the position of those living in the oil-producing communities.

The executions of Ken Saro-Wiwa and eight fellow Ogonis on November 10, 1995, provided a catalyst for nations worldwide to condemn the situation in Nigeria. In particular, the alleged human rights abuses by the military government have sparked a fierce debate about the current political and economic climate in Nigeria. Worldwide condemnation of the executions has highlighted the need to understand the underlying issues that ignited the problem. In particular, confusion over the roles and responsibilities of the government and multinational corporations operating in the Niger Delta has led many oil-producing communities to speak out. Concern relating to environmental degradation has also been voiced within the country and outside by international organizations. Against this background of political and humanitarian debate it is, however, important not to lose sight of the fact that the environment must be seen in cultural as well as physical terms.

NOTES

1 Data for this article were collected while conducting anthropological fieldwork in Oloma Village, Bonny, for 12 months in 1983 to 1984.

2 For a model of an Eastern Delta fishing community before European contact, see R. Horton (1969: 37–58). See also E.J. Alagoa (1970: 319–329; 1971: 269–278).

3 See A. Jewett, Chapter Two, in *Change and Continuity Among the Ibani* (unpublished PhD thesis, Cambridge University) for an overview of the decline of Bonny in the 20th century.

4 See Tumini Dagogo Waribor (June 1976).

REFERENCES

Afiesiama, S (1985) 'Medical Aspects of the Mangrove Environment.' (Abstract) B. Wilcox and C. Powell (eds) *The Mangrove Ecosystem of the Niger Delta*. Nigeria: University of Port Harcourt.

Alagoa, E J (1971) 'The Development of Institutions in the States of the Eastern Niger Delta.' *Journal of African History* 12,2: 269–278.

Alagoa, E J (1970) 'Long Distance Trade and States in the Niger Delta.' *Journal of African History* 11: 319–329.

Alagoa, E J and T Tamuno (eds) (1989) *Land and People of Nigeria: Rivers State.* Nigeria: Riverside Communications.

Earl, K. (1962) 'Bonny.' Nigeria Field.

Ekoriko, M (1996) 'How Safe Are We?' Special Report. *Newswatch* (January 8).

Green, K. (1982) 'Oil and Gas Industries in Bonny: A Critical Appraisal.' *Ogolo Magazine* 1.

Horton, R (1969) 'From Fishing Village to City-State: A Social History of New Calabar.' M Douglas and P Kaberry (eds) *Man in Africa.* London: Tavistock Publications.

Jewett, A (1988) 'A Contemporary Ethnography: Change and Continuity Among the Ibani-Ijo of Coastal Nigeria.' Unpublished PhD thesis. University of Cambridge.

Odu, E A and A M A Imevbore (1985) 'Environmental Pollution in the Niger Delta.' B Wilcox and C Powell (eds) *The Mangrove Ecosystem of the Niger Delta.* Nigeria: University of Port Harcourt.

Onuoba, G (1985) 'Oil Pollution and the Brackish Environment.' B Wilcox and C Powell (eds) *The Mangrove Ecosystem of the Niger Delta.* Nigeria: University of Port Harcourt.

Waribor, T (1976) 'Spatial Implications of the Oil Terminal in Bonny.' Unpublished BA thesis, University of Nsukka, Nigeria.

Webber, H (1931) Intelligence Report on the Bonny Tribe of 1931. Typescript.

Wilcox, B H R and C B Powell (1985) *The Mangrove Ecosystem of the Niger Delta.* Nigeria: University of Port Harcourt.

Chapter 5

The Movement in Bhopal And Its Lessons

Satinath Sarangi

INTRODUCTION

As a participant-observer in the struggle of survivors of the Bhopal disaster, I wish to consider its successes and failures over the last 10 years. This stocktaking is intended mainly to arrive at a general understanding of the initiatives needed to confront other situations like the Bhopal disaster. Given the waves of liberalization sweeping through the Indian subcontinent, the increasing deployment of extremist technologies in the countries of the South, and the growth and spread of toxic capital in most of the 'undeveloped' world, the recurrence of Bhopal is a real possibility and the lessons from the movement in Bhopal could help us prepare for such an eventuality.

Many of the shortcomings of the Bhopal movement can be explained, although not justified, by the unprecedented nature of the disaster. The people who found themselves surrounded by Union Carbide's poison clouds and ran in panic in the direction of the wind (instead of against it) were not the only ones to be confused by the shock and suddenness of calamity. As subsequent events have shown, the activists who sought to confront the disaster were as much taken by surprise and equally lacking in direction. It is possible, with hindsight and a conscious distancing of oneself, to identify some of the problems in the activists' response to the disaster.

In the following pages, I present a description of the struggle of the Bhopal survivors, outlining some of the major problems and possibilities in the last 10 years. Recommendations are made by positing 'what would have been' against 'what has been.' For the sake of brevity, details about the disaster and its aftermath have been avoided (see BGIA, 1992; Pearce and Tombs, 1989). Although these observations relate to the particular situation in Bhopal, they are most likely to be relevant to communities in most of South Asia, which share a common social, cultural, and political context and, more significantly, common perpetrators of industrial crimes.

BACKGROUND

The city of Bhopal (population close to one million in 1984) is divided into three areas. The old city, established during the reign of the Nawabs, forms the northern part; the new city, with government offices, ministers' bungalows, and manicured parks, lies in the middle; the industrial township surrounds a government-run engineering industry further south. These areas are distinct from each other, with so little interaction between them that they could as well be three different cities. The people exposed to the poisons from Union Carbide's pesticide factory on December 2–3, 1984, were residents of the city of old Bhopal.

A substantial section of the population of old Bhopal is composed of first- and second-generation immigrants, driven out of their homelands in neighboring districts as a result of the introduction of mechanized agriculture to their villages and other 'development' projects. Over 75 percent of the people who were later to be exposed and incapacitated earned their livelihood through daily wage labor and petty business. Women, particularly among the Muslim poor who formed over 35 percent of the population, did piece-rate work in their homes and were cut off from the world outside their communities and families. A strong sense of community pervaded across religious lines. Considering that at least 100,000 of the people were settled in what the government prefers to call 'illegal slums,' togetherness in the community was a necessary condition of survival.

During the 1950s, as a part of the then national policy of organizing the geography of the country, Bhopal was made the capital of the newly formed state of Madhya Pradesh. The location of state authority in the city subsumed all political articulation within the language of party politics and generated social interventions toward creation of vote banks by slum-level petty leaders. Compared with other Indian cities, old Bhopal had very few industrial units and a negligible history of militancy among the industrial workers, who numbered about 8,000 in 1984. Associations of workers were modern in form, but feudal tendencies persisted in their activities. The general population of Bhopal had remained largely untouched by the pre-1947 freedom movement against British rule, and organizations among nonindustrial workers were rare. In terms of the modes of usurpation, exercise, and coping with power, Bhopal was in a premodern, 'pre-political' situation.

The modern industrial disaster and the popular response to it in its aftermath brought about substantial changes in that situation. Not all of these changes, as subsequent years have shown, were conducive to regaining power by the people.

SPONTANEOUS PROTESTS

The collective response of the survivors over the last 10 years appears to have gone through several distinct phases – spontaneous protests in the immediate aftermath, organized under middle-class leaders for the first two years – and formation of survivors-led organizations. The first started with an angry march and the gathering of over 1,000 survivors at the factory gates of Union Carbide on the morning of the disaster. They had hardly any information on who was running the factory or how it was run, and even less on its hazardous nature. When the marchers reached the factory, a decision was taken to burn it down. The factory officials in panic spread a rumor that the gases had started leaking again. In confusion, the crowd fled away from the factory, to be joined by hundreds of others along their way, in a reenactment of the previous night's mass panic. Spontaneous collective protests, mostly leaderless, continued in different communities without any overall intercommunity organization. In small groups, survivors demonstrated at government offices, calling for medical care, monetary assistance, and the immediate hanging of the killers of Bhopal whose names, and particularly that of the chairman of the corporation, were widely known within the first three days. Upon declaration of the government's plan to utilize the highly toxic methyl isocyanate (MIC) gas that was left in the tank, in an exercise ironically named Operation Faith, widespread fear and chaos again arose after December 10, 1984. Over 400,000 survivors left Bhopal in less than two days and a small fraction opted to stay at the government relief camps set up in new Bhopal. The camps provided a place for survivors from different communities to come together and protest against the near absence of government efforts to provide relief and care. Hundreds of people marched to the governor's residence on December 16 and then again two days later. A small number of external activists played a role in facilitating collective decisions and action. By the end of the month, these activists were to abrogate more powers to themselves and to initiate the second phase of the movement in Bhopal, in which spontaneous protests found encouragement only on rare occasions.

ORGANIZED RESPONSE

Within the first week of the disaster, about 30 individuals, with varying leftist persuasions, met in two groups to found two organizations – Nagarik Rahat Aur Punarvas Committee (NRPC) and the Zahreeli Gas Kand Sangharsh Morcha (ZGKSM or Morcha for short) – with clearly distinct emphases. Although a few locals were involved in the founding of the organizations, external and new-Bhopal activists played a dominant role in outlining the respective 'politics' of the organizations. For NRPC, provision of relief and rehabilitation was to be the main focus. The Morcha, or more correctly its leaders, stressed the need for a political organization of the survivors that would take up issues of justice, scientific information, medical care, legal interventions, and others. Although there was reason and space for both organizations to coexist and support each other's work, internecine conflicts started brewing almost from their inception. The NRPC viewed Morcha as doing politics instead of providing help, and the Morcha thought of NRPC as a bunch of reformists with dubious motives. Of the two, the Morcha was to become the much larger organization, casting decisive influence on the turn of events in the aftermath of the disaster. Within the first month,

NRPC was overwhelmed by the resource and infrastructural requirements of providing direct relief and soon took to organizing survivors for demonstrations. Meanwhile, government repression of Morcha activists was making them consider strategic relief initiatives for more legitimate articulation of political demands. Yet, six months were to pass before the two organizations came together and even then it was only briefly successful.

INTERNECINE CONFLICTS

The issue of a united stand and a common understanding between organizations in Bhopal became further complicated with the involvement of trade union activists from Bombay. One of the major reasons for discord was their emphasis on transforming the Carbide factory into a worker-controlled soy-milk production facility and on generating employment for over 600 factory workers who were rendered jobless due to its closure. This, according to the leaders of the survivors' organizations, demonstrated insensitivity toward the affected people, who would rather have the factory erased. The possibility of alternate employment generation, combining the skills and needs of both workers and people in the communities, was left unexplored.

LACK OF DEMOCRACY

The survivors who lay divided had little to do with the internecine feuds and very little power over decisions made by their respective leaders. The Morcha leaders did mention 'democratic participation' as one of their priorities, but, in practice, a Stalinist interpretation of these words was followed. The interests of the community-level traditional leaders, who formed an intermediary layer between the leaders and the common survivors, coincided with such interpretations and there were no serious reflections on the structural aspects of the organizations. Men and particularly women survivor activists, who demonstrated unusual courage and commitment, were largely denied opportunities to exercise decision-making powers. As the number of active individuals dwindled from well over 10,000 in January 1985 to fewer than 2,000 in January 1986, due to such exclusivist policies, the Morcha leaders recruited and depended upon slum-level leaders, who were not averse to using unethical means to bring people for demonstrations.

NARROWING DOWN OF ACTIVITIES

During the formation of the Morcha and in the few months following it, a wide range of activities was planned. Details were worked out for generation and dissemination of information, documentation, scientific and medical research, fund-raising, and other activities. Some of these were actually put into practice.

Surveys to assess medical and economic damages were carried out; scientific information on the leaked chemicals was collected and some of it disseminated through fliers. Morcha activists set up poster exhibitions in different communities to educate survivors on the medical consequences of exposure, and radical professional groups were assisted in carrying out epidemiological studies. NRPC, along with other support groups, organized a medical study on the effect of the gases on pregnant women. A follow-up study was not possible, however, since a legal battle ensued between the sponsors over ownership of data collected. Together with the Carbide workers' union and its supporter group, Morcha and NRPC founded a medical clinic in early June 1985. However, almost all of these positive actions were short-lived and devoid of any long-term perspective or commitment. They were wound up before they could be effective and by September 1985, marches and meetings became the only activities of the organizations. The clinic, managed to a large extent by a group of trained survivors, lost its autonomy and eventually its existence by mid-1986.

LACK OF SOLIDARITY LINKS

In the initial period following the formation of the Morcha, several social, labor, and environmental groups from the US and other countries offered help in fundraising and campaign activities. Though the Indian government has used international associations of mass organizations to discredit and defame them, given the international dimension of the disaster, it was perhaps possible to create publicly legitimate international solidarity on the issue. Such possibilities were, however, overlooked by the Morcha and offers of support from abroad were meticulously shunned.

A National Campaign Committee was formed by the Morcha in early 1985 and involved over 100 organizations from different parts of the country. As with the local organizations, the National Committee was structured along the lines of centralized political parties and at one time its deliberations included disciplinary proceedings against constituent groups that did not follow the party line or failed to implement programs to the satisfaction of the national leadership. Needless to say, the leaders of Morcha were also the leaders of the National Committee. Possibilities existed of involvement of sympathetic professionals and their organizations, but, given the narrow definition of struggle, there was little scope for them, unless they proved their credentials by affirming the political views of the leadership. The prevailing atmosphere of interorganizational conflicts and suspicion was also a deterrent to the involvement of supporters from outside Bhopal.

LACK OF AUTONOMOUS STRUCTURES

The narrowing of action priorities by survivors' organizations and their intolerance to independent initiatives precluded the setting up of autonomous structures that could focus on vital issues such as assessment of the damage caused by the disaster, scientific and legal research, monitoring of medical, economic, and social consequences, alternative employment generation, and public education. By the end of 1986, when most of the middle-class leaders and activists were gone and the organizations ceased to be functionally existent, the situation in Bhopal had lost its emotional appeal and a large section of its potential supporters.

THE ACHIEVEMENTS

It would be decidedly incorrect to say that the organizations formed by middle-class leaders did not achieve anything through their efforts. For one, they pressured a reluctant government into providing relief in cash and kind, recognizing the extent of injuries caused, and initiating medical care and economic rehabilitation. The extensive and informed media coverage that Bhopal received in the year following the disaster was possible, to a large extent, due to the efforts of these organizations. Credit is also due to them for introducing a culture of popular protest outside the political parties in Bhopal. However, as has been described above, because of the inability and refusal of the leaders to envision structures, activities, and solidarity links appropriate to the Bhopal situation, several possibilities remained unrealized. More significantly, an unprecedented opportunity for rebuilding through political subversive activity was lost.

SURVIVOR-LED ORGANIZATIONS

Left to fend for themselves after the exodus of the middle-class leaders and activists, the survivors were soon to organize themselves to continue with the struggle in Bhopal. Initially concerned with the immediate problems of jobs, pensions for the destitute, and the regularizing of employment rehabilitation centers, the four organizations that were formed were soon to take up medical care, monetary relief, criminal liability, compensation, environmental rehabilitation, and corruption by government officials as their rallying points. The organizations grew in strength and effectiveness, and two of them – Bhopal Gas Peedit Mahila Udyog Sangathan and Nirashrit Pension Bhogi Sangharsh Morcha – had over 10,000 members within the first two years of their formation. Although these organizations resembled the earlier ones in their size, range of concerns, and ability to pressure the government, as things turned out the resemblance did not end there. In fact, these organizations resembled the traditional Indian extended family in many of their features, and their leaders had even less respect for democratic functioning. Conflicts between organizations grew as their leaders competed with each other to be the sole representative of the survivors. Although they shared common concerns and their charter of demands differed only in their detail, they hardly ever came together. Given that their constituencies and focus of activities were quite distinct from each other, the objective conditions for independent existence and interorganizational cooperation were very much there. Such possibilities could never be realized, due to the petty squabbles among the leaders of the organizations. In contrast to the organizations formed earlier, women outnumbered men several times over. Defying the traditions of their respective religions and family bondage, Muslim and Hindu women survivors played an active and sustained role in the organizations. However, the two largest organizations came to be dominated by men with few scruples about usurping women's power for their personal glory.

LIMITING THE STRUGGLE

Although conscious of the need for research, documentation, and monitoring activities, the survivors' organizations in the third phase lacked the necessary skills and training to be able to carry them out. Dissemination of information was limited to the minimum required for immediate mobilization of people around particular issues. The involvement of large numbers of women presented the possibility of organizing their wide-ranging production skills into income-generating cooperatives. However, the organizations chose to depend upon, and pressure the government into, providing jobs for the Bhopal survivors. Even the closure of the sewing centers by the government in July 1992 did not prompt any initiatives for helping the survivors to become self-supported. With time, the two major organizations became involved with party politics and the popular response to the disaster reflected the traditional politics of Bhopal.

VICTORIES OF THE STRUGGLE

Given these serious shortcomings, the latter-day survivors' organizations have made significant achievements. Much-needed monetary assistance from the government, modification of the infamous settlement order, withdrawal of criminal immunity from Carbide and its officials, and most government relief and rehabilitative measures have been made possible through their legal and extralegal interventions. Above all, through their continuing marches and rallies demanding justice and a better deal for the survivors, they have kept Bhopal alive in the public mind.

CRISIS AND BREAKTHROUGH

The Bhopal disaster has rightly been construed as a manifestation of the crisis of the high-tech development policies pursued by the Indian government since the late 1950s. As has been described above, public response to the disaster showed up the crisis within the mass movements in the country. In the dominant economic paradigm, disasters are generally welcome since they give rise to needs for production of goods. For the people in the movement, while mourning such calamities is an essential human response, they need also to be viewed as possibilities for constructive political actions. The movement in Bhopal had the possibility of overcoming the dogmatic and parochial thinking, centralized decision-making, and patriarchal attitudes that pervade most of the mass movements across the country. Outlined below are the real possibilities of breaking through the crisis, so that the disaster could be turned against its perpetrators.

Evolution of appropriate forms of organization: Given the wide range of interventions required plus the spectrum of skills available and the various degrees of involvement that were offered, it would have been possible to evolve an organizational structure that encouraged autonomous collective initiatives and allowed individuals with different views to work together. This required a departure from classical centralized models of organization and a broader definition of political action. Democratic participation of the survivors in all decision-making was crucial for bringing about this organizational climate.

Generation and dissemination of information: Denial of information by Union Carbide and the Indian government's suppression of facts related to the causes and consequences of the disaster were, and still are, a major obstacle to establishing the extent of damage, the means of ameliorating injuries, and affixation of liability. It would have been possible for a group of professionals and nonprofessionals to carry out interviews, surveys, research studies, and analysis on a long-term basis, starting from the crucial period immediately following the disaster. The unavailability of scientific, medical, and legal information has caused much panic and confusion among the survivors. It would have been possible to equip survivors with techniques of information gathering and publicize such knowledge in accessible forms.

Relief and rehabilitation: The dependence of the survivors on government-run medical care and monetary assistance caused much damage to their personal dignity and led to much loss of control over their own lives. However, this need not have been so. The successful, albeit brief, running of the medical clinic and the few short-lived income-generating projects demonstrated the survivors' capabilities and enthusiasm in being self-supported in medical care and economic rehabilitation. Of course, given the magnitude of the disaster, it would be unrealistic to assume that the problems of all the survivors could have been addressed through such efforts. However, without question, even a few models of such initiatives could have gone a long way in reinforcing a sense of community and regaining lost honor. With a perspective that places emphasis on mutual cooperation and delegitimizes state control over individual lives, relief efforts would very well have been part of the Bhopal movement.

National and international solidarity links: The involvement of a transnational corporation that has a presence in 137 countries across the globe, and the sheer magnitude of the destruction caused, evoked responses of support from different parts of the country and the world. It would have been possible to build upon these responses and form lasting linkages among individuals and groups concerned with environmental, labor, human rights, health, gender, legal, and other issues. With the imposition of the New World Order in recent years, the need for collective action across national boundaries is being increasingly felt, particularly on issues of industrial hazards and the involvement of transnational corporations. Bhopal could very well have provided the impetus and basis for such counter-globalization.

In conclusion, rather than providing a model for future responses to industrial mega-disasters, the Bhopal movement offers many negative lessons. Although the suffering of the survivors continues in Bhopal and justice is far from done, it is no longer realistic to hope that a fresh beginning could be made. However, one ends with a note of optimism that the mistakes, to use a gentle word, in the activists' responses will not be repeated should another Bhopal occur.

REFERENCES

BGIA (1992) *Compensation Disbursement, Problems and Possibilities: A Report of a Survey Conducted in Three Gas Affected Bastis of Bhopal.* Bhopal: Bhopal Group for Information and Action.

Pearce, Frank and Steve Tombs (1989) 'Bhopal: Union Carbide and the Hubris of the Capitalist Technocracy.' *Social Justice* 16,2 (Summer).

Chapter 6

Ecocide, Industrial Chemical Contamination, and the Corporate Profit Imperative: The Case of Bougainville

Rosemarie Gillespie

THE SPIRIT OF THE LAND

In the beginning there was harmony, a resonance, between ourselves, nature, and the earth from whence we come and will return. Like a gentle mother, she gave us nourishment and protection. Her forests gave us shelter from the searing heat of the summer sun, and wood to keep the fires burning through the cold winter nights. We were at one with the spirit of the land.

Out of this harmony there emerged, as if from some poisoned seed, people whose love of power was greater than their love of life itself. They had lost the meaning of life. Hierarchy replaced harmony and the natural cooperation between peoples was replaced by coercion and violence. War, rather than reason, consultation, and consensus, became the final arbiter. Self-governing communities were replaced by nation-states, many of which used propaganda, terror, or both to maintain control over their subject peoples.

Greed and exploitation were proclaimed virtues. Corporate superstructures grew like parasites in the nation-states that harbored them. Through interlocking directorships and proliferation of subsidiaries, they eventually replaced nation-states as the dominant global power and brought governments to heel.

This paper was presented to the Permanent Peoples' Tribunal, London, November 29, 1994. The author thanks the extended efforts of Janine Oldfield, Susan Bailey, and Jeremy Greaney for their assistance on the manuscript.

Democracy was subverted by corporate dictatorships that wielded more power and money than their host governments. A global corporate empire is now emerging that is more powerful, less visible, and more dangerous than the former empires of nation-states.

Our struggle is both international and local. As the tentacles of the corporate empire reach further, more and more communities come under threat. When forced to fight for their survival, the people of these communities are often subjected to organized state violence in the name of 'law and order.'

Such is the case with Bougainville, an island ripped apart, first by a giant copper mine and then by six years of war. When the people moved to close the mine that was destroying their land and environment, the Papua New Guinea police were given orders to 'shoot to kill.'[1]

SACRED ISLAND

Bougainville is an island in the once peaceful South Pacific region, part of the Solomon Islands archipelago. The people of Bougainville have exercised sovereignty over their land continuously for thousands of years. They hold their land as their natural God-given inheritance, handed down 'since time immemorial,' to be preserved for future generations.[2] Bougainville is known to many as Meekamui, which means Sacred Island.

The European colonists of last century treated the people and their land as pawns on a global chessboard, as mere objects of trade, in a deadly contest for wealth and power. 'Blackbirding' [slave trading] was commonplace. Fiji, Vanuatu, and the Solomon Islands, including Bougainville, were raided by pirates. The young men were kidnapped, taken away in chains to work as slaves on foreign-owned plantations, severed forever from their land and their peoples.

In 1899 Bougainville was partitioned from the rest of the Solomon Islands by a deal struck between Great Britain and Germany. Bougainville was incorporated into what was then known as 'German New Guinea,' 800 kilometers away. Fifteen years later, Germany and Great Britain were at war.

Following Germany's defeat in World War I, Australia assumed control over Bougainville under a League of Nations mandate until the island was invaded by Japan in World War II. Following World War II, the Australian government resumed control of Bougainville under a United Nations Trusteeship.

Except during World War II, when Bougainville was of great strategic importance, these colonial powers showed little interest in the island until substantial copper deposits were identified in the mountainous Panguna area of Central Bougainville.

A BREACH OF TRUST

In 1963, the Australian Colonial Administration granted Conzinc Rio Tinto Australia (CRA), a subsidiary of Rio Tinto Zinc (RTZ), a Special Prospecting

Authority to explore the Panguna area. This was done without the permission of the Nasioi people, who owned the land. At the time, Bougainville was part of the United Nations Trust territory of Papua New Guinea administered by Australia. In breach of this trust, the Australian Administration granted CRA two prospecting licenses and a license to mine the land belonging to the Nasioi people against their will.

By granting exploration and mining 'rights' to CRA, the Australian government was giving the company land that belonged to someone else. This is contrary to the requirements of the trustee under the principles of the International Trusteeship system, or the League of Nations Mandate System that preceded it.

The trustee does not exercise sovereignty over the mandated or trust territory. Any 'rights' the trustee has are founded in obligations and are limited to what is strictly necessary to carry out the obligations under the trust.

Further, a fundamental principle of the trust relationship is that it is illegal for a trustee to 'absorb the property entrusted to him into his own patrimony.'[3] The Mining Ordinance passed in 1922, which transferred ownership of the minerals beneath the surface of the soil from the indigenous landowners to the Commonwealth of Australia, was a clear violation of this trust. At that time, Australia exercised control over Bougainville as part of a League of Nations mandate.

As Justice Evatt of the High Court of Australia stated,

> It is quite fallacious to infer from the fact that in pursuance of its international duties under the mandate, the Commonwealth of Australia exercises full and complete jurisdiction over the territory as though it possessed unlimited sovereignty therein...that the territory...has ever been assimilated or incorporated within the Commonwealth.[4]

Therefore, the Australian Colonial Administration had no legal basis for passing legislation that deprived the indigenous people of Bougainville of their land or property. This includes the transfer of ownership of the minerals below the surface of the soil from the indigenous landowners to the Australian government. There are therefore grounds for a claim for damages against the Australian government for breach of trust.[5]

Bougainville Copper Limited (BCL) was established as a CRA-controlled subsidiary to operate the mine. Between 1969 and 1972 (when mining operations commenced), the Australian Colonial Administration granted BCL leases over 12,500 hectares of land for the mine site, access roads, and waste. These land acquisitions, which in each case were vigorously opposed by the peoples whose lands were affected, also constitute a breach of trust by the colonial administration. Both the Nasioi and Nagovisi peoples were affected.

In Bougainville, land is owned on a clan basis and the landowners are women. Land is passed down from mother to daughter, who know well the boundaries of their land entitlements.

> *The right to use any piece of land must be sought from the*
> *female members of the clan. This is an idea conceived by our*
> *ancestors since time immemorial....*
>   *Everything in each particular piece of land or in the sky*
> *above and the earth beneath is respectively owned by each*
> *particular clan and not by another governing body. Whiteman,*
> *under the Mining Ordinance made in Australia, have introduced*
> *their foreign policies that are not in conjunction with the Local*
> *Land Ownership Policy. We do not agree with the foreign*
> *concepts of the land ownership policy as stated in the Mining*
> *Ordinance.*[6]

At no time did any of the women give permission for their land to be used for exploration or mining. From the beginning, the Nasioi people resisted CRA intrusion onto their land and treated the prospectors as trespassers.[7]

In 1965 they expelled the CRA exploration team and pulled down their camp, which had been erected on Nasioi land without their permission. The Australian Colonial Administration responded by jailing 200 Bougainvilleans, including elders, some of whom were beaten in custody.

In 1969 women at Rorovana refused to allow their land to be used for mine port facilities. On July 28, 1969, the Rorovana people were told they had to accept the administration's terms of $105 per acre plus $2 per coconut tree by August 1 or their land would be taken without compensation. The people rejected the ultimatum.[8]

One hundred specially trained and equipped riot police were flown to Bougainville to help the surveyors mark out the areas of land owned by the Rorovana people that BCL wanted. On August 1, surveyors, supported by police wearing gas masks and carrying truncheons, drove in the first concrete peg. Some of the women landowners broke through the police cordon and wrenched the peg out, triumphantly carrying it home.

On August 5, riot police carrying batons, shields, rifles, and respirators attacked a group of about 65 unarmed villagers, men, women, and children. The police fired a barrage of 150 teargas canisters at them, and the people stood firm. Then the police charged them with their batons, clubbing both men and women who were forced off their land.[9]

THE BOUGAINVILLE COPPER MINE: STATE-SANCTIONED DESTRUCTION OF AN ECOSYSTEM

State violence by the Australian Colonial Administration against the Bougainvilleans who resisted theft of their land for use by CRA contrasts starkly with the leniency the same administration afforded CRA and its subsidiary BCL. The Colonial Administration gave the mining company a three-year tax holiday, followed by four years of accelerated depreciation, and allowed the company to flush the chemical wastes and tailings into the Kawerong and Jaba Rivers. No environmental impact statement was required. Over a billion tons of chemical wastes and tailings were dumped into the river system, causing massive environmental damage.

BCL commissioned a number of consultant reports on tailing disposal and on the effects of tailings and overburden discharges into the Kawerong-Jaba river system. Initially the consultants advised against discharge of tailings into the river, accurately predicting massive deposition and extreme land degradation. A subsequent report stated that disposal into the river system was the least costly. Their predictions concerning land degradation were revised to suggest that the tailings would pass through the Kawerong and upper Jaba rivers to deposit at sea and on the flood plain adjacent to the coast. It was claimed that the tailings reaching the sea would be removed by ocean currents.[10]

This turned out to be patently false. The tailings were deposited in the Kawerong-Jaba river system (40 percent) and in the delta that formed at the mouth of the Jaba River in Empress Augusta Bay (60 percent). Very little material was transported away from the delta.[11]

DESTRUCTION OF AN ECOSYSTEM

The tailings spread out over an area of 4,000 hectares, turning fertile river valleys into wasteland. Lowlands near the coast were converted into chemically contaminated swamps as the Jaba River, laden with the toxic waste products of mineral processing, overflowed its banks. Whole forests died, with the branches of the dead trees pointing skywards like the fingers of a huge skeleton. Three thousand hectares of land were totally destroyed, covered with chemically contaminated tailings where nothing will grow. Thirty kilometers of the river valley system were converted into moonscape.

The Jaba River choked, became convoluted, and changed its course. Tailings accumulated at the mouth of the river and created an artificial cape covering 1,000 hectares and stretching several kilometers into the Empress Augusta Bay. The white sands at the mouth of the river were replaced by a huge expanse of gray-black tailings. Where there was once a plentiful supply of fish and shellfish, the area is now desolate, inhabited by crocodiles and water rats.

> *The beaches of Empress Augusta Bay will continue to be affected by tailings for the life of the mine and possibly longer and the evidence we have seen indicates that there would be a long, slow decline in the overall population of mussels in Empress Augusta Bay.*[12]

CHEMICAL CONTAMINATION: THE DISCHARGE FROM THE CONCENTRATOR

Discharge from the copper concentrator, which processed 130,000 tons of ore per day, poured directly into the Kawerong River, coloring the water green. Chemicals discharged into the river included dissolved copper, at concentration levels toxic to both plants and animals, and residual lime that rendered the river water alkaline. These alone were enough to kill all the animal and plant life in the rivers and turn fertile valleys into wasteland.[13] Aluminum, heavy metals such as mercury, cadmium, lead, zinc, and arsenic, contributed to the ecocide. Xanthate, ingestion of which is harmful, methyl isobutyl carbinol, which is a severe skin irritant in concentrated form, and polyacrylamide monomer, which is toxic and can be absorbed through the skin, were also discharged into the river.[14]

Chemical action and reaction between the chemical contaminants in the tailings have made revegetation impossible for many years, if ever. Vast tracts of tailings are still barren, devoid of vegetation five years after the closure of the mine.

AERIAL SPRAYING OF TOXIC CHEMICALS

Approximately 400 hectares of dense tropical rain forest were destroyed to make way for the mine itself. The larger trees were poisoned and the undergrowth was sprayed with herbicide. The chemicals used were: (a) tree poison, an arsenic pentoxide solution with a concentration of four pounds per gallon of water, and (b) the herbicide 'Bush Killer 80,' a mixture of 40-245T and 40-24D, both of which are toxic and teratogenic.

Aerial spraying commenced on August 18, 1969, and continued over a period of a month. No tests were carried out on the effects of the aerial spraying on the people who lived and worked in the area. One worker went blind. First trees, then crops were affected.[15]

AIR AND WATER POLLUTION

The mine, one of the largest open-cut operations in the world, dug a crater six kilometers long, four kilometers wide, and half a kilometer deep. Dust clouds from the mining operations combined with emissions from the copper concentrator to create a poisonous mix that polluted the air and increased the incidence of upper respiratory infections and asthma. The climate changed, crops were damaged, and trees no longer bore fruit. The fish in the rivers developed ulcerations and died.[16] Every trace of animal and plant life in the Kawerong and Jaba river valleys was extinguished.

Land animals were also affected. Birds left the area in search of a more hospitable environment. Possums and flying foxes, once plentiful in Panguna, the area of the mine, became scarce. The normal food supply, garden vegetables and fruits, supplemented by possum, flying fox, and fish, could no longer provide for the needs of the people, creating health problems.

THE RAPE OF THE LAND

The life and culture of the people are entwined with the land. As destruction of the land and environment by the mine spread, the culture, economy, and life of the people were ripped apart.

> *Land is our life. Land is our physical life-food and sustenance.*
> *Land is our social life, it is marriage, it is status, it is security, it*
> *is politics; in fact, it is our only world. When you take our land,*
> *you cut away the very heart of our existence. We have little or*
> *no experience of social survival detached from the land. For us*
> *to be completely landless is a nightmare that no dollar in the*
> *pocket or dollar in the bank will allay; we are a threatened*
> *people.*[17]

The Australian Colonial Administration and the CRA executives, being from an alien culture, could neither understand nor grasp the significance of this. For them, land was a commodity to be bought and sold. They had no sense of deep-rooted links between the people and the land. They just treated it as an exploitable resource. Ignorance was combined with arrogance, a common characteristic of colonial occupying powers that can impose their will through the use of force.

By forcing the mine on the Nasioi and Nagovisi people against their will, the Australian Colonial Administration was acting more like an occupying power than a trustee. In the meantime, the destruction of the land and pollution of the environment were undermining the health of the people. Deaths from upper respiratory infections, asthma, and TB increased. Many children had impaired hearing due to chronic middle-ear infections. Coughs and colds became commonplace, especially among children. Obesity, particularly among women, became common when they had to abandon their traditional diet for European tinned and packaged foods.[18]

This was just the tip of the iceberg, the smoke emission at the top of a live volcano. A deep sense of social malaise set in that expressed itself in clan tensions, depression, alcohol abuse, rage, traffic accidents, and incidents of violence – all distress signals of people severed from their roots. A pervasive sense of powerlessness spread like clouds of pollution across the valley as the mining operations continued to rape the land. Panguna became known as 'The Valley of Tears.'

> *We don't grow healthy crops any more, our traditional customs*
> *and values have been disrupted, and we have become mere*

> *spectators as our earth is being dug up, taken away, and sold*
> *for millions. Our land was taken from us by force: we were blind*
> *then, but we have finally grown to understand what's going on.*[19]

For over two decades, the cries of the people fell on deaf ears. The Australian Colonial Administration and the CRA executives did not understand Melanesian society, the system of land ownership, or the importance of women as custodians of the land. By overriding the women of the clan, by forcing mining on the people against their will, raping the land, environment, and culture, the Australian Colonial Administration had created a time bomb.

PAPUA NEW GUINEA'S POSTCOLONIAL LEGACY

This time bomb was handed over to Papua New Guinea (PNG) when it was granted formal independence by Australia on September 16, 1975. Bougainville had declared independence two weeks earlier, a move that was met with police violence from the newly created state of PNG, which paralleled the violence of its former colonial masters. Moses Havini, leading a demonstration, narrowly escaped death when police fired a teargas canister at his head.

At no time had Bougainville ceded its independence to any foreign power. Bougainville is geographically part of the Solomon Islands. The nearest island in the Solomons is only eight kilometers away, while the mainland of PNG is 800 kilometers. Prior to colonization, contact between the peoples of PNG and Bougainville was minimal. Bougainvilleans approached the United Nations three times, in 1962, 1968, and 1975, seeking to exercise their right to self-determination and were rejected each time.

The Australian government insisted that Bougainville be part of the newly formed nation-state of PNG. Having put in place an expensive top-heavy government and administrative system, ill-suited to the culture of the people on whom it was imposed, money was needed to maintain it. The Bougainville copper mine was expected to provide the revenue.

For CRA, its shareholders, and the PNG government, the mine was a multi-million dollar money earner, the 'Jewel in the Crown' of RTZ.[20] During its 17 years of operation, total dividends and other benefits to CRA and its shareholders totaled 2,341.7 million Kina (approximately 1,600 million pounds sterling). Total payments to the PNG government in taxes and dividends were 1,085.6 million Kina.[21]

A NEW GENERATION RISES

The people, who as children had witnessed the scenes of the 1960s, grew up and became the militants of the 1980s and 1990s. In 1987, a new Panguna Land Owners Association (PLA) emerged, led by younger, more educated men and women who strongly opposed the BCL mining operations. In March 1988, the new PLA organized a march of 500 landowners to BCL and lodged a petition demanding localization of employment and greater control of environmental degradation and pollution.[22]

On March 24, 1988, Mr Perry Zeipi, the Minister of the Environment in the PNG government, sailed down the Jaba River and described the amount of pollution as 'dreadful and unbelievable.' The minister observed that the river was full of all kinds of chemicals and wastes and aquatic life had been destroyed. The water was no longer safe for drinking and bathing. Although he expressed shock that this had been allowed to happen, he said his department could do nothing about it. Under the Bougainville Copper Agreement, the power to control and monitor environmental pollution was vested with the Department of Minerals and Energy.[23]

Bougainville Copper Limited failed to reply to the PLA petition. Two months later the PLA organized a one-day sit-down protest that temporarily stopped mining operations. BCL then engaged Applied Geology Consultants to do a survey of health, environment, and other effects of the mine.

The report avoided burning issues such as the effect of chemical pollutants on food crops, which is the mainstay to people. Instead of systematically comparing food crops in mine-affected areas with other areas of Bougainville, the consultants did a cursory survey and stated that all villages observed, both near and distant from the mine, had problems with their crops.[24]

Francis Ona, secretary of the PLA and a former surveyor with BCL, declared the report a 'whitewash.' A few days later, a quantity of dynamite was stolen from BCL stores. In November 1988, militants commenced blowing up power pylons and engaged in other acts of sabotage that forced the mine to close.[25]

In November 1988, Paul Tohian, then Minister for Police in the PNG government, issued an order for police to 'shoot to kill.'[26] The militants reorganized and formed the Bougainville Revolutionary Army under the leadership of Sam Kaouna. Francis Ona, spokesperson for the landowners, said that the people meant business and were prepared to die for their cause.[27]

Early in 1989, the PNG army was called in. It was also issued a license to kill. The human rights violations committed by the PNG army and police culminated in the St. Valentines Day massacre on February 14, 1990, in which both militants and civilians were killed, including a Uniting Church pastor.[28] These human rights abuses turned Bougainville against Papua New Guinea and the struggle to close the mine became a struggle for independence that the people won.

In March 1990, the PNG army and police left the island, defeated. The PNG Armed Forces imposed a military blockade on Bougainville in April 1990. On May 17, 1990, the people of Bougainville declared independence and established their Interim Government.

STATE VIOLENCE

How far will a nation-state go to force an unwanted and environmentally destructive mining operation on a people? The case of Bougainville highlights like a strobe light the nature of conflict between:

1   Corporate interests and the role of state violence in protecting these interests; and
2   The interests of peoples in protecting their land and environment from destruction by mining and its industrial by-products.

Bougainville is the first place in the world where an indigenous people have forced the closure of a mine that was raping their land and environment, and kept it closed. Prior to closure, the mine contributed 19 percent of government revenue and 40 percent of PNG's export earnings. At the time the mine was closed, it was worth A$862 million (431 million pounds) on the Australian Share Market.[29]

Investors were becoming nervous, as landowners on the mainland of PNG started to flex their muscles. Mining executives wanted to ensure that 'the problems on Bougainville don't come to other parts of the country.' They were concerned that there was increased talk among indigenous people, whose lives had been affected by mining operations, that other mine sites could become 'another Bougainville' unless demands for environmental protection or compensation were met. BCL Chairman Don Carruthers commented: 'The banks are not happy about lending in PNG...and I think that's a problem for any future projects.'[30]

The PNG government tried to isolate the Bougainville situation, saying it was not indicative of the PNG mainland. The government argued that there were racial differences between Bougainvilleans and the people of the mainland.

THE BLOCKADE OF BOUGAINVILLE

In April 1990, the PNG government isolated Bougainville by imposing a blockade on the island. The primary purpose of the blockade was to cut off medical and other essential supplies, thereby increasing the hardships of the people, in an attempt to turn them against the BRA. The strategy is outlined in a document leaked from the Intelligence Branch of the PNG Department of the Defense:

> ...the hardships of life without essential goods and services (that they had been so used to as one of the PNG's most developed provinces) grow worse each morning. This alone has had a great psychological effect on the NSP (Bougainville) population and is slowly but surely turning the population against the BRA. Should a complete cut in shipping services to the island eventuate (a blockade?), goods and services would come to a

complete standstill and it is only a matter of time (3–4 weeks?)
before Kaouna will be pressured to listen to the silent majority
of the province. Because of Kaouna's weakness as a strong
leader, he will most certainly succumb to the pressure.[31]

The blockade, which contravenes the Geneva Conventions of the Laws of War, is both an economic blockade and a medical blockade, and is still in force. The blockade prevents medicine, clothing, and other essential supplies from reaching the people behind the blockade. Deaths from preventable diseases continue to mount as a result. The local Red Cross in central Bougainville estimated that by November 1992 the blockade, through the lack of medicines and vaccines, had caused the death of more than 2,000 children.

Hospitals in the blockaded areas have been forced to close their wards due to lack of medical supplies. Seriously ill people trying to escape to the Solomon Islands in search of medical treatment are routinely fired upon if seen by PNG troops maintaining the blockade. Women and children have been most affected by the blockade.

The blockade has meant that pregnant women have died
needlessly in childbirth and young children have died from
easily preventable diseases. No babies born after late 1989 have
been immunized against killers like TB, measles, and whooping
cough. For many, the blockade has delivered nothing short of a
death sentence.[32]

The blockade turned more people against the PNG than the BRA, as the death toll from the blockade passed 5,000.

THE PNG ARMY RETURNS

Equipped with Australian-supplied mortar bombs, helicopters, guns, grenades, and ammunition, the PNG returned to Bougainville and attacked towns and villages. During 1993 and 1994 the situation deteriorated, the blockade was tightened, and the risk of illness, especially among babies and small children increased. Many civilians who fled their villages to avoid capture and detention by the PNG army took refuge in the mountains.

The colder climate particularly affects small children, already at risk due to the shortage in clothing. Mothers have no clothing to wrap newly born babies. Without antibiotics, many babies die of upper respiratory infections.

The blockade also keeps out journalists and human rights organizations. In the absence of public scrutiny, PNG troops continue to commit human rights violations with impunity.[33] Human rights violations and war crimes committed by the PNG Armed Forces include the following:

1   Aerial bombardment of civilian targets;
2   Wanton killing and acts of cruelty;
3   Burning of houses and villages;
4   Making the civilian population or individual civilians the object of attack;
5   Outrages upon personal dignity, rape, and humiliating and degrading treatment;
6   Perfidious use of the Red Cross emblem; and
7   Pillage.

An estimated 500 civilians have been killed as a result of violations of the laws of armed conflict by PNG troops. Some examples are given below:

Case 1: Ken Savia, the Minister for Health in the Bougainville Interim Government, was captured by the PNG Armed Forces on February 14, 1993. He was subsequently killed in custody. He was dragged around an unused parking lot tied to the back of a truck and died of the injuries received.

Case 2: 'When I did not return to the Tokiano Centre (a PNG-controlled concentration camp), PNG soldiers came to my village and shot dead my four sons, Raphael Morikei, Iamu Kubui, John, and Bana Kurai' [Statutory Declaration of Chief Andrew Purai of Buin, sworn January 1993].

Case 3: 'As the PNG soldiers approached the Kopani village, most of the people saw the army coming and ran away into the bush. An elderly couple, Mr. Peter Tapatomam and his wife, were shot and wounded as they were sleeping in their house. The soldiers stole K7,000 that belonged to Mr. Tapatomam, who was a Health Extension Officer. The PNG soldiers then burnt the village to the ground. Mr. and Mrs. Tapatomam were burnt alive in their house.'

Case 4: 'In September 1992, a man called Peter from the Laguai village was seen carrying a packet of rice to his village. He had left Turiboiru at the allotted time to go to his food garden. He was spotted by PNG soldiers as he passed the PNG army base at Buin town. They captured him and put in the back of a truck. On their way back to the base, they dropped him off the back of the truck and onto the bitumen road. He broke one of his legs. He was dropped at the junction of the road leading to the Buin Health Centre and the road to Kangu Beach.

The PNG soldiers then picked Peter up off the road and put him in the back of the truck again. They drove the truck in the direction of Wally Sito's store and while the vehicle was moving dropped him off the truck again. The store is just in front of the PNG army barracks in Buin. When he fell on the road his skull split open and he died instantly. The PNG soldiers picked him up again and took him down the Kangu Road until they reached the crossroads near Laguai village. They put him face down on the log and put the packet of rice on his back. They then sprayed his body with bullets.'

Case 5: 'A squadron of PNG Armed Forces surrounded the Okogupa village in the Aita area of Wakunai. The village is built on the top of a hill and is near the PNG army camp at Wakunai. The PNG armed forces captured a whole family and some other residents of the village.

The PNG army lined the people up in two lines and asked them what they were doing. Someone had reported to the PNG army that the village had been celebrating the independence of Bougainville from Papua New Guinea.

The father of the family, Silus Ausi, the chief of the village, admitted they had been celebrating independence. PNG army officers shot him in the head in front of this family. His wife and five children were shot by the PNG Armed Forces next. Then all the other people in the village were lined up and shot. The PNG army then burned the village to the ground.'[34]

The United Nations Commission on Human Rights and the Sub-Commission for the Prevention of Discrimination and the Protection of Minorities have passed resolutions calling on the PNG government to immediately lift restrictions on the flow of medical and other humanitarian supplies into the areas under military blockade, to permit the Special Rapporteur on Extra-Judicial and Summary Executions and the Special Rapporteur on Torture to go to Bougainville to investigate and report on allegations of human rights violations there.[35] The PNG government has refused to comply with these resolutions.

In the meantime, the killing continues and PNG is on the verge of bankruptcy.[36] Papua New Guinea is fighting a war it cannot afford and cannot win. Why?

LAWS IN CONFLICT

The nation-state of Papua New Guinea, created 19 years ago as an amalgam of former colonial territories, was hastily constructed with hierarchical Western-style political and legal structures superimposed on the traditional system of autonomous self-governing communities. The constitution of PNG, drawn up by Western or Western-trained lawyers, in many respects was found to be inappropriate or ill-adapted to the needs of the majority of communities who retained their traditional land-based economy, customary laws, and village government.

Customary land laws, which stipulate that the landowner owns everything above and below the soil, are in conflict with state-imposed law, which claims the minerals below the surface of the soil to be the property of the state. The traditional relationship between the people and the land on which they rely for sustenance is powerful and enduring. 'Land is life' is the common thread linking the peoples of the Pacific. The Panguna landowners, in a 1992 statement to the then Prime Minister of PNG, drew attention to this:

> *The Prime Minister of Papua New Guinea, his government, and*
> *people must recognize the unquestionable fact that we are both*
> *of Melanesian race and culture. Mr. Wingti, as a Melanesian*
> *you must be aware that the roots of every Melanesian person,*
> *man and women, our very identity, our being, our culture is*
> *based on the land and the environment. Therefore the fight to*
> *save our land, our environment, and our livelihood is not only to*
> *save the people of Bougainville. It is a fight to uphold the land*

rights of all Melanesians, including the people of your land,
Papua New Guinea.[37]

The success of the Bougainvilleans in closing the mine that was destroying their land, their environment, and their culture gave other Melanesian people on the PNG mainland confidence and courage to take similar action. In 1992, people in the highlands of PNG closed a gold mine owned by CRA at Mount Kare. In 1994, Torres Strait islanders declared they would use 'whatever means' available to protect the strait from mining, including violence if necessary. 'We are totally dependent on our marine resources for sustenance and maintenance of our traditional way of life and livelihood,' Mr Getano Lui, chairman of the Torres Strait Islands Coordinating Council, said. The council's position is that the current ban on mining should be extended indefinitely. Traditional inhabitants of both sides of the Australian/PNG border hold the same position.[38]

The struggle of indigenous people in the Pacific to protect their land from mining and logging is spreading. This is perceived by mining companies and international lending institutions as a threat to 'development.'

Following the closure of the mine at Mount Kare, a ministerial delegation from Australia, including Foreign Affairs and Trade Minister Senator Gareth Evans, flew to PNG to meet with government leaders. The message was conveyed that the PNG government must protect Australian investments and be seen to protect those investments. The Australian government offered aid funds to assist with the formation of a Rapid Deployment Police Force to counter any more actions directed at foreign mining operations.

This force soon developed into a paramilitary force that works in conjunction with PNG troops.[39] Using Australian-supplied Iroquois helicopters (flown by Australian and New Zealand pilots) as gunships, they strafe Bougainville villages. This aerial bombardment violates the conventions on the conduct of armed conflict. The war on Bougainville is in effect a proxy war being fought by the PNG armed forces and police to protect Australia's strategic and economic interests in the region. Papua New Guinea troops are being asked to fight a war to protect overseas mining interests and give the appearance to prospective foreign investors and lending institutions that their investments in PNG are secure.

In June 1994, the PNG navy and air force went on strike for a brief period. Discontent among the PNG Armed Forces is spreading, while the Bougainville Revolutionary Army is committed to protecting the rights of the people to their land and their way of life. They have a strong sense of purpose, as summed up in a recent statement by Sam Kaouna:

> *Six years ago this struggle re-erupted in earnest, now becoming*
> *an armed struggle. We were only forced to defend ourselves*
> *from Papua New Guinea armed forces. We did not initiate the*
> *war, and merely responded in our duty to defend you, our*
> *people and our inherent rights to our land, and our right to*
> *self-determination.*

We have stood committed to you, and by you, in all circumstances of this war; and along with many of your sons/daughters that have now fallen. Thousands more have died as the consequences (like the blockade) of this uninvited war to our shores. We have stood selflessly to defend and protect you. To continue with our political struggle not only here, but also within the international community, and to the United Nations.

For more than forty thousand years we have been a part of our land. Without it we cannot be whole; it is our culture, our religion, our life. To take away our land is like taking the bones out of a man's legs – he cannot walk any more. They (PNG and international interests) came and took our land without asking, destroyed it, and tore it apart, poisoned our streams, and made our people sick.

They were all greedy for money and the copper that we had – they tried to break us down. They sent the soldiers in to kill and rape and burn, and force us to surrender this land of Bougainville.

But God helps those that are persecuted unjustly. Too, the ghosts of all our dead and of our enraged ancestors stand with us firmly here. You can break our bones, but you can never break our spirit. The land of Bougainville is ours. We will not give up this land.[40]

A VISION OF THE FUTURE

At the core of the struggle is the determination of the people to protect their land, to restore the harmony that once existed between the people, the land, and environment. Despite the suffering that they have endured through the six years of a bitter war, the hope and belief remain that their island paradise, once lost through greed and exploitation, can be restored once more. The 1993 Christmas address to the people of Bougainville by President Francis Ona reflects these aspirations:

While we celebrate Christmas and New Year I ask everyone to think about a very special theme, the environment, our coastline, our plains, rivers, and mountains – this total ecosystem we call Bougainville. This environment protects us from the enemy, feeds and shelters us, grows our food, and breeds our wildlife. We must shelter and protect it from now on. We have been fighting a bloody war for the last five years, while others like PNG have exploited and tried to destroy our land. We must make sure that we do not lose what we have suffered to protect, our customs and culture, our trees and wildlife, the rivers and environment, to ensure that Bougainville is true to its name as our tropical paradise.

If this land can shelter and protect us for the last five years under a blockade unprecedented in our life and experience, then we should value our natural environment far more than copper and gold. We will stop whoever the enemy may be, whether it be a mining company, organisation, or another country. We will not allow our river to be polluted, be it by Australian companies, or our forests logged by Japanese companies.[41]

NOTES

1 'Police Shoot to Kill at Copper Mine.' *Sydney Morning Herald* (December 8, 1988).

2 See Statement of the Joint Declaration of the Buin Council of Chiefs, south Bougainville, January 4, 1993, in 'Krai Bilong Bougainville' (p 46); Statement of the Birong-Etta Council of Chiefs, central Bougainville, November 27, 1992 (*Ibid*: 40).

3 (1950) International Court of Justice (ICJ) 128 p 149. (Advisory opinion on International States of South West Africa – Namibia.)

4 (1937) 58 CLR 528 pp 581–582.

5 Peter Dunidi, *Indigenous or Aboriginal Land Rights to Property – A Papua New Guinea Perspective* (Utrecht: International Books, 1994: 28).

6 Thomas Koronaro, National Coordinator of Chiefs of Bougainville, 'Basic Ideas Behind the Bougainville Revolution' (November 1992).

7 R. Bedford and A. Mamak, 'Compensation for Development,' *Bougainville Special Publication* No 2, Christ Church, Aotearoa (New Zealand), University of Canterbury (1977: 7–10).

8 Papua New Guinea *Post-Courier* (July 28, 1969).

9 *Daily Mirror* (August 6, 1969).

10 *Environmental, Socio-Economic Public Health Review: The Bougainville Copper Mine, Panguna* (Applied Geology Associates Limited, 1998: 3–7).

11 *Ibid*: 3.11.

12 *Ibid*: 5.35.

13 *Ibid*: 5.18.

14 *Ibid*: 5.20.

15 *Ibid*: 5.28.

16 *Ibid*: 5.29.

17 J. Dove, T. Miriung, and M. Togolo, 'Mining Bitterness,' in P. Jack (ed) *Problems of Choice: Land in Papua New Guinea's Future* (Canberra: Australian National University Press).

18 *Environmental Socio-Economic Public Health Review. The Bougainville Copper Mine, Panguna* (Applied Geology Associates Limited, 1988: 4.28).

19 W. Hiambohn, 'Landowners Resort to Sabotage in Panguna.' *Pacific Islands Monthly* (January 1989: 16–19).

20 Roger Moody, *Plunder* (Partizans/CAFCA, London and New Zealand, 1991).

21 Bougainville Copper Limited Annual Report 1992.

22 David Myndman, 'Digging the Mines in Melanesia.' *CS Quarterly* 15,2 (1988: 34).

23 *Papua New Guinea Post-Courier* (Friday, March 25, 1988).

24 *Environmental Socio-Economic Public Health Review, op cit,* p. 5.36.

25 Myndman (1988: 34–35).

26 'Police Shoot to Kill at Copper Mine.' *Sydney Morning Herald* (December 8, 1988).

27 Myndman (1988: 35).

28 *Sydney Morning Herald* (August 3, 1990).

29 'Bougainville Says It Is Committed to Panguna.' *The Age* (August 19, 1994).

30 'PNG Riches at Risk,' by Glenda Korporal. *The Bulletin* (February 13, 1990).

31 'An Intelligence Resume for Contingency Planning for North Solomons Province,' Department of Defence, Defence Intelligence Branch, NSP Cell, April 1990 (Confidential).

32 Atu Emberson-Bain, 'Cries from the Mothers of the Land.' *Pacific Islands Monthly* (April 1993: 25).

33 'Papua New Guinea: Under the Barrel of a Gun: Bougainville 1991 to 1993.' Amnesty International (November 1993).

34 Rosemarie Gillespie, *Australia's Role in Arming Violators of Human Rights: The Case of Papua New Guinea and Bougainville* (August 1993).

35 United Nations Economic and Social Council E/CN.4/Sub.2/1994/L38, August 19, 1994, as amended.

36 Rowan Callick, 'PNG to Sell Down Its Mine and Oil Holdings.' *Financial Review* (November 10, 1994).

37 Rosemarie Gillespie, 'Resolution of the Panguna Landowners, December 18, 1992.' *Krai Bilong* (Bougainville, August 1993).

38 'Islanders Fight for Ban.' *Sydney Morning Herald* (November 3, 1994).

39 Centre for Independent Journalism, 'Badge of Dishonour.' *Snoop* (1993).

40 Statement by General Sam Kaouna of the Bougainville Revolutionary Army (October 1994).

41 1993 Christmas Address by President Francis Ona in 'Bougainville: Voices from Behind the Blockade,' compiled by Rosemarie Gillespie (July 1994).

Chapter 7

Environmental Security and Displaced People in Southern Africa

Meena Singh

WHAT IS UNIQUE ABOUT SOUTH AFRICA?

South Africa is often described as a dominant country in the African continent, a 'world in one country,' and the country with the highest level of inequality (for the latter, see, eg, Wilson and Ramphele, 1989: 18). One of the last African countries to be freed from white minority domination, its position a year and one-half after the first democratic election, although representing hope for the majority of black South Africans, remains precariously locked in a government of National Unity. For over a century, South Africa has enjoyed the status of a superpower in the subregion and has therefore significantly shaped the character of many neighboring countries. Drawing on the cheap and abundant labor from the Frontline States, South Africa treated with indifference the lives of its work force and their abandoned families.

The land area of South Africa makes up only 4 percent of the total for Africa, with its population accounting for 6 percent of the African total. Yet South Africa boasts that it generates roughly 17 percent of the GNP of the continent: 40 percent of industrial output, 45 percent of mining production, and 83 percent of steel production (*South Africa Yearbook*, 1989–1990). South Africa did not, however, gain its powerful position in Africa without control over and destruction to its neighbors. In pursuing an aggressive policy of destabilization of countries sympathetic to the liberation movements opposing apartheid, South Africa has been responsible for the slaughter of wildlife and deforestation of valuable teak plantations in Angola (in exchange for arms and military support to UNITA), and the deforestation in Zambia, Mozambique, and Malawi that was caused by concentrations of internal refugees resulting from South African support for rebel movements (McCallum, 1991: 168; Pogrund, 1991: 163–165).

With the euphoria of South Africa's first democratic elections in 1994, came the legacies created by a long era of apartheid rule. Despite the supposed affluence in South Africa, it is still very much a reality that children eat food gathered in toxic waste dumps, workers die in factories and mine accidents that could have been prevented, communities choke on the pollution-filled air they breathe, and peasant farmers die of starvation during times of drought.

An environmental justice network forum launched in 1994 has been directed at linking environmental and social justice issues, challenging the abuse of power that results, on the one hand, in the majority of poor people being denied access to natural resources and suffering the effects of environmental damage while, on the other hand, big industry, large commercial farms, and a small minority of the population enjoy easy access to and abuse scarce resources such as water. This may be illustrated by the fact that while South Africa produces 60 percent of Africa's total electricity output, over 60 percent of South Africans (80 percent of whom are black) do not have access to this basic service. The majority of households in Soweto still use coal since it is cheaper and therefore more readily accessible. Air pollution levels over Soweto have been described as among the worst in the world, exceeding the safe limits identified by the World Health Organization (eg, Kgomo, 1991: 120).

Policies regarding the importation of toxic wastes, the role of transnational companies, and workers' rights to safe working environments had been lax. Thus, shortly after the creation of the Government of National Unity in May 1994, local press headlines were dominated by a scandal of toxic waste importation by the Ministry of Environment. The promotion of trade in international toxic wastes by the Department of Environment not only undermines efforts of African countries to prevent such imports, but it is also a direct assault on the lives of many poor people forced to live in dangerous proximity to such wastes.

The budget of the Department of Environmental Affairs reflects the style of the old regime, with 60 million rands allocated for plant and animal protection, and a mere three million rands for pollution control (*Environmental Justice Networker*, 1995: 2).[1] Following criticism of the lack of consultation with regard to environmental policies, the Ministry of Environment and Tourism is presently engaged in a process of drafting a Green Paper for Environmental Policy. A clause on internalizing 'externalities,' such as the pollution generated by SASOL (the state-owned oil-from-coal and chemical producing corporation), reflects a concern with addressing issues previously ignored by environmental policies. For the first time in South Africa, an attempt is being made to view the environment in a holistic way, to encourage the incorporation of traditional knowledge in conservation efforts, and to safeguard the rights of citizens to safe drinking water and clean air. The draft policy document will be circulated for discussion in all provinces and via a democratic process; comments and suggestions will be taken on board, making for a healthy process of policy formulation. Such changes in the *modus operandi* of government ministries lend hope for an emerging democracy such as South Africa, where notions of participation and 'bottom-up approaches' become transformed into practice.

Water scarcity still poses one of the most serious threats to security in semiarid Southern Africa. When we envisage water scarcity, we imagine droughts and disturbing images of thin animals and parched earth. Much more threatening to the water supply, however, is the alarmingly excessive consumption of water that goes largely unnoticed.

Within this context of a country riddled by contradictions, I would like to explore the theme of displaced people and the likely future scenario if the situation is not urgently addressed. The region of Southern Africa, which is at present undergoing dynamic changes, will provide the framework in which the displaced people will be examined.

ENVIRONMENTAL SECURITY AND CONFLICT

Environmental security is inextricably linked to development, since poverty and environmental destruction go hand in hand. The causes of environmental displacement will be explored by viewing environmental degradation in relation to poverty and development. Unequal access to resources often implies that scarce resources are in great demand. From the work of Myers (1986, 1989a) and Homer-Dixon (1994), it has been possible to identify resource scarcities as important contributing factors in violent conflicts. In the case of the recent war in Rwanda, land scarcity played a significant contributing role (Kane, 1995: 6). While it has been pointed out (eg, Myers, 1995: 13) that resource scarcities do not necessarily in themselves lead to social unrest, they exacerbate poverty by widening the gap between the majority poor and the elite in a society, and the unrest that ensues raises national security alarms. Once social unrest begins, particularly in undemocratic societies where neither human rights nor the legal mechanisms for addressing grievances are secure, such unrest may spill over into neighboring countries, thereby threatening the security of the region as a whole. By addressing the root causes of social unrest, not only may we avoid conflicts that would otherwise develop, but we tackle the very security issues that affect the lives of millions of people who need clean water, fertile land, and fuelwood resources for their daily subsistence.

I wish to clarify 'who' really are environmental victims. Anyone can become an environmental victim by a random process of natural disasters striking in any place regardless of who inhabits the area. Anecdotal evidence from South Africa can better illustrate the point I am trying to make: inclement weather may lead to landslides in Kloof (a hilly and green suburb of Durban) and floods along the Umgeni and Umvoti Rivers in Natal's north coast. Both areas will have 'environmental victims.' Under apartheid laws, however, the former would have affected middle-class white residents and the latter black shack dwellers. While the residents of Kloof had chosen the area for its outstanding natural beauty, they would have the resources to pay for good architects and would have insured their property and belongings and therefore would not lose their livelihoods. The shack dwellers, on the other hand, would have chosen the river banks because the location was *itself* a livelihood resource, providing a base close to the city or enabling the cultivation of food on the fertile alluvium. In the event of a disaster, without any insurance or job protection they would lose everything they possess. So, it is indeed possible for anyone to become an 'environmental victim,' but when we speak of victims, like the shack dwellers in Natal, we need to recognize that their *vulnerability* to becoming environmental victims may be greatly reduced by appropriate policies and human action.

In contrast to the threats to regional security during the Cold War period, the security of neighboring states is not now threatened by powerful armies and military occupations. The threat is more often from unarmed, hungry, unemployed, and frequently ethnically divided people. The solution therefore cannot be a military one. This new scenario demands a different approach to security, which can only be effective if we have accurate data and a thorough understanding of the causes that generate such conflict. Following the 1992 elections in Angola, renewed conflict, exacerbated by a severe drought, claimed the lives of more than 100 people per day, until humanitarian aid became available to those lucky enough to have access to it. In South Africa, conflict over land and water resources continues despite the positive changes at the political level.

As populations dependent on scarce and diminishing resources grow, competition for resources may generate conflict. Food scarcity leads to price increases, thereby widening cleavages in society. Elite groups may become more powerful, and group identity is reinforced as competition accelerates. This may manifest itself in ethnic conflicts. Much more data is required to understand the population and consumption picture for the Southern African region.

RESOURCE CONFLICTS

Among the most common causes of conflict, particularly in developing countries, are land scarcity, unequal distribution of land, land degradation, and increased population. All of these factors are interlinked. In South Africa, land reform is addressing, to some extent, the disenchantment with unequal access to land created during the apartheid era. Experience from elsewhere, notably El Salvador and Mozambique, serves to illustrate that unless emerging democracies address the issue of land reform, violent unrest is likely to follow (Binswanger and Deininger, 1994: 12). It has been observed that in places as far apart as the Philippines and Lesotho, the lack of access to fertile land has forced the migration of peasants onto steep marginal lands and resulted in acute soil erosion, declining yields, and growing poverty (Myers, 1989a: 26; Singh, 1994: 20). Interestingly, in the case of both Peru and the Philippines, support for the underground revolutionary armies was strongest among upland peasants (Claussen, 1994: 41). This serves to illustrate the direct link between environmental factors and national security issues.

Another resource that is scarce and the source of much conflict is water. The historic conflict in the Middle East, which to this day is still centrally concerned with water, will stand as the clearest example of resource scarcities that generate conflict. Even now, access to and future use of the West Bank aquifer remains a point of contention in the Middle East. Rivers are by nature a shared resource, as they often define boundaries between countries. Access to water has generated conflicts among many nations in Africa: Ethiopia and Sudan; Sudan and Egypt; Cameroon and Nigeria; Burkina Faso and Mali, etc. During periods of water scarcity aggravated by droughts, thousands of people have been forced to migrate, not only from country to country (the usual focus of news headlines), but also within countries. South Africa is not free from water troubles either: being a semiarid country, many conflicts in South Africa are rooted in the competition for this scarce and precious resource. South Africa must rely on the few rivers and underground sources for its water needs. There are presently around 520 dams, most of which are severely silted, and it is fairly 'normal' for commercial farmers to drill a borehole on their farms. There was no law prohibiting the extraction of ground water, so the only constraint would have been a financial one. It follows, therefore, that in times of drought when surface waters ran dry, it was the majority of poor rural farmers who became the first victims. The problem is not, however, limited to periods of drought. Harmful pesticides, often banned elsewhere (such as DDT), contaminate surface and ground water and no penalties have been imposed on offenders. As mentioned earlier, including such externalities into a system of taxation is being addressed in the new environmental policy document.

Linked to both land and water issues is the topic of forestry. As the demand for land increases, more forests are cleared to make way for crop production. Not only does forest clearance result in profound hydrological changes, which may affect precipitation patterns, but deforestation also induces accelerated soil erosion. The clearance of forests for fuelwood is insignificant compared to the scale of commercial afforestation and logging in South Africa, and in the latter case, common property resources, including wild herbs, fruit, and game are destroyed. So devastating is the consequence of afforestation in South Africa that plantations have been described as 'green deserts,' since unlike natural forests, they do not encourage biodiversity (Cooper, 1991: 186). With the protective tree layer (and its complex root system and leaf litter) removed, rainwater-generated runoff is increased and flash floods are common. Runoff also removes valuable topsoil and eventually deposits sediment down slope. Soil loss in South Africa has been estimated to be approximately 400 million tons per annum, and soil erosion has been cited as one of the greatest environmental problems facing Southern Africa (Verster, 1992: 181). Refugees and internally displaced people in Mozambique, Malawi, Zimbabwe, Zambia, and Ethiopia, who are forced by their desperate situation to seek shelter and energy, have removed trees. This has resulted in increased soil erosion, which produces an almost moonscape environment (McCallum, 1991: 168; Gallart, 1994: 26). In Haiti, where 50 percent of the country is affected by accelerated erosion, soil accumulates in the streets of Port-au-Prince and has to be cleared by bulldozers (Claussen, 1994: 41).

While the Rio conference highlighted, among other things, the need for sustainable development, the Cairo conference drew important linkages between poverty, women's education, and fertility rates. The key issue of access to resources has received surprisingly little attention. Dasgupta (1995) highlighted the links between population, poverty, and the environment, and showed how the need for extra hands will only be reduced if and when the poor have access to cheap fuel, drinking water, and improved social and economic security.

Coupled with environmental sustainability should be social sustainability – which means that human institutions should be in place to manage the resource base. The net economic value of the resource is an important criterion in the management of resources. To the extent that people identify the value of resources through net social welfare, the more likely will there be sustainable resource use and conservation (Cooper et al, 1995: 3). Translated into policy, what this entails is enabling local participation in a real way to govern access to resources. With all its overused and misused connotations, the lesson of avoiding the top-down approach still applies today.

ENVIRONMENTAL REFUGEES

The main definition of refugees, as people who have a 'well-founded fear of persecution for reasons of race, religion, nationality, membership of a particular social group or political opinion,' emerged as a result of the refugees generated by World War II (Harrell-Bond, 1995: 5). Resettlement was seen to be a permanent solution. Due to the obvious displacement of millions of people in Africa because of severe droughts, it is not surprising to note that the Organization of African Unity (OAU) in 1969 adopted a broader definition for refugees that included involuntary environmental or economic migrants (Myers, 1995: 22). Environmental refugees have been defined as 'people who fear that for environmental reasons they may not remain alive unless they migrate' (Zaba, in Myers, 1995: 28).

Countries have gone to war over the question of sovereignty of resources and self-determination. Many new environmental problems are symptoms of old resource disputes. There is a close link between military and environmental security – both are essentially concerned with access to natural resources. The military approach has always been the acquisition and defense of natural resources in the name of 'national security.' Throughout history, in seeking to maintain access to and control over resources, military options have been employed.

The OAU Refugee Convention, by placing the interests of the state over that of refugees, sent a strong signal of territorial integrity and noninterference in the internal affairs of member countries (Harrell-Bond, 1995: 7). This noninterference is presently the topic of debate among the Southern African Development Community countries. For example, the formation of the Association of Southern African States represents a direct step toward building regional mechanisms for conflict resolution and peacekeeping.

With the growing refugee crises in the 1980s, refugees began to be seen as a threat to international security. Intergovernmental bodies such as the United Nations Office of High Commissioner for Refugees (UNHCR) had often failed and donor countries shifted funds from intergovernmental bodies to NGOs. Africa harbors the world's largest refugee population, with six million refugees and 15 million internally displaced people. Among the environmental factors contributing to migration are soil erosion, droughts and water shortages, floods and cyclones, a decline in wood supply, and, as in the case of the former Soviet Union, pollution. There are an estimated 18 million cross-border environmental refugees and another 20 million people internally displaced, living in temporary refugee-like conditions (Claussen, 1994: 41).

DISPLACED PEOPLE IN SOUTHERN AFRICA

There are an estimated 1.5 million Mozambican refugees, of whom 800,000 have been repatriated by the UNHCR in its largest program ever undertaken in Africa. Since approximately 80 percent of Mozambicans are employed in the agricultural sector, land is a crucially important resource. However, there are an estimated one million land mines laid randomly in Mozambique. Devastated by 16 years of war, the crippled economy and land-mine infested agricultural fields offer little hope for the population. Faced with such a reality, it is understandable that migration to neighboring countries is growing.

People moving from rural areas in the Cape to the outskirts of Cape Town make up one of the fastest growing internally displaced groups in South Africa. Many of the displaced people were made redundant from white farms and were faced with the daunting choice of returning to impoverished homelands or trying to find a better life in the city. Since this phenomenon has only really started exploding in the 1990s, there is an absence of data and very few studies on the topic.

The case of people displaced as a result of the Highland Water Scheme in Lesotho poses another angle to the growing refugee problem in the region. Having parallels with the well-known Narmada Dam project, the human and ecological costs of the Water Scheme require research to understand the nature and extent of both human and environmental side effects.

At present, the UNHCR only recognizes the traditional meaning of 'refugees.' By improving understanding of the diverse causes of displacement, it will be possible to improve the relief offered to displaced people, as well as to address the root causes.

FOCUS FOR THE FUTURE

It must be recognized that the growing numbers of displaced people are causing serious concern. The growth in numbers of people fleeing their homes is often not due to any complex inexplicable cause, but is usually a result of a search for natural resources such as water and fertile land. Many of the refugees come from countries devastated by the destabilizing role played by the former apartheid South African government. It is not surprising, therefore, that there is a strong sentiment, both in the Frontline States and within South Africa, that South Africa should play a role in the reconstruction and peace process in the region. The regeneration of economic growth in the region is intimately linked with peace and security. Reducing peoples' vulnerability to environmental problems and natural hazards is a starting point. Poverty accelerates population displacement. By addressing some of the root causes, such as collapsed economies and diminished natural resources, South Africa will be playing an important part in redressing the migration of people.

NOTE

1 The rand is valued at around 21 and one-half cents US.

REFERENCES

Binswanger, H P and K Deininger (1994) 'South African Land Policy: The Legacy of History and Current Options.' Paper prepared for the World Bank.

Claussen, E (1994) 'Environment and Security: The Challenge of Integration. An Address to the Woodrow Wilson Centre's Environment and Security Discussion Group.' *Environmental Change and Security Project Report* 1,40: 3.

Cooper, D (1991) 'From Soil Erosion to Sustainability.' J Cock and E Koch (eds) *Going Green*. Cape Town: Oxford University Press: Chapter 12.

Cooper, D, S Fakir, and D Bromley (1995) Land Reform and Management of Environmental Impact. Unpublished discussion paper, Land and Agriculture Policy Centre, Johannesburg.

Dasgupta, P (1995) 'Population, Poverty, and the Local Environment.' *Scientific American* 272,2: 26–31.

Environmental Justice Networker (1995) *Quarterly Newsletter of the Environmental Justice Networking Forum* 6: 2.

Gallart, I (1994) 'Boundless Refugees.' *Refugees* 2,96: 26–27.

George, S (1992) *The Debt Boomerang*. Boulder: Westview.

Harrell-Bond, B (1995) 'Refugees and the International System: The Evolution of Solutions.' Paper delivered at conference on The Third World After the Cold War: Ideology, Economic Development, and Politics. Oxford (June 5–8).

Homer-Dixon, T (1994) 'Environmental Scarcities and Violent Conflict: Evidence from Cases.' *International Security* 19,1: 5–40.

Kane, H (1995) 'The Hour of Departure: Forces That Create Refugees and Migrants.' *Worldwatch Paper* 125.

Kgomo, E (1991) 'Access to Power, Smoke over Soweto.' M Ramphele and C McDowell (eds) *Restoring the Land*. Cape Town: Panos: Chapter 11.

McCallum, H (1991) 'From Destruction to Recovery.' M Ramphele and C McDowell (eds) *Restoring the Land*. London: Panos: Chapter 16.

Myers, N (1995) *Environmental Exodus. An Emergent Crisis in the Global Arena.* Climate Institute: USA.

Myers, N (1989a) 'Environment and Security.' *Foreign Policy* 74: 23–41.

Myers, N (1989b) 'Population Growth, Environmental Decline, and Security Issues in Sub-Saharan Africa.' A. Hjort af Ornas and M.A. Mohammed Salih (eds) *Ecology and Politics: Environmental Stress and Security in Africa*. Scandinavian Institute of African Studies.

Myers, N (1986) 'The Environmental Dimension to Security Issues.' *The Environmentalist* 6,4: 251–257.

Pogrund, B (1991) 'Exporting the Damage.' M. Ramphele and C. McDowell (eds), *Restoring the Land*. London: Panos: Chapter 15.

Singh, M V (1994) 'Geological, Historical, and Present-Day Erosion and Colluviation in Lesotho.' Unpublished PhD thesis, University of Cambridge.

South Africa Yearbook (1989–1990) *Official Yearbook of the Republic of South Africa.* 15th Edition, Pretoria.

Verster, E (1992) 'Soil Erosion.' R. Fuggle and M.A. Rabie (eds) *Environmental Management in South Africa*. Cape Town: Juta and Co: Chapter 10.

Wilson, F and M Ramphele (1989) *Uprooting Poverty: The South African Challenge.* Cape Town: David Philip.

Zetter, R (1991) 'Labelling Refugees: Forming and Transforming an Identity.' *Journal of Refugee Studies* 4,1: 39–62.

Part Three

Solutions

Chapter 8

Good Neighbor Agreements: A Tool For Environmental and Social Justice

Sanford Lewis and Diane Henkels

INTRODUCTION

A community is – within limits – the master of its own environment and economy (*Schad* v. *Borough of Mount Ephraim*, 101 S.Ct. 2176 [1981]). Today, however, communities face a dilemma: all too frequently, the drive for economic welfare sacrifices public health and damages the environment. As the health and environmental hazards of industrial production become publicized and as downsizing and layoffs have escalated out of control in the US, communities have come to be more aware of the negative role corporations may play in undermining community welfare. Because there is little real corporate accountability for decisions that affect local communities, citizens groups throughout the US have organized to combat some of the detrimental effects of exploitative industrial practices. The demands of these groups vary from place to place; in some instances, the emphasis is on environmental concerns, while in others it is on jobs and economy-related concerns. In a few communities, both types of concerns have emerged, in tandem.

Communities have applied both legal and nonlegal tactics to increase industrial accountability. Some of the legal approaches that have been effective in increasing community control over its health and environment include zoning, permits, and NGO-company contracts. A separate economic accountability movement has attempted to build accountability for promises of jobs by placing new conditions on corporate subsidy agreements.

These accountability strategies are increasingly coming together in the form of citizen groups' efforts to build NGO-company contracts into their community empowerment strategy. These 'Good Neighbor Agreements' evolved originally as a nonlegal tool for developing a partnership between companies and communities as a response to this community welfare dilemma.[1]

The purpose of this article is to explore the value of Good Neighbor Agreements. The first part will briefly describe the political context in which Good Neighbor Agreements emerged as a tool for community empowerment. Next, it zeros in on the different types of Good Neighbor Agreements, distinguishing them by the legal and nonlegal enforcement mechanisms. That section discusses alternative dispute resolution and good faith clauses, which serve as legal handles to many of these contracts. A brief discussion of the relationship between Good Neighbor Agreements and public policy in contract law concludes the section on enforceability. Section three identifies ways to augment the effectiveness of Good Neighbor Agreements and increase their acceptability and use by communities and corporations.

SKETCHING COMMUNITY EMPOWERMENT IN THE 1990S

It is no longer a secret that economic development in the United States has generated as a by-product an enormous amount of pollution and hazardous waste. In 1986, according to Environmental Protection Agency's Toxic Release Inventory, the waste created by the chemical industry's top 50 products amounted to 539 billion pounds of toxins and hazardous substances discharged into the environment (Commoner, 1992: 89). In the last decade, global conferences have formally recognized industry's detrimental effect on the environment and called upon each country to preserve the environmental integrity of the future while raising current living standards (Rio Earth Summit, Agenda 21, 1992). Meanwhile, the public is increasingly aware of the effects of industrial production on the environment and the public welfare. Despite corporate public relations efforts, polls show that a large number of people in the United States are growing increasingly distrustful of anything corporations say (Meeker-Lowry, 1995: 76).

The US government has made attempts at responding to the crisis, but has been generally unable to address the environmental and health hazards endured by local communities at the hands of corporations. Over the last quarter of a century, Congress has passed scores of statutes piecemeal in reaction to highly publicized crises (eg, Love Canal, Bhopal, the Exxon Valdez oil spill). However, regard for how each specific emergency response could be melded into a coherent environmental management system has been insufficient (Futrell, 1994a: 17). Starting in the 1970s, a series of legislative initiatives regulated, controlled, and monitored toxins, pollution, worker safety, and the like (Hawken, 1993: 108). Some observers have suggested that this 'piecemealism' has resulted in a checkerboard of conflicting, confused over-regulation for some activities and gaps where major environmental insults go unchecked by law (Futrell, 1994a: 17). For instance, different standards for the same hazardous chemicals are promulgated by the EPA and the Occupational Safety and Health Administration (*Ibid*).

Inefficient though they may be, these regulations have been viewed by polluters as government mechanisms for stifling their profitability. As a result, corporations have not sat idly by watching these dramatic challenges to their power go unchecked (Hawken, 1993: 108). With the growth of environmentalism, industry's political action committees launched corresponding lobbying efforts. The corporate lobbies have wielded influence by aggressive campaign donations in support of politicians who support their positions. Lobbying also takes other forms of influence-building. For instance, from 1989 to 1990, US House members took nearly 4,000 privately funded trips, often to resorts and vacation spots (Levine, 1992: D3). Two-thirds of these were paid for by corporations and trade groups (*Ibid*). During 1995, it appeared to many that Congress had begun to undertake a task of entirely neutralizing environmental regulations. The House of Representatives approved an appropriations package for the EPA and other federal agencies that prevents the enforcement of many sections of the Federal Water Pollution Control Act and the Clean Air Act, and weakens enforcement of other environmental regulations (Citizens Clearinghouse for Hazardous Waste, 1995: 7). However, public sentiment in the US remains solidly in favor of continued protection of the environment; as a result, some of the worst provisions proposed during 1995 were buffered by Senate responses and a presidential veto. Besides exerting their political muscle on government, many corporations have responded to communities' expressions of their environmental concerns by 'greening' public relations. Some companies have established public panels to address environmental or safety concerns and advanced these as a model for involvement of the public or the work force in key environmental decisions (Lewis, 1992: 2–56). The Chemical Manufacturers Association's 'Responsible Care' program is the leading driver of this activity (*Ibid*: 2–57). CMA launched 'Responsible Care' in response to the deepening crisis of public confidence, as well as to the slumping self-images and morale of many personnel in the industry itself after Bhopal. Under this program, CMA encourages member companies to establish community advisory panels (*Ibid*). However, most of the panels' members are hand-picked by the corporation or its consultants, agendas are often set by the company, and critics are kept out or outnumbered 10 or more to one (*Ibid*: 2–58). The panels also generally are not provided with the independent technical support needed to evaluate corporate performance. Thus, the role of these panels in serving as an accountability mechanism has been less than one might expect. Some examples indicate that corporate America has responded to the dilemma with some substantive changes, especially reduced pollutant emissions at many plants; however, industry's 'self-policing' is insufficient (Hawken, 1993: 108).

The development of 'socially responsible investing' demonstrates the inherent challenge of self-policing. In their 'double bottom-line' approach, for instance, Calvert Social Investment Fund demonstrates the tenuous balance between the twin goals of profit and social responsibility. In this approach, the fund measures returns in traditional financial analysis first (Calvert Group, 1995:

V). Then, if the company is determined to be of interest financially, it is evaluated for its social and environmental policies and actions (*Ibid*). Primacy of the profit motive virtually precludes adequately prioritizing community health and welfare. This approach is probably leading to increased investment in the 'most green of the dirtiest' industries in America, such as Sun Oil and General Motors. These two companies, both notorious polluters, have endorsed a 'green pledge' known as the CERES Principles, which has been endorsed by social investors. Yet the two companies and many other CERES endorsers continue to engage in demonstrably destructive environmental operations that contradict the high-sounding language of the code. In short, despite the 'green' trend in the United States, government and corporate response to community environmental concerns remains limited and does not coincide with individual community needs for sustainable development.

Rather than relying on top-down government control to address specific needs, communities themselves are learning how to supplement the need for direct government or corporate assistance in addressing community development. The emerging environmental justice movement, for instance, has engendered a shift in local leadership as women, people of color, and indigenous people play a more active role in their communities (Collin and Collin, 1994: 1173). This movement has continued to expand as race has been shown to be the best predictor for the location of a hazardous or toxic waste site – better than income, topography, or hydrology (*Ibid*: 1175).

In addition, communities now have a little more information for attending to local business issues because of the federal Community Right-to-Know and the 1990 Toxic Pollution Prevention Act (Sobol, 1991). The Right-To-Know law requires manufacturers to report their emissions to air, land, and water of over 300 toxic chemicals (Emergency Planning and Community Right-to-Know Act, 42 USC. ss. 11001–11050 [1988 and Supp. V 1993]). The Toxic Pollution Prevention Act requires that any facility that is required to report data must also report on its toxic pollution prevention (Pollution Prevention Act, 42 USCA ss. 13101 to 13109). The growth in available information has provided a powerful tool for exposing the truth of environmental degradation. For example, information has exposed environmental racism.

Thus far, tools that have been useful in increasing community empowerment have included both legal and nonlegal approaches. Information dissemination and boycotts are examples of nonlegal tools that have been used quite effectively to encourage company accountability (Meeker-Lowry, 1995: 98). A community may also resort to several forms of legal recourse. Zoning, for instance, has enabled communities in the US to control industrial development within their locales (*Village of Euclid* v. *Ambler Realty Co*, 272 US 365 [1926]). Under nuisance law, a party may sue for harm caused by another's polluting activity, and a court may require a cessation altogether of the operation (*Boomer* v. *Atlantic Cement Co*, 362 N.E.2d 968 [1977]). Citizen suit provisions in various environmental statutes have also provided a vehicle for citizens to force federal agencies to comply with federal pollution standards (Percival et al, 1992: 995). However, the Clean Water Act and the Emergency Planning and Community

Right-to-Know Act have been found not to authorize citizen enforcement suits for past violations that have been cured by the date the suit is filed (*Atlantic States Legal Foundation, Inc* v. *United Musical Instruments*, 61 F.3d 473 [1995]). This restrictive precedent would constrain the future use of citizen suit provisions if it is followed in other courts.

Contract law provides a possible tool for problem solving and legal recourse for community groups. The law provides a remedy for the breach of a contract, or set of promises, the performance of which the law may recognize as a duty (Pollution Prevention Act, Restatement [Second], Contracts s. 3 [1979]). The private nature of contractual agreements provides an avenue for legal enforcement that can be as flexible and creative as the parties intend, but that remains legally binding.

GOOD NEIGHBOR AGREEMENTS

Good Neighbor Agreements are instruments that provide a vehicle for community organizations and a corporation to recognize and formalize their roles within a locality. The purpose of these agreements is to foster sustainable development in a community by reconciling economic development with the community's welfare, including the health of its environment and its individual members. Since the first such agreement was signed in 1978 in Worcester, Massachusetts, several agreements have been signed in the US

As distinct from other methods that seek to increase corporate accountability, Good Neighbor Agreements seek to promote broadly defined sustainability. The Good Neighbor Project, a leading proponent and support organization for the establishment of Good Neighbor Agreements, defines 'sustainable' industry as operations that are 'clean, stable, and fair' (Lewis, 1992: 4). Fairness in this context means that 'human health, environment, labor resources, and the capital resources and materials within a local community would be treated in a manner to ensure their continued viability for the long term' (*Ibid*). A variety of industry sectors have entered Good Neighbor Agreements in the US, including chemical plants, oil refineries, and foundries. Though several agreements have arisen after industrial accidents, others are negotiated before such a crisis has occurred, or in response to chronic issues such as pollution emissions or job concerns. The philosophy common to all Good Neighbor Agreements is the industry's and community organization's mutual acknowledgment of the need to build a relationship responsive to community and industry needs.

The Process of Forging a Good Neighbor Agreement in a Nutshell

Forging and implementing a Good Neighbor Agreement is a several-step process that requires the commitment of a citizens group made up of members of the community and of a plant manager, in particular. The process proceeds as follows. First, members of the citizen group meet, discuss, and delineate the issues they would like to resolve with the company. This early stage may also involve identification of additional stakeholders who should be brought into the process of development of the agreement – especially the potential role of organized labor, as well as other civic organizations and community leaders.

After identifying the issues and potential solutions, an initial meeting with the company management takes place, followed by a joint assessment of the situation by the citizens group and the company. Over a period of successive meetings, the parties further clarify issues and the relevant details involved, toward the formulation of principles and provisions for inclusion in a formal agreement. The parties then sign and ratify the contract. Finally, the process of implementing the agreement terms begins, or in some cases, continues.

The Provisions of Good Neighbor Agreements

Various types of conditions have been negotiated in Good Neighbor Agreements. Some of the key terms that have been sought or negotiated have included the following:

(1) *Community access to information*: A company will place on reserve at a local library specified information. This is defined differently in the various agreements. Good Neighbor Agreement requests and provisions have included information required to be filed under state and federal law, results from environmental and safety audits and inspections, plant safety manuals and procedures, corporate annual reports and SEC filings, and a list of a plant's workers with their addresses. Although many federal environmental statutes require that information reported be made publicly available, only those members of the public who are specifically aware of the statute and the disclosure requirement have ready access to the information (Bagby et al, 1995:14 *Va. Envtl. L.J.*. 225, Part 6). Even the most diligent investor would have a difficult task uncovering the range of needed environmental information concerning a particular firm (*Ibid*: 225, conclusion).

(2) *Right to inspect the facility*: Depending on its content, an inspection clause may permit community members to inspect a plant and be accompanied by an expert and a plant worker of the community's choice. Such a provision may be particularly strong because the law does not require that a plant routinely allow community members into a facility to conduct a physical inspection (Interview with Rick Abraham, Texans United, concerning the Rhone-Poulenc Good Neighbor Agreement, October 1995). Similar types of inspection conditions (rights to accompany government inspectors and for a union to have its own inspection capacities) are commonly adopted in labor unions' collective bargaining agreements.

(3) *Accident preparedness*: A company must prepare a plan for procedures it will undertake in case of accident and make this plan available for review and input by the public. A chemical accident may pose severe hazards to the commu-

nity, yet existing and proposed federal regulations contain no explicit requirements for involvement of neighbors and the community in the planning process
(Lewis, 1993: 83).

(4) *Pollution prevention*: A company will plan to reduce its use of toxics or
its toxic waste and emissions over a scheduled period. Various experts, including
in many cases specially retrained retired engineers, can go through a plant and
develop pollution prevention recommendations (Jo Haberman and Amy
Middleton interviewed by Paul Orum, Working Notes on Community Right-to-
Know, Working Notes on Our Right-to-Know About Toxic Pollution,
November-December 1994, Appendix C-1). These experts must be accountable
to the community and work force, not to the management of the company; how
the funding is raised to pay for them may be one of the topics of negotiation.

(5) *Good jobs, local jobs, union jobs*: The company may commit to gearing
its hiring and training processes to community needs by recruiting local people
for new openings. Strides can also be made toward unionization of the work force
through neutrality commitments and agreement to a simple 'card-check' election
process for determining if the work force decides to unionize.

(6) *Local economic needs*: The company may commit to establishing a
special community benefits fund, with discretionary spending to be determined
and overseen by the affected stakeholders. Expanded funding of local infrastructure needs such as roadways may be part of the program.

(7) *Citizen group concessions*: In return for company commitments such as
those described above, members of a citizens group may settle ongoing litigation
or permit challenges, end protests or negative publicity, or even generate positive
publicity about the company. The citizens group also may commit to protect a
company's trade secrets, through specific provisions on trade secrets protection.

The Range of Good Neighbor Agreements:
Enforceable or Commemorative

The form and content of Good Neighbor Agreements have varied according to
the philosophies of the citizen groups involved, the corporate culture of the
company, and the forces motivating the parties to agree.

Non-Enforceable Good-Neighbor Agreements

Early Agreements – Citizen Inspections: The phrase 'Good Neighbor
Agreements' was coined in neighborhood-based campaigns in the early 1980s
that resulted from community groups' inspections of local industrial facilities. In
these campaigns, community groups negotiated an informal 'right' to inspect a
local industry. After winning such an inspection, they sought subsequent negotiation of a Good Neighbor Agreement that would consist of follow-through action
commitments based on the recommendations that emerged from the inspection.
In more recent years, the concept of a Good Neighbor Agreement has begun to
evolve in various other directions.

Minnesota Model – Reducing Nonbinding Goals to Writing: Citizens for a Better Environment, a Minnesota environmental watchdog group, bases the Good Neighbor Agreements it facilitates on a relationship-building model in which the agreements contain no legally binding language. Community members and management from a 'polluter' company sit down and discuss the community's pollution concerns and other problems before there is a crisis. The goal of these dialogues is to establish mutually agreed-upon pollution reduction goals that go beyond the legal requirements (Doerr, 1994) and to commemorate those goals in a Good Neighbor Agreement.

A Good Neighbor Agreement between People of Phillips (Minnesota) and Smith Foundry is an example of CBE's nonadversarial facilitation (Smith Foundry Good Neighbor Agreement with People of Phillips and Citizens for a Better Environment, signed in October, 1995). The Smith Foundry is an example of an industry that, while usually functioning within legal guidelines, still may be polluting the neighborhood. According to the Minnesota Pollution Control Agency (MPCA), the foundry, which produces 'gray' metal, a type of heavy metal used in the production of metal products, conformed to PCA standards. However, the MPCA received over 20 complaints from area residents about odor coming from the foundry. The foundry was cited by OSHA in 1988 for several violations of employee safety standards, such as exposing workers to respirable silica in excess of the permissible limit. In 1989, there were complaints of white dust and black soot being blown from the building (Sobol, 1991).

In April 1995, CBE helped area residents organize and enter into a Good Neighbor Agreement with Smith. 'The agreement did not focus only on pollution prevention, but also dealt with employment issues in the community' (Jo Haberman, Citizens for a Better Environment, interviewed on October 10, 1995). One such issue arose out of concerns that the number of Native Americans employed at the foundry was disproportionately low in comparison to the percentage of Native Americans living in the community. Agreement negotiations revealed that the Native Americans living in town were unable to learn of foundry openings listed at the foundry's screening service in the suburbs. A relocation of the service seems to have resolved the employment issue.

Six months later, the groups are due for a follow-up meeting to assess the foundry's progress, the results of which CBE predicts will be positive for the people of Phillips. In addition, the signing of the agreement will have generated excellent publicity for Smith. As an outcome of negotiations and follow-up meetings, the foundry adopted a five-year approach to pollution prevention. Under the plan, pollution prevention would fit into the business' existing framework (*Ibid*).

According to CBE, there were two key factors to the success of this agreement, like all the Good Neighbor Agreements they facilitate. One was the fact that the owner of Smith Foundry was personally very committed to cooperating with the community to reduce pollution and improve employee relations. The other was Phillip's 'extremely sophisticated' neighborhood organization (*Ibid*).

The CBE example raises a potentially troubling issue of enforcement: What happens if the company doesn't fulfill its obligations under the agreement? Although the Minnesota groups have not yet had to confront this issue, other communities have been 'burned' by nonbinding agreements that have been discarded by company officials – for example, when the plant's manager has changed. If a company purposefully disregards an agreement, in the context of a nonbinding agreement the recourse of the citizens group is limited to becoming more adversarial, such as launching a campaign of negative publicity or challenging permits or licenses. The voluntary non-enforceable approach only works as long as the company and community place sufficient value on their relationship to keep to their commitments.

Essential to continued compliance is regular communication. The Smith agreement provides for meetings, 'as needed, but not less than twice a year,' but requires no written accountability. However, CBE agrees that agreements should provide a mechanism for yearly reports as a means of maintaining this communication and of informing the parties of changes affecting the contract. A regular report would also assist the community in keeping track of the company's activities even after the citizen group has disbanded or moved on to other projects (*Ibid*).

Enforceable Good Neighbor Agreements

In contrast to the above approaches, most Good Neighbor Agreements currently sought or reached throughout the US are legally enforceable. In some situations, a Good Neighbor Agreement is linked to an environmental permitting process. Local governments issue a wide range of permits for construction, digging, filling, and many other activities. Most companies need some form of local permit to operate. These permits can be used as handles giving citizens groups leverage in confronting a company (Lewis, 1990: 252–253). Good Neighbor Agreements may also serve as a settlement agreement in the aftermath of an industrial accident.[2] Some require that alternative dispute resolution be the mechanism used to resolve disputes under the agreement. Litigation and forum selection clauses have also been specified as enforcement tools in Good Neighbor Agreements.[3] Finally, many Good Neighbor Agreements require that parties negotiate and perform their obligations in 'good faith.'

LEGALLY BINDING APPROACHES: EXAMPLES

Approach 1 – Oversight Agreements: An example of an oversight agreement emerged at the Rhone Poulenc plant in Manchester, Texas. Manchester sits along the notorious Houston Ship Channel, home to the nation's largest concentration of petrochemical companies. Like so many communities under the stacks of major polluting industries, Manchester is a predominantly minority community (Hispanic). In June 1992, a serious accident occurred at the plant – a release of poisonous sulfur dioxide. At least 27 people were sent to area hospitals. The Manchester community decided to take action. With the assistance of an environmental organization, Texans United, the community won an agreement that gave the community specific rights never before recognized in Texas.

Rhone Poulenc agreed to pay for an independent environmental audit by an expert selected and supervised by a panel of community residents and a statewide organization, Texans United. Among the features of this oversight agreement are:

- The committee was selected by the community, not the company. Elsewhere, corporations have been hand-picking the membership of advisory committees to which they will ostensibly be accountable. This agreement set a new direction for local communities by keeping the designation of a representative group in the community's hands, rather than the company's.
- The agreement requires a broad audit including review of regulatory compliance, safety training, accident prevention, emergency response, waste analysis and information systems, monitoring programs, and waste minimization practices. In contrast, some companies have tried to limit local citizen oversight to a quick walk-through tour of a facility, followed by a slide show of issues that the company's PR department wishes to highlight.
- The agreement requires public disclosure of company documents in a public library, including hazard assessment and risk analysis, lists of accidents, upsets, near-misses, and corrective actions, as well as waste minimization and reduction plans;
- The company commits to 'negotiate in good faith' on the audit recommendations;
- Citizens are entitled to accompany the auditor and conduct other inspections by appointment;
- The agreement is legally binding because it is integral to the firm's operating permit. As such, it can be enforced either by local citizens or by state officials.

Approach 2 – Union Collective Bargaining Agreements: Labor unions have a long history of on-site tracking of corporate performance on occupational safety and health issues. Unions' 'safety stewards' are rank-and-file workers with the training to watchdog occupational health and safety issues that arise on the shop floor. Stewards are aided by professional industrial hygienists who work for the local or international unions. Union health and safety committees discuss any problems identified and raise the issues in negotiations with management or in communications with appropriate government oversight bodies.

One of the most advanced environmental oversight precedents for organized labor emerged at Harvard Industries, in New Jersey. There, the United Auto Workers negotiated the establishment of a 'hazard prevention' committee. The union's committee has a right to shut down any operation in the plant that presents a danger to worker health or safety or to the environment.

Approach 3 – Specific Corporate Commitments: In contrast to the above examples of establishing more effective 'stakeholder oversight processes,' some of the new agreements establish specific corporate commitments to environmental or safety goals. For example, Chevron Refining is the biggest industry and polluter in Richmond, a predominantly low-income African-American community in Contra Costa County, California. Chevron has had innumerable accidents at the site and has been cited for serious violations of almost every conceivable environmental law. The West County Toxics Coalition, with the support of the statewide organization Citizens for a Better Environment (CBE), has been working to change this. After struggling for 10 years on numerous fronts, including protests, pressure on elected officials, permit challenges, and shareholder resolutions, the company finally agreed to a Good Neighbor Agreement committing to:

1   Install 350 'leakless' valves in the new project and retrofit 200 to 400 valves in the existing refinery;
2   Continue to reduce toxic emissions from the refinery beyond the 60 percent achieved between 1988 and 1992;
3   Contribute two million dollars to a local health center;
4   Install sirens and computers, train emergency workers, and establish and fund a city Emergency Services coordinator position for five years.

Approach 4 – Toward a More Comprehensive Approach: The Chevron agreement differs from past resolutions in that until recently, most agreements that have been reached have focused either on environmental or economic concerns. Yet a new and important trend is the formation of coalitions consisting of both economically and environmentally affected populations, ie, workers and plant neighbors, who are prepared to make joint demands in both arenas. The Unocal agreement reached in Rodeo, California, exemplifies this powerful new approach.

In September 1994, Crockett and Rodeo, California, residents were inundated by two separate chemical releases due to leaks from the Unocal Refinery in Rodeo. The first involved a brown chemical substance, the second a spill of the potentially deadly chemical hydrogen sulfide that hit the Hillcrest School in Rodeo, sickening scores of children and teachers.

Unocal was unresponsive to community concerns and complaints after both incidents. As community outrage and demands for action grew, there were several public meetings and strategy sessions by community leaders, environmental groups (CBE-California), and labor unions. The strategy that resulted was one intended to force the company to upgrade the plant, preserve jobs, and give the community and work force more ability to safeguard activities on the site. In the end, the company was forced to sign a legally binding 'Good Neighbor Agreement' in order to receive land use approvals that were a precondition to continued operations. What sets the Unocal agreement apart from most others is the breadth of issues that the community required Unocal to address. Following are highlights.

Environmental and Health Issues

- Unocal committed to test and install an improved air pollution monitoring system. All data collected will be made available to the public.
- Unocal will fund an independent audit of the refinery. The audit will cover the refinery emergency response plan, emergency notification procedures, safety management program, and the results of the Process Hazards Analyses performed as part of the Process Safety Management Program.
- A community-based Audit Committee will oversee the independent audit, including selection of the auditor. The committee's composition was determined in the agreement.
- Unocal is responsible for deciding whether and how to implement any of the recommendations contained in the final audit report.
- Unocal agreed to monthly monitoring of valves and pumps to achieve on-site emissions reductions for volatile organic compounds (VOCs). Results of the tests will be available to a Community Advisory Panel.
- Unocal agreed to fund an independent health risk assessment, and to fund a medical clinic for the diagnosis and treatment of people affected by the Unocal Catacarb release.
- Unocal contributed funds for an Emergency Response Van that will provide mobile, on-site medical services during chemical emergencies.
- Unocal agreed to establish a database of health effect information, including recommended evaluation and treatment measures, for chemicals used at the refinery.
- Unocal made a commitment to implement and fund a community-based information and notification system that provides information about unusual events and other items of interest that occur at the refinery.
- Unocal agreed to install a permanent monitoring station to detect sulfur compounds at the Hillcrest School and to provide training to teachers and students on how to respond to a chemical emergency.
- Unocal pledged to spend $30,000 per year for nine years to further vegetate appropriate areas of its property.
- Unocal agreed to construct a bike path through its property.

Economic Issues

- Unocal made a long-term financial commitment to the Vocational Training Program at the local high school.
- Unocal agreed to announce new job opportunities at the refinery in local newspapers, schools, and community organizations and to give hiring preference to local applicants when all other hiring factors are determined equal, and to work with the Building Trades Union to promote local hiring on construction jobs.
- Unocal committed $4.5 million to Contra Costa County to be dedicated for

improvements and/or upgrades to the local transportation infrastructure within 1.5 miles of the refinery.
- Unocal agreed to redesign its Reformulated Gasoline Project to avoid the use of anhydrous ammonia and to replace all bulk deliveries of anhydrous ammonia with aqueous ammonia at the refinery by December 31, 2001.
- Unocal promised $300,000 annually for a period of 15 years to benefit funds for two local communities and for the school district's vocational training program. Funds are to be used for appropriate projects of general benefit to the community in the areas of environment, recreation, economic development, community infrastructure projects, community services, and community functions.

Aftermath of the Unocal Agreement: Did the Agreement Address All It Needed To?

Several post-agreement developments at Unocal provide further food for thought. It has come to light in a government follow-up investigation and in a public statement by the work force that Unocal had allegedly failed to heed repeated work force warnings that the plant was operating dangerously. Workers said that they warned lower-level management, but stopped pressing the issue, fearing reprisals if they continued to press the issues after they were ignored by their supervisors. According to 15 workers in the plant's OCAW union newsletter:

> *We were not willing to jeopardize our jobs by individually insisting on the shutdown of a unit making a quarter of a million dollars daily when the company and all their experts said it was safe to keep it going.*

The Unocal agreement contains a clause to protect workers who speak up in the course of an audit against employer retribution. It also provides for confidential worker consultations with the independent auditor. The independent audit undertaken under the agreement noted that the company appeared not to be effectively utilizing even its own preexisting participatory processes (safety committee) as a means of following through on identified safety measures. Perhaps the checks and balances provided by outside scrutiny will serve to hold management more accountable with regard to safety issues, where a prior internal process failed to do so; the proof of this, however, will come in the longer-term implementation of the agreement.

About two months after the Unocal agreement was signed, the plant experienced another serious accident. Many of the residents who were sickened in one of the earlier incidents were now evacuated for several days. Local officials began to reconsider whether they really needed to close the plant down after all, until it could be proven safe. Yet the desire to preserve jobs led them to stop short of closing the plant. Instead, they ordered a further county review of accident prevention measures.

CONCLUSIONS

(1) Neighbors and workers are winning more control over corporate activities through these agreements. Although these agreements are no panacea for the ills that corporations impose on local communities, they can represent significant advances in community empowerment. The strength of this approach is that a community may begin to exert much greater sovereignty over the activities that occur within its borders. Local residents and workers who are considering a campaign for such an agreement would do well to ask whether and how they may actually improve corporate activities or community oversight beyond the weak federal and state regulatory system. What may they have to put up with if such rights and commitments are not attained? Can the community also establish some broader reforms that address the underlying problems of locally operating corporations, rather than only struggling through the issues on a case-by-case basis?

(2) Because the strategy is experimental, it has potential for innovation and refinement. There are opportunities and needs to apply the concepts developed in these agreements in new contexts. Examples of areas of active exploration by grass-roots groups and leaders include multiplant agreements, corporation-wide agreements, and linking the broad terms of such agreements to new plant approvals by local governments. The range of terms and conditions in the agreements is subject to broad expansion and experimentation, as each community develops agreements suited to their economic and environmental needs.

For agreements to yield the greatest possible benefits, worker participation must be secured. Participation processes in these agreements often contemplate worker involvement, but the potential for applying really independent work force views is almost impossible in the absence of a unionized work force. The presence and active participation of a union appear to be a necessary precedent to a truly tripartite process and to in-depth stakeholder understanding of plant issues and processes. Unionization of a plant, or a commitment to employer neutrality in union organizing, may become a central element of some of these agreements in the future – thereby expanding the potential for new community-labor alliances.

Further consideration is also merited as to the potential to apply some of the content of such agreements (both participatory rights and the corporate commitments and incentives) to public policy discussions regarding regulatory reform, sustainability, fair trade, and the right to know.

(3) Legally binding agreements create predictable kinds of benefits and dilemmas. Although some communities have entered into nonbinding agreements with corporate officials, based on longstanding or recently emerged relationships with management personnel, there is reason to be concerned about the viability of such agreements. Other communities have insisted on legally binding and enforceable agreements, because they are aware that personnel at these facilities, even plant managers, come and go, and their nonbinding commitments often may go with them.

There are many scenarios under which such agreements can be made enforceable, provided that the community has built the power needed to force the corporation into a binding agreement. After 10 years of grass-roots experimentation with this strategy, it is apparent that no corporation has signed a binding agreement unless the community or work force had established a bottom-line reason why the management needed to do so – for example, because it could alleviate some costs of delay brought on by community resistance to specific permits.

Even a binding agreement does not necessarily mean that the firm will in reality be a 'good neighbor.' Corporations that enter into these agreements are often multinational corporations operating at multiple sites. Thus, not only are these corporations not 'people' except in the fictitious sense awarded by some courts, but they are also not really 'neighbors.' Often they are far from 'good'; many corporations that have signed agreements continue to endanger their community and work force. Some, such as Unocal, have also interpreted certain agreed-upon obligations in the narrowest possible manner, and have even delayed implementation of other clauses. Such actions are undertaken in striking contrast to the neighborly spirit of the agreement. Informed by such experiences, we suggest that a 'corporate-community compact' may be a more appropriate and neutral term for describing these agreements. These agreements are simply as strong as what a community insists upon, given the range of circumstances that it faces; a corporation should not necessarily be labeled a 'good neighbor' simply because it persuaded locals that they are better off with an agreement than relying solely on federal or state bureaucrats.

(4) Corporations still 'call the tune' in most communities. Although there have been some striking successes, numerous communities have unsuccessfully sought such agreements with corporations and have lost the fight. This should come as no surprise to anyone acquainted with the power wielded by industry within such communities. It requires mustering of extensive political and legal power to lay down such new rules; many corporations have grown larger in size and power than some states and even some nations. Big corporations act like '800 pound gorillas' who know they are free to decide where and how they will 'sit down.'

People who wish to change this situation must find whatever leverage is available to support local pressure to negotiate. For instance, federal and state officials can and should be encouraged to support local citizens to effectively negotiate with companies by withholding approvals or assessing enforcement penalties until local needs are met; unfortunately, those agencies often serve as a 'buffer' that protects corporations more than the communities placed at risk. These agencies negotiate for placing only the most minimal conditions on corporate behavior, which corporations may hide behind rather than really being accountable to neighbors and workers.

Finding the right level at which to govern corporate behavior is an important challenge for activists, lawyers, and policymakers. These agreements are a supplement, not an alternative, to effective federal and state regulation and enforcement; they also cannot solve national and international policy gaps such as the worker job losses that may occur when major environmental or economic policy decisions by government and corporations lead to a phase out of particular operations.

Other tools are needed – such as new laws that grant local, affected citizens nonnegotiable *rights* – to oversee industries that endanger them and to assure job and income security when dangerous or antiquated operations must be closed. New institutions are also needed to undertake periodic public review of an entire corporation's behavior and to impose new corporation-wide conditions or take disciplinary action when corporations act contrary to the public good. Today's local agreements are merely one emerging chapter in a much larger 'book' of strategies for corporate governance that will need to be written from the grass roots in the coming years.

NOTES

1 The first Good Neighbor Agreement was formed in 1978 between Worcester, Massachusetts, and Fair Share and Standard Foundry. Source: James O'Connor, interview question (October 1995).
2 According to Denny Larson of California's Communities for a Better Environment, the political leverage that the Crockett/Rodeo Coalition and Shoreline Environmental Alliance citizen groups exercised in opposing Unocal's permit renewal evened the playing field between Unocal and the community.
3 An agreement drawn with Formosa Plastics Corporation identifies litigation as the primary enforcement tool. A contract between Intel Corporation and the Corrales Residents for Clean Air and Water specifies that all disputes be resolved in the district court for Sandoval County.

REFERENCES

Bagby, John et al (1995) 'How Green Was My Balance Sheet? Corporate Liability and Environmental Disclosure.' 14 *Va. Envtl.LJ.* 225, at Part 6.

Calvert Group (1995) Calvert Social Investment Fund. Calvert Group.

Citizens Clearinghouse for Hazardous Waste (1995) Everyone's Backyard. Washington Politics.

Cohen, Gary and John O'Connor (eds) (1990) 'Local Campaigns and the Law.' *Fighting Toxics*. Washington, DC: Island Press.

Collin, Robin and Robert Collin (1994) 'Equity as the Basis of Implementing Sustainability: An Exploratory Essay.' 96 *W.Va. L. Rev.* 1173.

Commoner, B. (1992) *Making Peace with the Planet*. New York: The New Press.

Doerr, Lisa (1994) Minnesota Program Director, Citizens for a Better Environment, 'How TRI Can Drive Pollution Prevention.' TRI Data Use Conference.

Emergency Planning and Community Right-to-Know-Act (1988–1993) 42 USC. ss. 11001–11050.

Futrell, William (1994a) *The Economy of Commerce*. New York: HarperBusiness. (1994b) 'Law of Sustainable Development.' The Environmental Forum (March/April): 17.

Hawken, Paul (1993) *The Ecology of Commerce*. New York: HarperCollins.

Henkels, Diane (1995) Interview with Rick Abraham, Texans United.

Levine, A (1992) 'Join Congress, See the World – On Corporate America's Tab.' (From Public Citizen's Congress Watch.) San Francisco Chronicle.

Lewis, Sanford (1993) 'Community Safety and Inspection and Audit Programs and Policies.' New Solutions.

Lewis, Sanford (1992) *The Good Neighbor Handbook: A Community-Based Strategy for Sustainable Industry.* Waverly, Mass.: The Good Neighbor Project.

Lewis, Sanford (1990) 'Local Campaigns and the Law.' Gary Cohen and John O'Connor (eds) *Fighting Toxics.* Washington, DC: Island Press.

Meeker-Lowry, Susan (1995) Invested in the Common Good. East Haven, Conn.: New Society Publishers.

Orum, Paul (1994) Interview with Jo Haberman and Amy Middleton, Working Notes on Community Right-to-Know, Working Paper on Our Right-to-Know About Toxic Pollution: Appendix C-1.

Percival, Robert et al (1992) *Citizens Suits to Enforce Environmental Regulations, Environmental Regulation Law, Science, and Policy.* Boston: Little, Brown and Company.

Rhone-Poulenc Good Neighbor Agreement (1992) Agreement with Texans United and Manchester's Community Advisory Committee.

Rio Earth Summit (1992) *Agenda 21.*

Smith Foundry Good Neighbor Agreement (1995) Agreement with People of Phillips and Citizens for a Better Environment, signed in October.

Sobol, Morley (1995) Unocal Good Neighbor Agreement with Crockett/Rodeo Coalition. Shoreline, Environmental Alliance and CBE-California.

Sobol, Morley (1991) 'Can Smelly Businesses Be Good Neighbors?' The Alley.

US Government (1990) *Pollution Prevention Act 42* USCA ss. 13101 to 13109.

US Government (1979) Restatement (second). Contracts s. 3.

Legal Cases:

(1995) *Atlantic States Legal Foundation, Inc.* v. *United Musical Instruments.* 61 F.3d 473.

(1977) *Boomer* v. *Atlantic Cement Co.* 362 N.E. 2nd 968.

(1981) *Schad* v. *Borough of Mount Ephraim,* 101 S.Ct. 2176.

(1926) *Village of Euclid* v. *Amber Realty Co.* 272 US 365.

Chapter 9

The Occupational Health Needs of Workers: The Need for a New International Approach

Françoise Barten, Suzanne Fustukian, and Sylvia de Haan

Workers represent an important group in a population. If, as the UN Universal Declaration of Human Rights declares, all people have a right to the highest level of health attainable, then surely the health of those who produce all valued products used by society is of basic concern. Yet, workers are one of the most vulnerable groups in the population. The effects of the health hazards they face are often added to those of poor living environments, poor nutrition, and unsatisfactory housing.

Workers' health status usually reflects the general health conditions of the population. At the same time, their working conditions influence the socioeconomic status, health status, and living environment of their dependents. This is particularly true for developing countries where, for the majority of workers, survival depends on work undertaken in exploitative conditions, with low incomes and unhealthy working conditions.

In many developing countries, rapid industrialization has occurred without adequate provision for the protection of workers. Their health has become an increasingly serious issue, as modern industrial and agricultural methods rely more heavily on hazardous substances. This has led to an increase in exposure to a wide range of occupational health hazards.

While concern for the health and ecological effects of air, water, and soil pollution has resulted in greater controls in developed countries, many governments of developing countries, under pressure from structural adjustment programs and the debt crisis, have offered their resources and communities as 'pollution havens' for industrial development. By shifting hazardous production processes to locations where little or no environmental regulation exists, manufacturers avoid investing in equipment and procedures necessary to control hazardous exposures. Combined with lower wages, taxes, and energy costs, this contributes to higher profits. It is the workers and people living in the surrounding communities who pay for this gain through exposure to disease-producing substances.

The past few decades have witnessed a rapid growth of the urban population in the South that has created pressure on the employment market as well as on the city environment. The increase in the number of job seekers has not kept pace with the growth of the formal sector and the chance of finding a regular paid job in a city has become even more limited.

Many households in Third World cities confront the challenge of survival through a complex system of informal activities, varying from street vendors to activities in small-scale industries. Exposure to occupational health hazards is of very little concern in this unregulated informal sector. Furthermore, poor working conditions may not only create health hazards for workers, but may also have an effect upon the health status of people living in the neighborhood of a small-scale factory.

Since many workers in small-scale industries are poor, they also show the disease patterns of the urban poor. This has implications for the development of occupational standards for exposure to toxic substances. Standards based on those used in the North are often inappropriate to the work situation in developing countries for a number of reasons:

1　The high prevalence of epidemic diseases reduces the resistance of those infected (Michaels et al, 1985: 536–542);
2　The length of the working day in the South is much longer – standards are often based on the 40-hour work week common in the North. Hence, Third World workers will receive, on average, much higher levels of exposure (*Ibid*);
3　The standards do not take into account differences in climate, nutritional status, or genetic predisposition (Rossiter and El Batawi, 1987: 3–11).

IMPACT OF INFORMALIZATION

The informalization of industry is one of the key developments of the 1990s; small-scale enterprises are growing faster than any others in developing countries, providing opportunities for survival to the poor and profit to the industrialists (Ghai, 1991). A clear distinction has often been made between formal and informal sector activities. However, this distinction has been criticized as research in several countries has highlighted the strong links between the two sectors. The functioning of small-scale industries is often closely connected to larger industrial plants, with small-scale enterprises providing larger industries with products essential to their operation (Portes et al, 1989). By shifting out of the formal into the informal sector, the payment of fixed overheads and workers' benefits are eliminated.

There appears to be a difference, however, between the number of occupational health hazards found in small-scale and large-scale industries. These differences may be explained by two factors. The first is the need for survival by workers in small-scale enterprises, who may consider occupational health hazards of less importance than the urgency of earning a living. Without the protection of labor regulations or access to free and adequate health services, workers in the informal sector are at significant risk from work-related diseases and injuries.

Second, the activities of small-scale industry generally fall outside the scope of the authorities. In many countries, small-scale enterprises are often legally exempt from labor regulations, including health and safety (WHO, 1992). Most laws regulating occupational health and safety apply only to medium- or large-scale industries, usually identified by the number of workers employed, normally over 25 to 50. For example, the Philippines is introducing the 'Law of 20,' in which enterprises with 20 workers or under will be exempt from most existing labor laws, in the expectation that this will encourage more enterprises and generate jobs (Reverente, 1992).

Christiani (1990: 393–401) gives several characteristics of the informal sector that indicate that occupational health may be a severe problem for workers in small-scale industries. Informal-sector workers are often very young (children) or very old (grandparents), and include reproductively active men and women – many of whom are pregnant. There is thus a strong link to maternal and child health considerations.

Children and young people make up a large and growing percentage of the informal work force. Millions of children, some as young as five years old, spend their time in economically productive activities that deprive them of formal education, good physical health, and psychosocial well-being. Accurate figures are impossible to obtain, as child labor is illegal in most countries and therefore goes unrecorded. Nevertheless, United Nations' estimates for 1981 pointed to 145 million children under the age of 15, rising to 375 million by the year 2000 (Lee-Wright, 1990).

Where it is illegal and hidden, child labor is outside the range of protective legislation. A child's wage, for example, may be half that of an adult's. Children are also more susceptible than adults to accident, injury, and occupational disease. Small, weak, and inexperienced workers are more at risk from dangerous machinery and materials, heavy weights, and the heat of industrial processes (Michaels et al, 1985). They are also more prone to poisoning and respiratory complaints caused by a multitude of airborne hazards. Examples of the health effects of child labor are not hard to find: tens of thousands of children work in the glass industry in Firozabad, India, and are exposed to excessive heat, noise, accidental burns, and cuts and lacerations caused by broken glass. They work through the night, often with no break for rest or food, and have a high incidence of tuberculosis (Mohan, 1992). In many countries worldwide, tourism and the sex trade rely heavily on child workers and child prostitutes.

LINKS BETWEEN WORK AND THE LIVING ENVIRONMENT

Benavides (1992) argues that most small-scale industries do not have a significant impact on the environment. On the contrary, it can be argued that these industries do, in fact, make a significant contribution to environmental contamination at the local level, ie, in the neighborhoods of small-scale industries. Such contamination can have a serious impact upon the state of health of the people living in these neighborhoods (Barten, 1992). In these situations, distinctions made between general health hazards and the more specific hazards of industry are rather artificial.

The number of small-scale industries in developing countries continues to mushroom, as the shortage of foreign currency forces governments to promote self-help enterprises (Nriagu, 1992: 1–37). Invariably, there are few restrictions or controls on what these operations discharge into the environment and quite often the homes and the surrounding play areas are contaminated with toxic metals. The fact that many people live where they work predisposes them to frequent (and potentially high levels of) exposure to metallic wastes and other hazards that result from such small-scale and cottage industries, obscuring the distinction between occupational and environmental exposure.

Workers themselves rarely distinguish between occupational and nonoccupational illness, although they are acutely aware that much of their physical well-being stems from bad working conditions (Shukla, 1991: 597–603). In India, a study was carried out among tannery workers. The tanneries were stratified on the basis of the tanning process (chrome, vegetable, or mixed) and hide processing capacity (large, medium, or small). The medical profile of the study population was divided between occupational and nonoccupational morbidity. However, many kinds of morbidity existing in the study population tended to be more embraceable in the WHO concept of 'work-related' disease, rather than the narrower concept of 'occupational' disease (Jeyaratnam, 1992). The former concept suggests that the causes are multifactorial and may be work-related, but not necessarily directly. For example, diseases such as tuberculosis or asthma may be aggravated, accelerated, or exacerbated by workplace exposures or conditions.

INFORMAL SECTOR IN TANZANIA

An important factor influencing the health of people involved in informal sector work is the insecurity of the working situation. Although the informal sector absorbs and maintains a fast-growing urban labor reserve and contributes significantly to the gross domestic product in many developing countries, national policies aimed at supporting and stimulating the sector are often lacking. In Tanzania, the informal sector is considered a threat and a nuisance by both government officials and the formal sector, since it operates outside official controls, occupies substantial sections of valuable urban land, and defies the official version of development (Schultz, 1995). This often results in incoherent local government measures against informal sector operators.

In Dar-es-Salaam, a consequence of this attitude is insufficient land allocation for informal sector activities by the government, resulting in unofficial occupation of land by informal sector workers. In many cases, they can only protect themselves through a high concentration of their activities, usually in districts with a high population density. From an ongoing study in Dar-es-Salaam, the authors note that this contributes to the plethora of problems that such densely populated areas already have: insufficient garbage collection and inadequate sanitary facilities and water supply that cause problems both for workers and the surrounding community.

Furthermore, a range of hazardous activities is carried out in these districts: small-scale industries such as wood workshops, metal workshops, and garages are set up close to places where women are cooking and selling food. Therefore, besides the hazards of their work, people are exposed to many other hazardous activities carried out in their home environment.

The lack of land allocation also causes an insecure situation for informal sector workers since they can be chased away from their premises any time. This does not stimulate the operators to invest in their enterprises and thereby improve the occupational and environmental conditions. Any investment is seen as a waste of money. The lack of permanent premises also makes it difficult to obtain credit, and leads to job insecurity and low incomes. To what extent these problems affect the mental health of informal sector workers and their productivity is virtually unknown (ILO, 1993). The effect on the health of workers' families is also not considered.

It has been suggested that, even when workers and operators in informal sector workshops were aware of health and safety issues, these were not their priority concern (Ibid). It is clear from the study that the struggle to provide the basic needs of life causes a daily burden for workers and their families in Dar-es-Salaam. The exposure of workers and their families to occupational and environmental risks is therefore not chosen voluntarily, but seen as the only possibility to maintain a basic living.

FAILURE OF THE EXISTING SYSTEM OF OCCUPATIONAL HEALTH CARE

Although the cottage factories and sweat shops of the informal sector employ only a very small number of workers each, collectively they represent the vast majority of industrial workers in all developing countries. Still, they lack any kind of organized health service and are entirely dependent on inadequate local health facilities. The same is generally true for agricultural workers.

One of the most important failings in the current approach to occupational health problems is the predominance of a medical-technical and reactive approach. Occupational health problems are theoretically preventable and are not primarily technical. Although they often involve technical data, the origin and persistence of occupational health problems have fundamentally more to do with the social relations of production (Schilling and Andersson, 1986: 6).

Unfortunately, equity in health is still merely seen in terms of access to medical services, rather than in terms of all aspects that determine health, such as work, housing, food, water, etc. At the district level of the health system, analysis of the district's health needs and problems seldom includes an assessment of industrial hazards, workplaces, and work processes, nor are they generally carried out with the participation of workers and other community members. At the primary care level, information on work hazards is rarely collected routinely in terms of exposure levels, etc, while an intersectoral approach is often lacking.

The occupational and environmental health problems of workers, particularly in the informal sector, present a challenge to health and labor ministries to develop a new approach. The model in the North of moving occupational health from the health ministry to the labor ministry is inappropriate in a situation where most workers are unorganized, are women and children whose health needs cannot be separated into 'home' and 'work,' and where industrial processes may affect not only workers' health, but also that of the population living nearby. This is illustrated by the following evidence.

In Kingston, Jamaica, Matte investigated the risk of lead poisoning among household members exposed to backyard battery repair shops. These shops are involved in the repair or rebuilding of lead-acid car batteries and are usually located on the same premises where the owner/operator and his family live. The survey found a high risk of elevated blood lead levels among subjects living in backyard battery repair shops, and found that the risk was not attributable to general environmental contamination of urban Kingston (Matte et al, 1989: 874–881). Disturbances in neurologic and systemic functions have been identified at levels that were once thought not to be a cause for concern (ie, 10 to 25 micrograms per deciliter). There is strong evidence that low-level exposure impairs cognitive development in children, and long-term effects of childhood exposure have been reported.

Cottage factories for melting lead and repairing and recharging batteries are to be found in all cities of the South. In Managua, the capital of Nicaragua, the total number of these cottage factories was estimated at 200 in 1989; by 1993, the total number exceeded 300 (Morales, 1994). In 1985, the Regional Commission on Occupational Health of the Ministry of Health of Nicaragua carried out a study of 133 workers in 42 of these cottage factories; 64 workers had high levels of lead in their blood, with a range of 36 to 164 micrograms per deciliter of blood, and an average of 74 micrograms per deciliter (MINSA, 1985). Moreover, the commission detected 16 cases of lead poisoning among children living in these cottage factories; three children – less than six years of age – died of lead poisoning.

The commission described the cottage factories as follows: 'The cottage factories are very small places, with an earthen floor, where residuals of lead are piled up and there is no periodic cleaning. The melting process of lead is realized by a totally artisanal method, with poor ventilation and no facilities for personal hygiene. Food and water for daily consumption are kept without any protection in the working places, where they are also consumed by the workers. In some cottage factories the risks are even higher, because they are situated in the owner's house or near public food selling places, exposing in an excessive way the members of the worker's own family (children, women) and the neighborhood' (*Ibid*).

In May 1987, a four-year-old child died of lead poisoning in the Managua neighborhood of Domitila Lugo; two other children of the same family also had to be admitted to a hospital because of suspected lead poisoning. They all lived in a one-room house, partly built of old car batteries, where their father melted lead (Barten, 1992). Following a visit to this cottage factory, it was reported as follows:

> *The work was carried out in a corner of a one-room shelter of approximately 4 x 4 m², constructed of planks and corrugated iron. In the same room there was sleeping accommodation. The surroundings were clearly polluted with the remainders of batteries. A sample of soil collected from the front yard of the house, situated at a distance of 300 meters from a battery plant, contained 20 times the acceptable concentration of lead. A family had lived there until a child died of lead intoxication (Zwennis, 1987).*

The data suggest that, in Managua, a considerable problem of increased lead exposure and risk of lead poisoning exists not only among workers, but also among the general population – particularly among young children. Of 1,474 people tested since then in various sites throughout Nicaragua, the average blood lead level was 59 micrograms per deciliter of blood (microg/dl), six times higher than the acceptable level in North America (Morales, 1992; CDC, 1991).

THE COLOMBO STATEMENT

Evidence such as this clearly indicates that the negative environmental impact of small-scale industries is of major significance, affecting not only workers, but also the general population, particularly the more vulnerable groups such as children and women. Since the scope of occupational health services is limited to workers, mainly those in large-scale industry, the implications for the community are not of primary concern to occupational health institutions (Christiani, 1990: 393–401). A broader approach is necessary, while a reduction of the occupational health hazards should also reduce the environmental health hazards.

Such an approach was suggested at the First Conference on Occupational Health in Developing Countries held in Sri Lanka in 1981. The Colombo Statement, issued by the conference, highlighted three key issues: the provision of health for neglected working populations in agriculture and small-scale industries, the situation of migrant workers, and the need for occupational health training in developing countries. It stressed the integration of occupational health services with primary health care (PHC). Because PHC advocates an integrated and comprehensive approach to the health needs and problems of working populations, with a focus on equity and workers' participation in decision-making processes (WHO, 1978), it has the potential to improve the health status of both workers and populations living in industrial zones.

Before this can be achieved, however, health authorities need to be more aware of the health conditions of workers. District health systems need to be strengthened and reoriented toward health promotion, prevention, and protection. Attention is needed to ensure that the integration of occupational health with PHC goes beyond the establishment of another separate, vertical technical program (Macdonald, 1993). For example, health promotion aims to work with people in the 'settings' of their everyday life, focusing on building up 'healthy workplaces' or 'healthy neighborhoods,' rather than focusing on people at risk from specific conditions or already in contact with the health services (Ashton and Seymour, 1988). Establishing local information systems can promote links between environmental/occupational health data and health conditions; local resource centers have proved to be important tools in mobilizing all possible sectors.

Since the conference in Sri Lanka, several alternative approaches have been developed to meet workers' health needs. One is to integrate public health services with occupational health to cover workers in small-scale industries. A district health center, with responsibility for the population in an industrial area, would thus expand its services and provide both occupational and PHC services for these workers (El Batawi and Husbumrer, 1987: 288–292). This requires a number of steps, including the routine analysis of the work environment and training district health workers to identify work-related health problems. An effective referral system to other levels of the health system, with skills in a range of work-related diseases and injuries, is also essential.

Another approach is to take an integrated occupational/PHC service to the workplace; health workers treat certain conditions on the spot, or refer them either to a local health facility or to an occupational health unit, established as a referral center. In Botswana, workers considered this to be the most acceptable, since they got the care they needed without loss of work time (Rojas, 1990; 108–113). This approach also allows a stronger link between the health system and the employer, with the opportunity for regular assessment of working conditions.

Establishing a comprehensive approach relies heavily on the involvement of an active, organized, and informed work force working in alliance with its community. Worker participation is essential to ensure 'healthy workplaces': discussing health problems, identifying opportunities for change, planning and organizing strategies for prevention and control, and playing a role in the surveillance of risks and monitoring of enforcement of laws and regulations.

Many workers' organizations have set up their own occupational clinics or run mobile clinics at workplaces or community venues. Some worker-based health schemes, such as the one run by the Ray Alexander Workers Clinic in South Africa, are committed to a PHC approach and address wider community health needs (London, 1993: 1521–1527). In this way, unemployed and informal sector workers are covered, thus promoting equity and preventing the problem of providing health services for the skilled work force alone. However, this can only be an interim response; many of those involved with such schemes advocate that these clinics should be integrated into a national health service based on PHC.

In Nicaragua, for example, explicit attention to workers' health began after the victory of the Sandinista Revolution in 1979. An innovative approach was taken by establishing primary care teams at area level, involving health workers, a local union representative, and *brigadistas obreros* (worker-volunteers with responsibility for occupational health within a specific factory). Inspections and health screenings were carried out by the teams, with support from the occupational health specialist of the regional team. Results were then discussed with the factory directors; a start was thus made in improving factory conditions.

For many people living in the *barrios* of Managua's industrial zone, occupational and environmental health became important issues as they came to learn of the potential pollution hazards from the factories in their *barrios*. Due to their heightened awareness and concern, particularly following the deaths of the three small children from lead poisoning, the level of priority given to occupational and environmental hazards was high. Unfortunately, workers' health no longer appears to be a priority for the new government, as the workers' health program set up during the former Sandinista government has ceased to exist. Increased poverty has also meant that the network of cottage workshops has expanded and they are visible all over Managua. Despite this, awareness and concern about the lead poisoning hazard among workers and the general population are still strong: in September 1994, people living near the FANABASA battery plant demanded its closure following the discovery of more people, including children, with high blood levels (*Barricada*, September 1994).

AN INTERDISCIPLINARY APPROACH

Developing an adequate response to work-related health needs will thus require an interdisciplinary approach, involving not only the health sector, but also other ministries, employers, workers, and communities. No one sector is able to respond in isolation; for example, in most countries the health sector is not officially responsible for ensuring that health and safety regulations are being met by employers. Therefore, each group has a specific contribution to make, which, when coordinated by the public health sector, can offer a comprehensive response to workers' health needs.

The most important first step is to raise awareness about the issue among a wide range of interest groups: government health services and other relevant agencies, employers (both large and small), development agencies and research institutes, and, most importantly, among workers and communities themselves. Workers' health activists, such as the Institute for Occupational Health and Safety Development in the Philippines and the Industrial Health Research Group in

South Africa, argue that improving health and working conditions will only be realized through the persistent efforts of workers themselves, as both governments and employers give workers' health a very low priority.

The assessment of occupational and environmental effects of small-scale industries and the eventual improvement of workers' health thus require a political approach that takes into account the social and environmental context of the worker and the workplace. Occupational and environmental health problems associated with industrialization are becoming as prevalent in the South as in the North. As witnessed in Nicaragua, any move to change and improve workers' health requires, above all, a political commitment to recognize this as a right.

To challenge the effects of the dominant development model of the 1990s, with its prime focus on economic growth and the marketplace, the highest priority should be given to the protection of workers' health at both the national and international policy levels. The requirements of future occupational health policy can be stated in eight key points:

1   Involve workers' organizations in the strategic planning process of health development at the district and municipal levels, eg, ensure that 'healthy workplaces' is on the agenda of healthy city processes;
2   Put occupational health on the wider agenda of urban development;
3   Consider the specific vulnerability of workers in informal sector activities;
4   Consider the vulnerability of child workers and women of reproductive age;
5   Consider that 'occupational' health hazards are only one among many other (often interrelated) environmental health hazards. Low-income urban communities are often exposed to a wide range of other hazards related to poor living environments. The combination of exposure to hazards in the living and working environment may enhance vulnerability;
6   Consider that standards applied in the North may not be valid;
7   Develop integrated approaches at municipal/district level involving all relevant actors/sectors;
8   Occupational health should be developed within primary health care at the primary care level.

REFERENCES

Ashton, J and H Seymour (1988) *The New Public Health: The Liverpool Experience.* Milton Keynes: Open University Press.

Barten, Françoise (1992) 'Environmental Lead Exposure of Children in Managua, Nicaragua: An Urban Health Problem.' Unpublished PhD thesis. Nijmegen University.

Benavides, L (1992) Hazardous Waste Management for Small-Scale and Cottage Industries in Developing Countries. Paper presented at the International Workshop on Planning for Sustainable Urban Development – Cities and Natural Resource Systems in Developing Countries, Cardiff (July 13–17).

CDC, Centers for Disease Control (1991) Preventing Lead Poisoning in Young Children:

A Statement by the Centers for Disease Control. Atlanta, Georgia.

Christiani, D (1990) 'Occupational Health in Developing Countries: Review of Research Needs.' *American Journal of Industrial Medicine* 17: 393–401.

Colombo Statement on Occupational Health in Developing Countries, Sri Lanka (1981) *Journal of Occupational Health Safety* 2,6 (Aust Nz 1986).

El Batawi, M and C Husbumrer (1987) 'Epidemiological Approach to Planning and Development of Occupational Health Services at a National Level.' *International Journal of Epidemiology* 16,2: 288–292.

Ghai, D (ed) (1991) *The IMF and the South: The Social Impact of Crisis and Adjustment.* London: Zed Books.

International Labor Organization (ILO) (1993) Selected Papers on Occupational Safety and Health in the Informal Sector in Tanzania. Geneva: African Safety and Health Project.

Jeyaratnam, J (ed) (1992) *Occupational Health in Developing Countries.* Oxford: Oxford University Press.

Lee-Wright, P (1990) *Child Slaves.* London: Earthscan Publications.

London, L (1993) 'The Ray Alexander Workers Clinic – A Model for Worker-Based Health Services in South Africa?' *Social Science and Medicine* 37,12: 1521–1527.

Macdonald, John (1993) *Primary Health Care: Medicine in Its Place.* London: Earthscan Publications.

Matte, T et al (1989) 'Lead Poisoning Among Household Members Exposed to Lead-Acid Battery Repair Shops in Kingston, Jamaica.' *International Journal of Epidemiology* 18,4: 874–881.

Michaels, D et al (1985) 'Economic Development and Occupational Health in Latin America: New Directions for Public Health in Less Developed Countries.' *American Journal of Public Health* 75,5: 536–542.

MINSA (Ministerio de Salud, Regional III) (1985) *Informes del Departamento Regional de Salud Ocupacional 1985.* Nicaragua: Ministerio de Salud.

Mohan, R (1992) Protection of Working Children in India: Examining Adequacy of the Welfare Measures. London: London School of Economics, unpublished dissertation.

Morales, Carlos (1994) Personal Communication. Managua, Nicaragua: Centro Nacional de Higiene y Diagnostico, Ministerio de Salud.

Morales, Carlos (1992) *Assessment of Prevention of Lead Poisoning in Nicaragua: A Model Program for Developing Countries.* Managua, Nicaragua: Ministerio de Salud.

Nriagu, T (1992) 'Toxic Metal Pollution in Africa.' *The Science of the Total Environment* 121: 1–37.

Portes, A et al (1989) *The Informal Economy. Studies in Advanced and Less Developed Countries.* Baltimore, MD: Johns Hopkins University Press.

Reverente, T (1992) 'Occupational Health Services for Small-Scale Industries.' J. Jeyaratnam (ed) *Occupational Health in Developing Countries.* Oxford: Oxford University Press.

Rojas, P et al (1990) 'Nurses Bring Primary Health Care to Industrial Workers.' *World Health Forum* 11,2: 108–113.

Rossiter, C and M El Batawi (1987) 'The Working Environment.' *Industry and Environment* 10: 3–11.

Schilling, R and N Andersson (1986) 'Occupational Epidemiology in Developing Countries.' *Journal of Occupational Health Safety* 2,6 Aust Nz.

Schultz, M (1995) 'The Informal Sector and Structural Adjustment-Strengthening Collective Coping Mechanisms in Tanzania.' *Small Enterprise Development* 6,1.

Shukla, Abhay, S Kumar, and Ferco Ory (1991) 'Occupational Health and the Environment in an Urban Slum in India.' *Social Science and Medicine* 33,5: 597–603.

World Health Organization (WHO) (1992) *Our Planet, Our Health. Report of the WHO Commission on Health and Environment.* Geneva: WHO.

World Health Organization (WHO) (1982) *Review on Occupational Health Services in Small-Scale Industries in Developing Countries.*

World Health Organization (WHO) (1978) *Primary Health Care. Report of the International Conference on Primary Health Care.* Alma Ata, USSR.

Zwennis, Wim (1987) Report on a Visit to the Ministry of Health and the National Institute of Hygiene and Epidemiology in Managua, Nicaragua. MBL, TNO, The Netherlands.

Chapter 10

Introduction to the *Charter of Rights Against Industrial Hazards*: For Communities, Workers, and Protection of Their Environment

Barbara Dinham

The world has now acquired ample evidence of industrial and environmental hazards. Lessons must be learned from these experiences so that those who have died and suffered will not have done so entirely in vain. So judged the Third Tribunal on Industrial Hazards and Human Rights, after hearing evidence in Bhopal from the victims of the industrial disasters in October 1992. The *Charter of Rights Against Industrial Hazards* (see Annexe) is based on a series of tribunals and aims to provide workers and communities with a common agenda.

The four tribunals on Industrial Hazards and Human Rights have listened to evidence from survivors, community groups, and workers around the world, as well as from professionals and experts, and, together, their evidence has shaped a new Charter that is intended to set standards for protecting people and their environment from hazards arising from all aspects of industrial production. The Charter has been shaped by the evidence presented to the tribunals and many others to whom it has been circulated for consultation, to address the failure of industry, government, and professional services to meet the needs of those affected by industrial hazards. Whether a hazard is dramatic and affects many, as in the case of Bhopal, or is the result of smaller-scale regular or irregular toxic emissions, common principles of justice need to be applied, common standards established, and common guidance provided on proper medical, legal, social, and economic action to take so as to prevent or redress the wrongs.

The resulting Charter presented below forms the basis of an international convention for presentation to the United Nations for formal recognition by governments. The Charter also calls on community groups, trade unions, public interest organizations, and individuals to assert these rights as a duty in order to improve standards and protect communities and workers, as well as their living and working environment.

Despite the diverse situations and experiences of survivors and other affected groups who presented evidence at the tribunals, a remarkable similarity characterized the problems they encountered and the absence of the support they needed to deal with problems arising from industrial hazards. Although approaches will change according to particular circumstances and problems, broad principles can be established and general needs identified. These charters must be taken up now to ensure that communities, workers, and their environment are safeguarded from the harmful impacts of industrial processes.

The *Charter on Industrial Hazards and Human Rights* was drafted in the spirit of learning from the past so that a more humane future may be possible. It is a people's statement, not an official document. Unlike most human rights documents, its content was not determined by diplomatic compromise. Rather, its substance, and hence its authority, derives directly from the collective experience of those who have been forced to live with the consequences of industrial hazards.

The hearings on industrial hazards and human rights took place in New Haven (US, 1991), Bangkok (Thailand, 1991), Bhopal (India, 1992), and London (UK, 1994). Nearly five years in the drafting, the Charter was based on evidence presented at the first three sites and was then discussed at a parallel session to the London hearings that was attended by witnesses and other community, victim, and worker groups. This draft was circulated widely around the world for further consultation and the final text reflects a great deal of consensus from these sources. The charters thus reflect the experience and work of many diverse groups and individuals concerned with industrial hazards, human rights, the plight of affected people, and the impact of hazards on the environment. These tribunals brought the impact of industrial production into the arena of human rights abuses. They heard evidence from victims' organizations, communities, workers, women's groups, and public interest groups. The London session also heard evidence from lawyers, medical experts, scientists, economists, academics, and occupational health and safety specialists who helped form the guidelines for the best practices.

At the New Haven tribunal, the Permanent Peoples' Tribunal considered three draft charters – on the rights of workers, communities, and victims. The drafts were based on existing principles of human rights law, interpreted in the light of industrial hazards. At the final hearing in London, the three charters were consolidated into one document, which was then circulated to a large number of experts and nongovernmental organizations from all parts of the world. The final version was approved by the Permanent Peoples' Tribunal (PPT) in early 1996. Thus, although the Charter is drafted in legalistic language, its content directly reflects the views of those with immediate experience of industrial hazards in a wide variety of settings.

The tribunals have taken place under the umbrella of the PPT, which was formed as an independent forum to examine violations of the rights of peoples and to suggest remedies for such violations. The PPT provides a panel of judges that hears evidence directly from those affected by human rights abuses. The members include eminent jurists, writers, statespeople, artists, and scientists from all parts of the world.

Established in 1979 by the Lelio Basso International Foundation for the Rights and Liberation of Peoples, the PPT is the immediate successor to the Bertrand Russell Tribunals on Vietnam and Latin America. In the tradition of the International Military Tribunal at Nuremberg, the PPT is an international public opinion tribunal that identifies and publicizes the systematic violation of fundamental rights, particularly in cases where national and international law fail to protect peoples' rights. The PPT is based in Rome, but its 75 judges come from all over the globe and include eminent persons whose reputations must be above reproach in art, culture, science, and politics, including a number of Nobel Prize winners.

Individual hearings are initiated by aggrieved groups and are normally heard by a bench of three to 11 sitting tribunal judges. Accused parties are invited to present their case at the hearings, and if they do not attend, the PPT appoints legal counsel to represent their case in a rigorous manner. The PPT applies principles of international law and is bound by the *Algiers Declaration of the Rights of Peoples* as well as by its own statute of operations.

As part of its mandate, the PPT supports the development of new standards and legal norms. With the Charter, the PPT aims to contribute new principles of justice to the existing body of human rights law. The Charter was placed before the United Nations and other international bodies for official consideration. Yet it is also based on the principle that official action is not enough: it calls upon individuals, community groups, trade unions, and public interest organizations to assert its rights as part of a common duty to take action against industrial hazards.

Despite the diverse backgrounds and experiences of those who testified – from survivors of industrial hazards, concerned community groups, and workers, to doctors, lawyers, scientists, engineers, and other experts who provided information on the organization and effects of industrial hazards – they told a common story. Industrial hazards are proliferating on a global scale and pose a serious threat to human life and health. Moreover, the existing economic, legal, and medical systems are not responding adequately to this feature of globalization. Victims' groups voiced a common demand for a system that protects them from death, injury, and persistent insecurity. Expert testimony highlighted instances of the best practices, but also described the main features of an international order in which hazards are promoted, traded, and protected without effective controls.

The *Charter on Industrial Hazards and Human Rights* does not bestow rights from above as a gift from the state. It is a set of demands from below, to be seized by individuals and groups acting in the context of particular struggles. The way in which it is interpreted and used will necessarily vary from one situation to the next, but it nevertheless articulates a universal vision of a world in which people are able to lead their lives without industrial hazards.

Chapter 11

Conclusion: The Dynamics of Future Change

Christopher Williams

Environmental victims are involved in a game in which the rules, players, and goal-posts are elusive and constantly changing. Winning in the short-term, by those who want to make a profit irrespective of the injuries, currently takes precedence over long-term fair play. Few policy forums exist within which the concepts presented in Part One of this book can be developed. None of the major injustices described in the case studies has been resolved. Although innovative strategies for improvement, such as the Good Neighbor Agreements, are shown to be effective, they are rare and unlikely to be taken up in the low-income countries where victimization is worst. The Charter from the Permanent Peoples' Tribunal will probably not be taken further as an instrument of international or domestic law. The dynamics of change, which will dictate the eventual utility of the environmental victims concept, are likely to arise in four main areas: science, law, public attitudes, and the human ability to develop new learning strategies.

CHANGING SCIENCE

It is an old adage that science is always changing, yet it is an adage that scientists frequently ignore, especially in relation to the so called 'safe' levels of exposure to environmental toxins. The notion of a 'safe' or threshold level of exposure, below which intake of a toxin is considered harmless, is fundamental to deciding whether or not an environmentally-mediated impact amounts to victimization.

Courts and public administrators treat 'safe' levels as if they are carved in stone, yet they are constantly changing.

If we examine the 'safe' levels for exposure to lead, analysed previously by one of the authors in this book (Barten 1992:23), we see that between 1971–1991 the graph falls dramatically like a stock market crash. The difference is that, unlike the financiers, the scientists, politicians and others entrusted with public protection do not perceive a pattern of this nature as indicative of what the future trend might be. The Romans knew that lead was an environmental poison, yet in 1997 we find the UK press reporting that one in ten children is likely to be suffering intellectual impairment because of lead pollution (Lean & Morgan 1997: 1). The author of the report, Dr Erik Millstone, points out that the current UK 'safe' level dates from 1983, since when the US and many other nations have introduced much stricter standards. During the same period the UK government was opposing EU proposals to ban leaded petrol.

Similarly, without the aid of modern science, mercury has been recognized as an occupational health hazard since observations of miners at the Almader mines in Spain 2400 years ago. The Mad Hatter in *Alice in Wonderland* was based on reality – 19th century hatters were considered to be 'mad' because of exposure to mercury used in the process of hat manufacture. This knowledge did not prevent the Chisso mercury poisoning at Minimata Bay, Japan, which was permitted to continue for many years because scientists claimed that the mercury was harmless. Efforts to control general mercury pollution, for example through burning coal in power stations, have been minimal.

It is not only governments which cannot grasp the significance of scientific trends. At the former Cavandish laboratories at the University of Cambridge, mercury contamination has been significant. In 1995 those given the responsibility to assess the risk declared that it was 'exceedingly unlikely' that anyone had suffered, or would suffer, harm. This conclusion, of course, leaves room for doubt, and the risk assessors publicly stated to concerned staff that they would respond to any further questions (Seaton 1995). Fundamental questions were then raised: Why was the downward trend in 'safe' levels not considered? What is the possible impact on the grandchildren of those now exposed (see later). Why were neurological impacts and the possibility of male mediated reproductive impacts not taken into account? These questions were straightforward but never answered, yet it had even been publicly acknowledged that omitting assessment of male-mediated reproductive impacts was a clear error which would be addressed. (It is a common failing in the male-dominated field of occupational risk assessment to forget that reproduction is not entirely to do with women.) The suggestion that the University should exercise a precautionary principle because 'safe' levels change was also not taken up. In contrast, at the same time in Paris, a number of university buildings were closed because of an asbestos hazard. Although there was no direct evidence of health problems, the precautionary principle was applied.

Then in 1997, a study of children in the Faeroe Islands who had consumed amounts of mercury well below the World Health Organization safety limits found the children to have suffered adverse effects (MacKenzie 1997:4). Prevailing 'safe' levels were, once again, it seems, too high.

The Cavendish laboratory at Cambridge is where Rutherford first split the atom and, of course, the safety of radiation is another area in which science is rapidly changing. The linear 'no threshold hypothesis' is now increasingly accepted – that all exposure to radiation, however small, poses a hazard (Chivian et al 1993:96). Until very recently scientific opinion held that exposure to radiation did not cause germ-line heritable impairments – that the grandchildren and further generations of those exposed would not be harmed. The opinion is based on data from Hiroshima and Nagasaki A-bomb victims, yet this has been challenged on the very simple basis that those victims received a high dose for a short period, and most contemporary exposures entail low doses over long periods (Roff 1995). In 1997 new research by Eric Wright at Harwell found a previously unknown pathway through which radiation can damage living cells. It is now concluded that:

> Radiation...may cause a much wider range of diseases than epidemiological studies predict...Worst of all, the small doses of radiation that millions habitually receive could be poisoning the human gene pool, wreaking damage on future generations...The public may well have been right all along (Edwards 1997:37).

Quite separately, there were also reports from a Cambridge scientist that 'epigenetic' changes in DNA had been observed for the first time. Until that point it had been believed that only changes in sequences of DNA could be passed to all future generations. Now it seems that effects on the way in which DNA works can also be inherited (Vines 1997:16). This is likely to create a major change in the understanding of heritable impacts. It might, for instance, explain why, during World War II, malnourished mothers had grandchildren suffering the effects of poor nutrition.

One irony of these examples is that the same university, Cambridge, produced the scientists who set in motion the radiation problem, the scientists who are at the forefront of changing what we know about the genetics of heritable effects, yet others who seem not to realize that science changes. In microcosm this is the pattern that pertains at national and global levels. Scientists, politicians and bureaucrats constantly fail to acknowledge the limits of scientific evidence and that opinion changes, usually in favour of stricter standards.

One of the first jobs for environmental victimology therefore is to generate a greater public awareness of this fact, so that public pressure is brought to bear on those whose current ignorance and inertia threatens human well-being. People with the responsibility to protect the public must quickly grasp that risk assessment is a dynamic process, and that the precautionary principle is now as important for the security of a nation's citizens from death and injury as is its police force or its army.

CHANGING LAW

Environmental law has been slow to embrace environmental victimization. As yet there are still few environmental statutes that directly aim to ensure human well-being. The current intent is to protect, in a vague way, 'the environment' with a hope that, as a spin off, we will be safe. Of the statutes that relate directly to human impacts, many *diminish* the rights of victims, others are so muddled that they are unworkable (Williams 1997:189). As mentioned in Chapter 1, the UK *Congenital Disability Act* (1976) intends to protect, and provide redress for, the unborn child in relation to radiation exposure. Yet if the child's parents were aware of the possibility of a workplace hazard, a claim cannot be made. How did those who drafted the law come to believe that the concept of 'contributory negligence' could be applied to a foetus? The only explanation is a muddled view that it is the parent and not the child who is the potential victim. The Act is clearly absurd, is frequently criticized in law books, and has hardly ever been used. Yet there are no plans to amend it.

Criminology has now started to show an interest in environmental crime. *Environmental Crime and Criminality* (Edwards et al 1996) provides a sound although almost entirely American discussion. But the criminology approach hits an immediate conceptual stumbling block – that most environmental victimization, although perhaps seen as morally wrong, is not yet defined as 'crime'. In addition, efforts to maintain that the ecosystem can be the 'victim' of environmental crime, proposed by Mark Seis (p 121–146), require long arguments which are contrary to the established view in 'interest theory', that only individuals and groups can have interests, and therefore rights, and therefore can be victims of criminal, civil or moral offences.

While domestic law and criminology amble into the field of environmental victimization, real life presents challenging new questions which demand immediate answers by courts. For instance, the link between exposure to organophosphates and a range of adverse neurological impacts is now hardly in dispute, yet those affected find that no law directly supports their case. But that is not where the problem stops. In 1992 a UK farm worker shot and killed his girlfriend's parents, and was sentenced to life imprisonment. Campaigners are now demanding a retrial on the basis that he was suffering mental impairment because of exposure to organophosphate pesticides. We have reached the point at which environmental victimization is not just a simple matter of perpetrator-victim cause-and-effect, but whether or not that effect can then constitute a defence or mitigation if the victim commits a crime as a result. Bearing in mind that virtually every human on earth has demonstrably been exposed to a range of environmental toxins, how will courts cope with the inevitable avalanche of defences of this nature? In the US, evidence provided by brain scans is now being used to defend those who claim their actions were caused by chemical impacts on their brain, and the Supreme Court has ruled that judges can now rule whether or not such scientific evidence is sufficiently reliable to be put before a court, irrespective of whether it has been peer reviewed (Motluk 1997:16).

On a national level there are occasionally indications of innovation. In Sweden it is proposed that pollution by synthetic chemicals should be banned if they are likely to *persist* in the environment. The introduction of this simple 'persistence' criterion would cut through the current problem of the expensive and complex testing thousands of chemicals each year for adverse human or ecological impacts. In other nations, progress is fuelled by innovative use of law by individual members of the public. Through individuals using the Indian Constitution – public interest litigation – the Supreme Court has held that the government is responsible for car pollution (*M C Mehta* vs. *Union of India*, 1991 AIR SCW 813). The victory is largely symbolic, but no democratic government wants to be seen as 'guilty' of such a significant form of environmental victimization. In the light of Chapter 3, it is interesting to note that in 1993, children in the Philippines (represented by their parents) initiated proceedings on behalf of themselves and future generations, in relation to government timber licensing agreements. After a Supreme Court ruling, the children were allowed to file the petition on the basis that the Philippines Constitution embodies the right to a 'balanced and healthful ecology' (s.16) and that the right to self-preservation is a fundamental right, even if unwritten, since the beginning of humankind.

At a global level, an ingenious concept, the 'planetary interest', builds on the established international relations understanding of the 'vital national interest' to propose how global governance might develop effective measures against the major threats such as ozone depletion and climate change (Graham 1998). This has the backing of around 20 named parliamentarians, from the spectrum of political beliefs, throughout the world. A key question, raised by Gwyn Prins in *The Planetary Interest*, is how do we *legitimize* actions by national governments or international organizations to address environmental and other global threats? Much of the necessary action, for example concerning car use, seems unlikely to achieve democratic support in the traditional sense. In Chapter 2 of *Environmental Victims*, Peter Penz provides more background detail about the question of legitimization, which also has relevance to a local view of strategies to address environmental victimization, and, as discussed later, to education.

There are a few islands of progress, but there is still little consideration of how to connect these islands – conceptualizations linking developments of domestic law, international agreements, and global governance. For decades we have known that many forms of environmental victimization, for example radiation exposure from weapons testing and power generation, do not respect our current conceptual or physical boundaries. So another task for environmental victimology is to break the parochial boundaries of its traditional intellectual predecessor and frame the local in the context of the global.

CHANGING PUBLIC ATTITUDES

In 1995, the oil company Shell decided to reverse a major decision to dump the obsolete oil rig *Brent Spar* in the North Sea, in response to opposition led by Greenpeace. It did so against the wishes of the UK government, and contrary to its own economic and scientific advice. Some areas of Greenpeace's own scientific evidence were then found to have been flawed, yet they still won the moral argument. The reason was that they had taken the debate away from the realms of science and law and onto a new level of public ethics – very simply they generated an agreement that it is wrong to use the sea as a dustbin. Shell detected a change in public attitudes, no doubt influenced by a few violent attacks on its petrol stations (Williams 1996:198), and opted for its own commercial version of the precautionary principle. The collapse of the UK beef industry in the space of a few days, following a very candid government announcement about BSE-CJD ('mad cow disease'), provided a striking reminder of why commercial entities are taking increasing interest in the volatility of public attitudes.

Of course this new-found awareness does not necessarily lead to greater integrity by companies – it might simply be used to plan new strategies for trying to manipulate or circumvent public attitudes. In 1996 the US company Monsanto wanted to introduce a new form of genetically-modified soya bean. The new variety is resistant to the use of a particular herbicide, Glyphosphate, manufactured exclusively by Monsanto. Aware of a probable public reaction against the use of genetically-modified products – on the grounds of unforeseen effects on personal health and unpredictable impacts on the general environment through the release of genetically-modified organisms (GMOs) and increased herbicide use – Monsanto chose to mix the genetically-modified produce with that grown normally. It was made impossible for buyers to purchase the pure produce, and for the public to use consumer choice.

Also aware of the probable negative reaction from the public, the UK supermarket Tesco put out leaflets headed 'Genetically modified Soya – THE FACTS'. Unsurprisingly the leaflets only gave one side of the facts, but also claimed that 'Processed soya beans grown on genetically modified plants...are indistinguishable in composition...from those made using conventional soya beans'. It does not take a geneticist to know that *processed* beans do not *grow* on anything – even genetically modified ones! But of greater curiosity is the claim that the GMO beans are 'indistinguishable'. If this were true there would be no point in introducing them – they are, of course, distinguishable by their new genetic make up. Tests developed for the Ministry of Agriculture, Fisheries and Food (MAFF) can detect a difference if there is just one genetically engineered soya bean in 100 beans (Motluk 1998:5). But these mistakes were in keeping with the general line the pamphlet promoted – that the genetically modified product is entirely safe and, in any case, cannot be separated from the standard crop.

Tesco was unrepentant about its error and stood by its leaflets. It also claimed that it was '*unable* to label those products that contain GMOs' and stated, 'We do not believe that it is helpful to customers to use statements such as, "may contain GMO" as this reduces customer choice...' (Proud 1997). In November 1997 it was announced by the food industry that all food products that *may* contain genetically-modified produce would be labelled as containing GMOs. Tesco was left looking less than straightforward in its dealings with the public – that unquantifiable but crucial commercial dynamic which underpins public attitudes, public trust, was put in jeopardy.

As negative public opinion spread throughout the US, Europe and the South Pacific, crisis management consultancies, which had been involved in managing the public perception of major incidents such as the Three Mile Island nuclear disaster, then became involved. They advised companies such as Tesco to avoid all discussion of the safety of GMOs with the public (Penman 1997:9), which, in the light of the 'FACTS' debacle was not unwise advice. But continued public pressure had pushed the food industry into a major U-turn about labelling (Laurance 1997:11). The fear within the food industry is probably that changing scientific opinion will most likely find that the genetically-modified products are not so risk-free, and that the industry will then suffer yet another major loss of public trust as it did over BSE-CJD. But any future problems are likely to be blamed on the supermarkets such as Tesco, which are familiar to the public, rather than on the more remote Monsanto. By labelling the products, the hope is probably that the food retail industry can at least try to claim that the public had choice whether or not to purchase the genetically-modified products, although the reality is that such choice is very limited.

The importance of the GMO example is that, as with *Brent Spar*, almost irrespective of the science or the law, it is the dynamics of public opinion around the world that have dictated the behaviour of otherwise powerful companies. What the food industry seems so far to have overlooked is that this might also extend to the public simply changing the rules of the game, as Greenpeace did concerning *Brent Spar*, concluding that large food companies cannot be trusted per se. Options are on the horizon. Sweden is considering becoming totally organic in its food production, as a nation. 'Made in Sweden' could become synonymous with: no need to check the small print on the labels to see if there is a risk from GMOs, pesticides, chemical fertilisers, food additives, or the host of other possible hazards. It is probable that some low-income countries will be able to follow suit, as the necessary labour is cheap and some regions have, so far, been too poor to be able to degrade their farmland with synthetic chemicals. The simplicity of the situation – shopping according to nation of origin – could bring about the demise of food companies and retailers and result in some countries, such as the US and UK, being seen across the board as 'dirty' food producers.

The globalization of the media means that, like the hazards, public attitudes do not now respect neat boundaries. The butterfly's wing effect, developed within chaos theory, may provide a more useful model for thinking about this global aspect of environmental victimology than the traditional perspectives, based on the incremental evolution of public opinion, which usually stop at the level of national surveys.

CHANGING LEARNING STRATEGIES

New learning strategies must therefore teach about the sociology and politics of scientific change, how the law should serve to protect environmental victims, and about the manipulation of public attitudes by powerful entities. Strategies must

163

go beyond the prevailing concept of environmental education, which is still largely just a development nature study combined with a little geography. At present, individual school teachers may take a more radical approach, but national curricula about the environment do not generally encourage children to challenge environmental victimization and think politically in the way that many adults now do.

In some settings, things are different. In Bhopal, apart from the obvious folklore about Union Carbide and the Indian and US governments, children are taught new forms of basic survival, for example that in the event of a factory exploding they should run *against* the wind. Although counter-intuitive, this is likely to get them out of the poisonous plume quicker, because the plume widens as it travels. As Satinath Sarangi indicates in Chapter 5, many of the Bhopal victims are thought to have suffered unduly because they did the opposite. In Chapter 3, Sharon Stephens describes how the Viola educational programs in Russia involve children in the process of resisting and redressing environmental victimization. But the Union Carbide disaster and Russian pollution are tangible threats and have had a clear impact on what children are taught. Most forms of environmental victimization are not so visible and clear-cut.

Environmental education will eventually need to address a problem that is more subtle than a response to obvious threats – how to develop the human perception of the new forms of 'invisible' environmental hazards. We have no innate information processing mechanisms to prompt a response to the threats posed by global climate change or PCB pollution, as we have to create a reaction to the risk posed by fire or stagnant water. The perception, assessment, and response to these new forms of hazard must stem *entirely* from how and what we learn. If environmental toxins took the form of slugs swimming in our tea or locusts pervading in the air we breath, perception of the problem would be innate and prompt immediate responses. They do not, and it is a major task of education to present invisible hazards to human perception in a manner that leads to a better questioning of arguments that are currently won solely on the basis of the visibility of the evidence.

One outcome of the absence of education of this nature is that social policy is often based only on the science that makes us aware of high-visibility, cost-related consequences. The fluoridation of drinking water in the UK is a good example. The evidence in relation to fluoride preventing tooth decay is easy to collect and disseminate. Toothache is an immediately unpleasant circumstance, which we would all rather avoid, and the savings to a health service of preventing decay are easy to calculate and present politically. So evident seems the argument, that the other side of the debate is rarely heard.

Fluoride is also a neurotoxin and a genotoxin. The Department of Health's own statistics show that between 1983–1986, cases of Down's Syndrome were 30 percent higher in fluoridated than non-fluoridated areas. Other similar evidence comes from research in Russia in the 1970s and more recently from the US. In China, a significant impact of naturally-occurring fluoride on the IQ of children has been identified (Woffinden 1997:28). China is not renowned for publicizing its environmental problems, but this is unproblematic in this circumstance because the source of the toxin is natural. People are not exposed because of deliberate government policy as in the UK. To this largely invisible evidence can be added one of those synergistic effects, highlighted in the introduction to this book. Fluoridated water dissolves the lead from lead pipes and so increases the exposure to those who drink it. This contributes, no doubt, to the statistic that '1 in 10 UK children are at risk from lead' mentioned at the start of this chapter.

Whoever is eventually found to be correct, the UK fluoride debate has so far been won on the basis of the visibility rather than the credibility of the evidence. The benefits and savings from avoiding a filling are clear and immediate. In contrast, long-term, mainly sub-clinical, and perhaps intergenerational, impacts of human intelligence are elusive and hard to put a cash-cost on. The US Environmental Protection Agency 'safe' level for fluoride is four parts per million; the UK government permits water authorities to add fluoride to a level of one part per million. The difference leaves little room for human error, or for the possibility that the 'safe' level is at present too high. Even if correct, the decision to put fluoride in the UK water supply is very hard to present as resulting from a legitimate democratic process, because one half of the evidence has never been presented to the public in a manner in which it can contribute to a balanced judgement.

The forest fires of 1997, in Indonesia and Malaysia, raise a broader question of legitimacy. In response, the Indonesian government introduced a state of emergency – a measure usually restricted to addressing military threats or serious domestic disorder. What are the grounds for legitimately using military measures to address environmental problems? One basis should be an identifiable change in public perception of environmental threats – that they can be equated with the traditional threats to national security. But that should not just be an unthinking evolution or state manipulation of public perception. It should arise from forms of education that give rise to more appropriate and effective ways to perceive and understand environmentally-mediated risk. If this does not happen, governments eager to find an excuse to use draconian measures for public control under the guise of environmental concern will not be challenged.

New learning strategies for educating the public about the appropriate perception of new risks are necessary to ensure that responses to environmental victimisation are democratically legitimized and do not themselves become yet another form of victimization. The comments of Ken Saro-Wiwa (Jr) in the Introduction to *Environmental Victims* provide an omen of the alternative scenario. Nigeria demonstrates what happens when power elites, not an appropriately educated populace, dictate whose version of security is going to underpin governance. And this applies at all levels, from municipality to the planet.

REFERENCES

Barten, Françoise (1992) *Environmental Lead Exposure in Managua, Nicaragua: An Urban Health Problem*. The Hague: CIP Gegevens, Koninklijke Bibliothek.

Chivian, Eric et al (1993) *Critical Condition: Human Health and the Environment.* Cambridge, Mass.: MIT Press.

Edwards, Rob (1997) 'Radiation roulette,' *New Scientist* (11 October).

Edwards, Sally, Terry Edwards and Charles Fields (1996) *Environmental Crime and Criminality: Theoretical and Practical Issues.* New York: Garland Publishing.

Graham, K (ed) (1998) *The Planetary Interest.* London: UCL Press. (Forthcoming)

Laurance, Jeremy (1997) 'Genetically-modified food to hit shelves in the new year.' *The Independent* (20 November).

Lean, Geoffrey and Andrew Morgan. (1997) 'One infant in ten has IQ reduced by lead.' *Independent on Sunday* (November 9).

MacKenzie, Debora (1997) 'Arrested development: official safety limits on mercury are too high to prevent damage before birth.' *New Scientist* (22 November).

Motluk, Alison (1997) 'What colour is innocence?' *New Scientist* (22 March).

Motluk, Alison (1998) 'Gene police could end up on the bean beat' *New Scientist* (31 January).

Penman, Danny (1997) 'Stay quiet on risks of gene-altered food, industry told.' *The Guardian* (August 6).

Proud, Rachel (1997) Unpublished correspondence from Tesco to the author.

Roff, Sue Rabbitt (1995) *Hotspots: The Legacy of Hiroshima and Nagasaki.* London: Cassell.

Seaton, Anthony (1995) 'Mercury contamination of the Old Cavendish laboratory.' Unpublished report to the General Board of the University of Cambridge.

Vines, Gail (1997) 'There is more to heredity than DNA.' *New Scientist* (19 April).

Williams, C (1996) 'Environmental victimisation and violence.' *Aggression and violent behaviour* 1(3): 191–204.

Williams, C (1997) *Terminus Brain: The Environmental Threats to Human Intelligence.* London: Cassell.

Woffinden, Bob (1997) 'Clear and present danger.' *The Guardian Weekend* (June 7).

Annexe

Charter of Rights Against Industrial Hazards

Permanent Peoples' Tribunal on Industrial Hazards and Human Rights

PREAMBLE

The Permanent People's Tribunal on Industrial Hazards and Human Rights,

Having convened four Sessions in New Haven, Bangkok, Bhopal, and London since 1991 to receive testimony and deliberate on issues relating to the right to life, occupational health and safety, environment protection, risk management, and damage reduction in the wider global context of hazardous production;

Having drafted over a period of four years a charter of rights designed to reflect the views and concerns of persons injured and distressed by industrial hazards, and having issued on the second day of December 1994 a Draft Charter for comment and discussion among individuals and nongovernmental organizations, including trade unions;

Following the Universal Declaration of the Rights of Peoples, the Universal Declaration of Human Rights, the International Covenant on Civil and Political Rights, the International Covenant on Economic, Social, and Cultural Rights, the Convention on the Elimination of All Forms of Discrimination Against Women, the United Nations Convention on the Rights of the Child, the Vienna Declaration and Program of Action of the World Conference of Human Rights, and other relevant international human rights instruments;

Guided by the Rio Declaration on Environment and Development, Agenda 21, the Draft Declaration of Principles on Human Rights and the Environment, the Draft Declaration on the Rights of Indigenous Peoples, and other relevant instruments for prevention of industrial and environmental hazards;

PERMANENT PEOPLES' TRIBUNAL (PPT), Via della Dogana Vecchia 5, 00186 Rome, Italy. Telephone: +39 6 65 41 468. Fax +39 6 68 77 774. The PPT on Industrial Hazards and Human Rights, hosted by The Pesticides Trust, Eurolink Centre, 49 Effra Road, London, SW2 1BZ, UK. Telephone: +44 171 274 8895. Fax +44 171 274 9084. E-mail: pesttrust@gn.apc.org.a.

Guided further by International Labor Organization conventions and recommendations, including the Convention on Freedom of Association and Protection of the Right to Organize, the Convention on the Right to Organize and Collective Bargaining, and the Convention Concerning the Prevention of Major Industrial Accidents;

Gravely concerned by the widespread diffusion of hazardous products and processes resulting in industrial practices that cause human, social, and environmental destruction, threatening in particular the habitat, life, economy, society, and culture of indigenous peoples;

Deeply concerned by the frequency of small-scale but harmful hazardous events, as well as the magnitude and nature of major industrial accidents, including the incidents in Seveso, Chernobyl, Bhopal, Basel, and elsewhere;

Concerned by the ineffectual national and international system of hazard prevention, post-disaster relief, medical and legal assistance, and legal accountability, which in their current forms have failed both to adequately prevent occupational and environmental hazards and to bring to account those responsible for worldwide deaths and injuries;

Noting that urgent action is needed to prevent future degradation to human life, animal life, and the environment and to adequately remedy the harms caused by industrial hazards;

Recognizing that the personal experience and repeated demands of community members and workers affected by hazards provide the most sound basis for the enunciation of rights;

Cognizant of the inherent limitations of national and international law, as well as the vital role of community organizations and people's movements in preventing and ameliorating industrial hazards;

Convinced that new national and international systems of prevention, relief, and legal accountability must be formulated and established;

Declares the Following:

PART I: RIGHTS OF GENERAL APPLICATION

Article 1: Non-Discrimination

1. Everyone is entitled to all the rights and freedoms set forth in this Charter, without distinction of any kind, such as race, color, sex, language, religion, nationality, political opinion or affiliation, ethnic or social origin, disability, age, property, sexual orientation, birth, income, caste, or any other status.
2. On account of the particular discrimination faced by women, both as waged and unwaged workers, attention should be given to the specific application of the rights stated below where women may be affected.
3. On account of their vulnerability and exploitation in the labor market, special protection should be accorded to children exposed to industrial hazards.

4. On account of the connection between low wages and hazardous working environments and the disproportionate impact of industrial hazards on racial and ethnic minorities, special protection should be afforded low-income groups and racial minorities.

Article 2: Relation to Other Rights

The rights in this charter and other human rights, including civil, political, economic, social, and cultural rights, are universal, interdependent, and indivisible. In particular, freedom from hazards, including the right to refuse hazardous employment and the right to organize against hazards, depends upon the full implementation of social and economic rights, including the rights to education, health, and an adequate standard of living.

Article 3: Right to Accountability

All persons have the right to hold accountable any individual, company, or government agency for actions resulting in industrial hazards. In particular, parent companies, including transnational corporations, shall be liable for the actions of their subsidiaries.

Article 4: Right to Organize

1. All community members and workers have the right to organize with other local communities and workers for the purpose of seeking to ensure a working environment free from hazard.
2. In particular, the right to organize includes:
   (a) The freedoms of expression, association, and peaceful assembly;
   (b) The right to form local, national, and international organizations;
   (c) The rights to campaign, lobby, educate, and exchange information;
   (d) The right to form trade unions;
   (e) The right to strike or take other forms of industrial action.

Article 5: Right to Appropriate Health Care

1. All persons have the right to appropriate health care.
2. In particular, the right to appropriate health care includes:
   (a) The right of individuals and groups to participate in the planning and implementation of health care;
   (b) The right of equal access of individuals and families to health care the community can afford;
   (c) The right to relevant health care services, including where appropriate access to hospitals, neighborhood clinics, specialist clinics, as well as the services of general practitioners, other medical professionals, and health care workers drawn from the affected community;
   (d) The right to independent information on the relevance and reliability of health care services and treatments including allopathic, homeopathic, nutritional, physiotherapeutic, psychotherapeutic, indigenous,

169

and other approaches;

    (f) The right to health care systems that recognize and take account of the different ways in which hazards affect women, men, and children;

    (g) The right to health education;

    (h) The development of national, regional, and international networks to facilitate sharing of information and experience.

Article 6: Right of Refusal

1.   All communities have the right to refuse the introduction, expansion, or continuation of hazardous activities in their living environment.

2.   All workers have the right to refuse to work in a hazardous working environment without fear of retaliatory action by the employer.

3.   The right to reject inappropriate legal, medical, or scientific advice shall not be infringed.

Article 7: Permanent Sovereignty over Living Environments

1.   Each state retains the right of permanent sovereignty over the living environments within its national jurisdiction. No state shall exercise this right so as to injure the health or living environments of its people, nor to cause damage to the environment of other states or of areas beyond the limits of national jurisdiction.

2.   Each state has the right and the obligation to regulate and exercise authority over hazardous and potentially hazardous enterprises in conformity with the interests and well-being of its people and their environment.

3.   No state shall be:

    (a) Refused external finance or assistance on the grounds of its refusal to import or establish hazardous products or processes;

    (b) Compelled to grant preferential treatment to foreign investment;

    (c) Made subject to external threats or coercive measures, whether military, diplomatic, social, or economic, intended to affect regulations or policies regarding hazardous production.

4.   Transnational corporations and multinational enterprises shall not intervene in the internal affairs of a host state.

PART II: COMMUNITY RIGHTS

Article 8: Right to Living Environment Free from Hazards

1.   All persons have the right to a living environment free from hazards. In particular, this right applies where hazards arise from:

    (a) The manufacture, sale, transport, distribution, use, and disposal of hazardous materials;

    (b) Any military or weapons application, regardless of national security.

2.   Any person has the right to raise a bona fide complaint to the owner or

occupier of an economic enterprise regarding activities of the enterprise that he or she believes are hazardous to the living environment.

3. Any person living in an environment from which it is impossible to eliminate a hazard shall have the right to protective safety systems necessary to eliminate any such hazard as far as possible. The owners or occupiers of the concerned hazardous enterprise may not refuse to provide the most effective systems available on the grounds of cost or inconvenience.

Article 9: Right to Environmental Information

1. All persons have the right to be given reasonable notice of any proposal to establish, expand, or modify a hazardous industry in such location or in such a manner as may put at risk public health or the living environment. To achieve the full realization of this right, the following steps shall be taken:

   (a) All states shall ensure that communities, individuals, and nongovernmental organizations have the right of access to full information regarding the proposal. This right shall be effective well in advance of official authorization and shall not be abridged by claims of commercial secrecy.

   (b) All states shall ensure that prior to official approval of any hazardous enterprise, independent and thorough assessments of the impact upon the environment and public health be conducted in consultation with the community. The methods and conclusions of such impact assessments shall be made available for public debate.

2. All persons have the right to be informed in their own language, and in a manner that they are able to comprehend, of any possible hazards or risks associated with any product or process used by any enterprise with which they may come into contact.

3. All persons have the right to be informed of the safety record of any economic enterprises whose manufacturing or industrial processes could affect their living environment, including the number of accidents, the types of accidents that have occurred, the extent of injuries resulting from such accidents, and any possible long-term adverse health effects.

4. All persons have the right to be informed of types and quantities of hazardous substances used and stored at the facility and emitted from the facility and contained in any final products. In particular, the right to information includes the right to regular toxic release inventories where appropriate. All persons living in the neighborhood of hazardous facilities have the right to inspection of factory premises and to physical verification of hazardous substances and processes.

5. All persons who live in environments in which they may come into contact with materials or processes that are known to be seriously hazardous and that emanate from the activities of an economic enterprise have the right to be examined regularly by an independent medical expert provided by the owner or occupier of the enterprise.

Article 10: Right to Community Participation

1. All persons have the right to participate in planning and decision-making processes affecting their living environment.
2. All persons have the right to planning and decision-making proceedings that are:
   (a) Public and open;
   (b) Accessible to all in timing and location;
   (c) Widely advertised in advance;
   (d) Not restricted by literacy, language, or format of contributions.
3. All persons have the right to express their concerns and objections relating to hazards associated with establishing, modifying, or expanding any economic enterprise.
4. All persons have the right to participate in the design and execution of ongoing studies to determine the nature of any hazards to the living environment resulting from an economic enterprise.

Article 11: Right to Environmental Monitoring

1. All persons have the right to regular and effective monitoring of their health and the living environment for possible immediate and long-term effects caused by hazardous or potentially hazardous economic enterprise.
2. All persons have the right to be consulted on the frequency, character, and objectives of environmental monitoring. The right to organize nonprofessional monitoring strategies, such as lay epidemiology, shall be protected. The rights of women, whose experience in providing health care may reveal otherwise unidentified consequences of hazards, are particularly affirmed.
3. Any person who bona fide believes that his or her community environment is endangered by the actions of any economic enterprise has the right to an immediate and thorough investigation, to be carried out by an independent agency at no cost to the person acting bona fide.

Article 12: Right to Community Education

1. All persons have the right to the effective dissemination of information regarding hazards in the community. This right extends to instruction based upon the best available information and standards, drawn from both national and international sources.
2. States shall take effective steps to provide for:
   (a) Clear and systematic labelling of hazardous substances;
   (b) Appropriate education of the community, including children, on hazardous products and processes;
   (c) Training of police, medical professionals, and other service providers on hazardous products and processes.

Article 13: Right to Community Emergency Preparedness Procedure

1. All persons have the right to an appropriate emergency preparedness

procedure. Such procedure shall include warning systems for impending dangers and systems for immediate relief efforts.

2. All states shall take steps to provide communities with adequate emergency services, including the provision of police, fire fighting, medical and paramedical facilities, and disaster management services.

Article 14: Right to Enforcement of Environmental Laws

1. All persons have the right to have their local environment adequately and frequently inspected by a trained environmental inspector who will rigorously enforce the law and take punitive legal action when serious breaches have taken place.
2. All persons have the right to environmental management legislation in compliance with the precautionary principle, so that where there are threats of serious or irreversible damage, lack of full scientific certainty shall not be used as a reason to postpone cost-effective measures to prevent hazards and environmental degradation.

Article 15: Rights of Indigenous Peoples

1. Indigenous peoples have the right to protect their habitat, economy, society, and culture from industrial hazards and environmentally destructive practices by economic enterprises.
2. Indigenous peoples have the right to control over their land and resources management of their land, which includes the right to assess potential environmental impacts and the right to refuse to allow environmentally destructive or hazardous industries to be set up on their land.

PART III: RIGHTS OF WORKERS

Article 16: Specific Rights of Workers

In addition to their rights as members of the community, workers have specific rights applicable to their working environments.

Article 17: Right to Working Environment Free from Hazards

1. All workers, both waged and unwaged, have the right to a working environment free from any existing or potential hazard arising directly or indirectly from the activities of any economic enterprise, in particular from manufacturing or other industrial processes.
2. Any worker has the right to raise bona fide complaints to the employer or any outside parties regarding conditions or practices in the working environment that he or she believes are harmful or hazardous without fear of retaliatory action or other discriminatory action by the employer.
3. Any individual working in an environment from which it is impossible to eliminate any hazard shall have the right to have provided, fitted free of

charge and maintained in fully effective order, protective safety devices, including personal protective equipment necessary to eliminate any such hazard as far as is possible. Employers may not refuse to provide the most effective equipment available on the grounds of cost or inconvenience.

4. All workers have the right to safe systems of work. All employers have the duty to devise, provide, maintain, and regularly update safe systems of work based on the best available information at all times.

5. No worker shall be subjected to exposure to a chemical, product, or process when a less hazardous one could be substituted.

6. Governments and employers are responsible for ensuring hazard-free working environments. The inaction by either employer or government shall not be an adequate excuse for a derogation of duty by the other.

Article 18: Right to Health and Safety Information

1. All workers have the right to be given reasonable notice of any proposed changes to their working environments that may pose a threat to worker health and safety.

2. All workers have the right to be informed in their own language, and in a manner they are able to comprehend, of any known health hazard associated with any substance, material, or process with which they come into contact during the course of their employment.

3. All workers have the right to be informed of the safety record of the work environment in which they are employed, including the number and type of accidents that have occurred, the extent of the injuries resulting therefrom, and any known long-term adverse health risks that result from the substances, materials, and processes used by the employer. Workers have the right to be regularly informed of the safety records of any economic enterprise affiliated by common ownership to the economic enterprise in which they work, and which uses any similar substance, material, or process to that used in their work environment.

4. All workers employed in hazardous work environments have the right to be examined by an independent medical expert provided by the employer at the commencement of employment and thereafter at periodic intervals defined on the basis of the most conservative estimate of potential risks, but in any case not exceeding one year and to be furnished with the resulting medical information.

Article 19: Right to Worker Participation

1. All workers have the right to participate effectively in management decision-making affecting health and safety.

2. All workers have the right to elect safety representatives. Such representatives have the right to participate in joint committees, composed of worker and management representatives in equal number, which meet regularly to address health and safety matters.

3. All workers have the right to participate in the design and execution of ongoing health and safety studies in their working environments to determine the nature of any risks to health and safety.
4. All workers have the right to establish and associate with community hazards centers and information networks. Governments and employers have a responsibility to support such organizations and programs.

Article 20: Right to Health and Safety Monitoring

1. All workers have the right to a work environment that is regularly and effectively monitored for possible harmful effects to the health and safety of the workers employed therein.
2. Notwithstanding the duty of employers to monitor working environments, the right of workers to seek independent or worker-based monitoring shall not be infringed. This right includes the right to regular monitoring for possible adverse, long-term effects that may result from contact with the substances, materials, or processes used in the working environment.
3. Any worker who bona fide believes that his or her health and safety is being or will be endangered by any substance, material, or process used in the work environment has the right to an immediate and thorough investigation, to be carried out by the employer, an independent agency, or by other means, at no cost to the worker.

Article 21: Right to Instruction and Practical Training

1. All workers in contact with hazardous or potentially hazardous substances, materials, or processes have the right to ongoing instruction and practical training regarding management of the hazard. The right to instruction and practical training based on the best available information, drawn from both national and international sources, is affirmed.
2. All workers and supervisors have the right to know and be fully instructed about the proper use and handling of any hazardous materials, the proper execution of any processes, the precautions necessary to protect health, safety, and the living environment, and any procedures that should be followed in the event of an emergency.

Article 22: Right to Workplace Emergency Preparedness Procedure

1. All workers have the right to an emergency preparedness procedure appropriate for the conditions or practices in their work environment, which shall include warning systems for impending dangers and systems for immediate relief efforts, with full-scale emergency preparedness rehearsals and desk top exercises to be held frequently.
2. Emergency preparedness procedures shall take account of the particular needs of individual workers, including those with visual, hearing, or mobility impairments.
3. All workers have the right to adequate emergency services, including

police, fire fighting, medical and paramedical facilities, and disaster management.

Article 23: Right to Enforcement of Health and Safety Laws

1. All workers have the right to have their work environments adequately and frequently inspected by a trained health and safety inspector who will rigorously enforce the law and take punitive legal action when serious breaches have occurred.
2. All workers have the right to adequate planning control legislation in compliance with the precautionary principle, so that where there are threats of serious or irreversible damage, lack of full scientific certainty shall not be used as a reason to postpone cost-effective measures to prevent hazards and environmental degradation.

PART IV: COMMON RIGHTS TO RELIEF

Article 24: Right to Relief and Compensation

1. All persons injured or otherwise detrimentally affected by any hazardous economic activity have the right to swift, comprehensive, and effective relief. This right applies to all persons affected by hazards or potential hazards, including persons not yet born at the time of injury or exposure, and those injured, bereaved, or economically and socially disadvantaged, whether affected directly or indirectly.
2. This right includes the right to fair and adequate monetary compensation, paid to cover all costs associated with hazardous or potentially hazardous activities, including the costs of:
   (a) Drugs, tests, therapies, hospitalization, and other medical treatments;
   (b) Travel and other incidental costs;
   (c) Lost wages, bridging loans, and other pecuniary loss;
   (d) Redundancy and unemployment in the case of plant shutdown;
   (e) Additional unwaged work, including health care, born by family and community;
   (f) Any purchase, measure, or lost opportunity caused directly or indirectly by hazardous processes or products; and
   (g) Environmental rehabilitation.
3. All persons affected by hazards have the right to effective and innovative policies to reduce, abate, or compensate for hazardous activities. To achieve the realization of this right, the steps taken by states and businesses shall include:
   (a) Plant shutdown;
   (b) Pollution abatements or cessation;
   (c) Guarantee by liable defendants to keep assets unencumbered;
   (d) Forced liquidation of the assets of a corporation whose liability is equal to or greater than its measurable assets;

    (e) Placement of corporate assets in annuity funds controlled by the persons affected or their representatives for the interests of persons affected;

    (f) Fair and adequate compensation for the costs of the medical monitoring of symptoms;

    (g) Other remedies that may be deemed to be necessary for the benefits of persons affected.

4.   Funds shall be established adequately to satisfy the claims for the persons affected and of those affected in future.

Article 25: Right to Immediate Interim Relief

1.   All persons adversely affected by any hazardous economic activity have the right to immediate and adequate interim relief to alleviate their injuries and suffering during the time that liability and compensatory damages are being determined. States shall ensure that all hazardous or potentially hazardous enterprises provide financial resources, through insurance or other means, adequate to cover potential interim relief costs.

2.   Where an economic enterprise fails to provide interim relief, it shall be the duty of the state to do so. Interim relief so provided will not be set off against any final compensation allowed by the court.

Article 26: Right to Medical Information

All persons immediately or subsequently affected by hazardous activities, including persons unborn at the time of the exposure to hazard, have the right to obtain relevant documents pertaining to injuries, including medical records, test results, and other information. This right may be exercised at the earliest opportunity and may not be made subject to delay or noncompliance by either government or industry. Such disclosure shall not be made in a manner so as to prejudice the affected person's right of access to any service, insurance, employment, or any social or welfare opportunities.

Article 27: Right to Professional Services

1.   All persons adversely affected by hazardous activity have the right of access to effective professional services, including the services of lawyers, journalists, scientific experts, and medical professions.

2.   Where questions of a scientific or medical nature are in dispute, all affected persons, or their representatives, have the right to genuinely independent advice, free from fear or favor. The right to seek independent or multiple advice is affirmed.

3.   Professionals and experts shall refrain from:

    (a) Giving advice on the basis of inadequate information or expertise;

    (b) Obstructing the efforts of workers and communities to seek information, conduct research, or gather data through lay epidemiology or other means;

(c)   Acting in concert against the interests of workers and communities.
4.   All professionals having control of any information concerning the health of any injured or hazard-affected person shall have a primary duty of care toward the well-being of that person. This duty shall at all times take precedence over any allegiance to any third party, including any government, professional organization, or commercial enterprise.

Article 28: Right to Effective Legal Representation

1.   All persons adversely affected by hazardous activities shall have the right to employ independent legal counsel.
2.   All states shall provide free legal representation and legal assistance by an independent legal expert, in any case where the interests of justice so require.
3.   In the determination of any suit, the persons affected shall be entitled to consolidate the claims under:
     (a)   The auspices of a workers' or community organization; or
     (b)   Class action laws in which the rights of any persons affected are determined in one action.
4.   All persons bringing or attempting to bring legal action have the right to inspect any relevant legal files held by their legal representative.

Article 29: Right to Choice of Forum

1.   All persons adversely affected by hazardous activities have the right to bring a lawsuit in the forum of their choice against alleged wrongdoers, including individuals, governments, corporations, or other organizations. No state shall discriminate against such persons on the basis of nationality or domicile.
2.   All states shall ensure that in the specific case of any legal claims arising from the effects of hazardous activities, any legal rule otherwise impeding the pursuit of such claims, including legislative measures and judicial doctrines, shall not prevent affected persons from bringing suit for full and effective remedies. In particular, states shall review and remove where necessary legal restrictions relating to inconvenient forum, statutory limitations, limited liability of parent corporations, enforcement of foreign money judgments, and excessive fees for civil suits.

Article 30: Right to Pretrial Documentation

All persons adversely affected by a hazardous activity and their representatives have the right to seek and receive relevant documents, records, or other information for submission in court or other independent tribunal or forum, for establishing individual, corporate, organizational, or governmental liability during litigation.

Article 31: Right to Fair Procedure

All persons adversely affected by hazardous activities shall have the right to a fair and public hearing within a reasonable time by an independent and impartial tribunal established by law. Included in this right is the right to the due process of law, including:

(a) The right to opt out of class actions;

(b) The right to a reasonable notice and communication before an out-of-court settlement in a civil suit is reached;

(c) The right to bring a lawsuit notwithstanding the period of limitation set by administrative, legislative, or judicial or any other means.

Article 32: Right to Freedom from Fraud and Delay

All persons adversely affected by hazardous activities shall have the right to be protected against fraud by corporations, government, or other organizations. Also prohibited is intentional delay or obstruction of the legal process, including:

(a) Declaration of bankruptcy;

(b) Abuse of the legal process to prolong adjudication;

(c) Fabrication of evidence.

Article 33: Right to Enforcement of Judgments or Settlements

All persons adversely affected by hazardous activities and their representatives shall have the right to enforce any judgment or settlement against the assets of the liable or settling party in any other countries and it shall be the duty of each state to provide under domestic law such comprehensive instruments as assist any of its citizens so affected.

Article 34: Right to Shift the Burden of Proof

1. Where there is prima facie evidence that death or injury was caused by an industrial hazard, the hazardous economic enterprise has the burden of proving that it was not negligent.

2. No person adversely affected by hazardous activity shall be subjected to excessive documentation requirements or strict standards of proof in establishing that the hazardous activity caused their illness or symptoms. The link between hazards and illness shall be presumed if the affected persons establish:

(a) They suffer from symptoms commonly associated with any harmful substance, or any component thereof, which contaminated the environment; and

(b) Either

   (i) They were present within the geographical area of contamination during the period of contamination; or

   (ii) They belong to a group of persons commonly identified as secondary victims, including the siblings, partners, children, or close associates of the original victims of the hazard.

Article 35: Right to Corporate or State Criminal Accountability

1. All persons who have suffered injury or death from industrial hazards have the right to a full criminal investigation into the conduct of the economic enterprise, any concerned government officials, and any other concerned individual or organization. The investigation shall be both immediate and rigorous and shall include an assessment of whether potential criminal offenses, including homicide or manslaughter, have been committed. Where sufficient evidence exists, prosecution shall be pursued promptly and vigorously.
2. Where criminal liability of a company and or individual is proved, such fines and/or prison sentencing are to be imposed as to have a punitive, exemplary, and deterrent effect.

Article 36: Right to Secure Extradition

Where a person accused of a criminal offense in connection with hazardous activities resides or is located in a state other than that in which the trial is being or will be conducted, the right to demand and secure the extradition of the accused to the trial state is hereby affirmed.

PART V: IMPLEMENTATION

Article 37: Corresponding Duties

All persons, individually and in association with others, have a duty to protect the rights set out in this Charter. Employers and government officers are under a strict duty of care in vigilant application of the rights. Special responsibility for the realization of the provisions of this Charter lies with trade unions, community groups, and nongovernmental organizations.

Article 38: State Responsibilities

All states shall respect and protect the rights of workers and communities to live free from industrial hazards. Accordingly, they shall adopt legislative, administrative, and other measures necessary to implement the rights contained in this Charter.

Article 39: Non-State Action

The absence of state action to protect and enforce the rights set out in this Charter does not extinguish the duties of employers, trade unions, nongovernmental organizations, and individuals to protect and assert these rights.

London, April 1996

Index